The End of
Globalization

The End of Globalization

Lessons from the Great Depression

◆ ◆ ◆

Harold James

HARVARD UNIVERSITY PRESS

Cambridge, Massachusetts

London, England

Library of Congress Cataloging-in-Publication Data

James Harold.
The end of globalization : lessons from the Great Depression / Harold James.
p.   cm.
Includes bibliographical references and index.
ISBN 0-674-00474-4 (alk. paper)
1. International economic relations.   2. International trade.
3. International finance.   4. Depressions—1929.   5. Financial crises.
6. National state.   7. Globalization—Economic aspects.   I. Title.

HF1359 .J35 2001
337—dc21   00-054157

◆ ◆ ◆

Preface

This book has had a long gestation. I began thinking about the subject in the mid-1980s while writing a book on the interwar depression in Germany. Much of the archival research was done in the late 1980s. In the 1990s I interrupted the project in order to write a more optimistic book, about the success of post-1945 monetary cooperation, based in large part on the archives of the International Monetary Fund. This book is a return to a gloomier theme, in which past endeavors at globalization conjure up ghosts that still haunt the present, however prosperous and secure we may feel.

My research was made possible by several institutions. Princeton University, apart from providing a wonderful setting in which to write, generously funded much of the archival research. In the final stages of the work I was a Houblon-Norman Fellow at the Bank of England and then a Fellow at the Historisches Kolleg in Munich. Being at the Bank of England in the aftermath of the Asia crisis afforded a unique opportunity to discuss the policy implications of some apparently very distant history. I dealt with many archivists in many countries and would like to thank all of them, but especially Henry Gillette of the Bank of England, Rosemary Lazenby of the Federal Reserve Bank of New York, and Professor Dieter Lindenlaub of the Deutsche Bundesbank. The Historisches Kolleg provided an idyllic work environment for completing the book. I thank Eva Giloi-Bremner, Karsten Jedlitschka, and Clara Oberle for careful and thoughtful research assistance.

I presented earlier versions of my argument in the following pages at seminars at various universities (Mannheim, Frankfurt, Princeton, Vienna) and in lectures prepared for the Deutsche Bundesbank and the Bank of England, for *Politeia* in London, and for the Bavarian Academy of Sciences, as well as at seminars organized by Robert Fleming and by the Herbert Quandt Foundation. I should like to thank the participants in those discussions, and especially Bill Allen, Axel Börsch-Supan, Christoph Buchheim, Gerhard Illing, Markus Ingenlath, Stanley Katz, Mervyn King, Sheila Lawlor, Dieter Lindenlaub, David Marsh, Kai Schellhorn, and Alice Teichova, who organized the events. The Mellon Foundation's Sawyer Program funded a year-long interdisciplinary seminar at Princeton in 1997–98 on "Western Economic Values and the Alternatives," whose regular participants and visiting speakers helped me clarify many arguments about the lessons learned from history. In April 1998 Princeton University organized jointly with the German Historical Institute, Washington, D.C., a two-day conference on the international financial system in the twentieth century. In June 1999 the Historisches Kolleg organized a colloquium of experts in this field to present their research and to discuss the subject in general. Those who attended and presented papers were Christoph Buchheim, Forrest Capie, Patricia Clavin, Barry Eichengreen, Gerald Feldman, Carl-Ludwig Holtfrerich, Albrecht Ritschl, Monika Rosengarten, Dietmar Rothermund, Robert Skidelsky, and Solomos Solomou. The colloquium was very skillfully managed by Elisabeth Müller-Luckner. By an agreeable chance, the colloquium coincided with the seventieth birthday of the great German economic historian, Knut Borchardt, who has been a longtime friend and mentor and to whom this book is dedicated.

In addition, I should like to thank Michael Bordo and Douglas Irwin for reading a near-final version of the manuscript attentively and offering valuable suggestions. It was a pleasure working with Ann Hawthorne and Jeff Kehoe of Harvard University Press.

Marzenna James has been a constant friend and inspiration. Without her patience and love I could never have undertaken this project. Maximilian, Marie Louise, and Montagu (who was born just as this book was completed) have all been sources of inspiration.

Princeton, New Jersey
November 2000

Contents

1 Introduction: The End of Globalization and the Problem of the Depression   *1*

2 Monetary Policy and Banking Instability   *31*

3 Tariffs, Trade Policy, and the Collapse of International Trade   *101*

4 The Reaction against International Migration   *168*

5 The Age of Nationalism versus the Age of Capital   *187*

6 Conclusion: Can It Happen Again?   *200*

Notes   *227*

Index   *255*

♦ ♦ ♦

Tables and Figures

Tables

2.1 Average annual long-term capital exports, United States and
Britain, 1919–1938   48

2.2 Short-term banking liabilities, United States and Britain,
1927–1930   50

2.3 Austrian budgets, 1928–1934   56

2.4 Banks' gross foreign liabilities as a share of international
reserves, various countries and years   99

3.1 British-Argentine trade, 1933–1935   150

3.2 Share of Brazil's total imports, 1913–1937   155

3.3 The bilateralization of trade, 1929–1935   165

4.1 Nominal wages of skilled male workers in 1929 as a share of
1926 wages, various countries   181

Figures

1.1 Correlation of journal articles on the Great Depression and
general economic conditions   27

2.1 Capital flows, 1924–1937   49

2.2 Pound and franc exchange rates relative to the U.S. dollar,
1924–1939   75

3.1 World production and trade, 1925–1937   103

3.2 Prices in international trade, 1921–1938   104

The End of
Globalization

1

•

Introduction: The End of Globalization and the Problem of the Depression

At the turn of the millennium, "globalization" has become a catchword used worldwide. Increasing economic interconnectedness has led to a profound political and social revolution. Old certainties are cast into doubt. The nation-state, the decisive driving force of the past two centuries, is dissolving under the pressure of a cross-national integration, which has developed with a dynamic and a momentum of its own.

Often we believe that this process is irreversible, that it provides a one-way road to the future. But historical reflections lead to a more sober and more pessimistic assessment. There have already been highly developed and highly integrated international communities that dissolved under the pressure of unexpected events. But in every case the momentum was lost; the pendulum swung back. In Europe, for instance, the universal Erasmian world of the Renaissance was destroyed by the Reformation and its Catholic counterpart, and separatism, provincialism, and parochialism followed. A more immediate (and perhaps more familiar) precedent is the disintegration of the highly interconnected economic world of the late nineteenth century.

No collapse, of course, is precisely like any other. In the following pages I will not be attempting to argue that the Great Depression of the twentieth century will be restaged in the twenty-first. But each collapse results from patterns of thought and institutional mechanisms that arise in response to a new and unfamiliar international or cosmopolitan world. The form of such reactionary resentment remains astonishingly similar over long periods.

The failure of the World Trade Organization ministerial meeting in Seattle in November 1999 gives some indication of the problems facing the interconnected world today. The major industrial states failed to organize a realistic agenda. They overburdened the trade talks with inappropriate demands about environmental and especially labor standards, which many developing countries interpreted as a new protectionism under another guise. Finally, they appeared to encourage the apocalyptic street scenes in which citizens of mostly rich countries, who might have been expected to see themselves as beneficiaries of globalization, rioted against the new economic order. Instead of serious trade talks, Seattle turned into a chaotic symbolic protest against the internationally diffused culture of McDonald's: the beginning of a new phase in two long-standing conflicts, the North against the South, and the rest of the world against Americanism. Both are battles in a conflict over globalism. Did the battle of Seattle set the tune for the new century?

This book explores the Seattle scenario—the circumstances in which globalism breaks down—by using a historical precedent, the collapse of globalism in the interwar depression. This collapse destroyed the financial power of the country, Great Britain, that had been the dynamic force behind the internationalization of the economy in the nineteenth century. It prompted, especially in Nazi Germany and imperial Japan, innovative but aggressive and exploitative approaches to a nationalist management of the economy that largely rejected the principles of globalism.

In contemporary discussions, two alternative paths to the autodestruction of the globalized economy have been identified. The first sees an inherent flaw in the system itself: in contemporary terms, the most frequently identified issue is the volume and volatility of capital movements. In this version, there may be a system, but it is inherently unstable and likely to produce radically destabilizing booms and busts rather than smooth development. The second explains the crisis of globalization in terms of the social and political responses and reactions it provokes. In this account, fear disrupts globalization.

First, then: can our system autodestruct? Many critics worry that an unreal financial economy has dwarfed the transactions of the "real" or "underlying" economy in which goods and services are exchanged. "Casino capitalism" builds up more bets on future outcomes than there are actual outcomes and diverts resources, time, energy, and emotions from real production and true satisfaction. The resources of official institutions, such as central banks, are hopelessly limited in relation to the enormous size of the currency markets. The international monetary system depends on the bets undertaken there, yet they create a great vulnerability. They can destroy countries as speculators scent a potential gain to be made in generating a self-fulfilling doomsday scenario. This was the story of the crisis that began in Thailand in 1997 and then swept across much of Asia. It is not just individual countries that are vulnerable. Ultimately, such bets might bring down the whole system, since they are predicated on a very narrowly conceived model of rationality.

A model for such a breakdown—in the eyes of many critics an anticipation of the final collapse of the financially integrated global economy—is to be found in 1998, with the collapse of the strategy adopted by the New York–based company Long Term Capital Management. That strategy had depended on what was termed a "convergence play": the increased convergence of interest rates in major economies, making residual risk premiums appear unjustified. When a global financial crisis seemed imminent, with the spread of crisis from Asia to Russia and Brazil, interest rates suddenly diverged, and the hugely leveraged positions built up by LTCM generated huge liabilities.

A major financial crisis can have systemic effects and catastrophically undermine the stability of the institutions that make global interchange possible. Such a picture, in which financial volatility destroys the system that was built up on the basis of a free flow of capital, has become increasingly worrying to many thoughtful analysts. Even thinkers close to the modern consensus about the desirability of liberalization have drawn back and wondered whether there might not be a case for controlling capital flows. When the Malaysian prime minister, Mahathir Mohamad, responded to the Asian crisis with such control measures, he was at first widely ridiculed. But the Malaysian economy stabilized, and gurus of the international economy such as Joseph Stiglitz—at the time chief economist of the World Bank—and Paul Krugman, then an MIT professor and a hot favorite for a Nobel Prize in economics, soon advertised their conversion to the cause of controlling capital movements.[1] This plea was supported by market practitioners, including some such as George Soros who appeared to be among the most favored beneficiaries of casino capitalism. At the height of concern about global financial meltdown, Soros predicted the "imminent disintegration of the global capitalist system," which would "succumb to its defects."[2] The diagnosis was shared by men who had held positions of great responsibility in the international economy, such as the former Federal Reserve Board chairman Paul Volcker. The British philosopher John Gray called for a "reorientation of thought," since free markets are "inherently volatile institutions, prone to speculative booms and busts."[3] According to this new uneasy critique of financial globalism, continued unregulated capital movements would be the mechanism whereby the liberal international order would destroy itself through its own contradictions (to borrow a phrase widely used in Marxist analysis).

The second path to disintegration lies not in the mechanism of the international order, but in the resentments that the injustices of the global economy may provoke. World injustice was the focus of the street protests in Seattle in 1999 and in Washington, D.C., in 2000. Thomas Friedman devoted a large section of his book on globalization to the "backlash." He explained: "What all the backlash forces have in common is a feeling that as their countries have plugged into the globalization system they are being forced into a Golden Straitjacket that is one-size-fits-all."[4] There are clear historical precedents. In particular, the economic historians Kevin O'Rourke and Jeffrey Williamson have recently discussed the "globalization backlash" engendered by the nineteenth-century wave of integration—both against goods markets and, most important, against international migration. In their analysis, globalization and the shifts in incomes that it entailed produced relatively speedy reactions—more trade protection, and control of immigration—that eventually strangled the process of integration. The consequence of a free flow of factors of production was that owners of land in previously land-scarce Europe lost, as did owners of labor in the previously labor-scarce New World. The European landowners and the New World laborers had substantial political power, which they increasingly used to limit the extent of globalization and of the troubling factor flows. O'Rourke and Williamson give a rational, interest-based account of how grievances against globalism build up. In an account of the nineteenth century with obvious and frightening contemporary echoes, they explain how trade and migration affected income distribution, and in particular how it contributed to a lowering of incomes for unskilled workers in dynamic countries of immigration (notably the United States).[5]

A third path—the one taken in this book—examines the same process from a less rational angle. It suggests that globalism fails because humans and the institutions they create cannot adequately handle the psychological and institutional consequences of the interconnected world. Institutions, especially those created to tackle the problems of globalism, come at particular moments of crisis under strains that are so great as to preclude their effective operation. They become the major channels through which the resentments against globalization work their destruction.

This book focuses on the institutions that evolved to handle globalization and its consequences: in the nineteenth century, above all tariff systems, central banks, and immigration legislation. The international world was then managed fundamentally by national institutions, in the framework of a nation-state that many conceived as a safety device or shield against the problems of the international economic order. In the interwar years, as the threat grew bigger, some governments believed that the globalization issues were better handled at an international level: by the League of Nations, its Economic and Financial Organization, the International Labour Organization, and the Bank for International Settlements. In the post-1945 era, a new set of international institutions handled the problems much more satisfactorily than did their predecessors,[6] but these have now become the targets for massive criticism from very diverse political and geographic groups: the International Monetary Fund and the World Trade Organization have become the whipping boys of globalization. Some commentators suggest another analogy: that the IMF or the WTO is like a church whose mission is maybe not to remove sin, but to make it psychologically bearable. Finance ministers on this account go into the confessional of IMF "Article IV surveillance meetings," recite ritual formulas about the ways in which they have erred, and are then reminded of the true doctrine from which they have strayed.[7]

A great part of this book is concerned with the experience of the world during the Great Depression of the late 1920s and 1930s. This was the time for testing of the first major phase of economic globalization: it was a testing so brutal that the system was destroyed, and the world reverted to autarkic or near-autarkic national economic management. It was only in the 1960s and above all since the 1970s that a global world economy was recreated.

Optimists argue that the depression was a once-only event, one that derived essentially from the consequences of the First World War. Since another sustained and large-scale international conflict of that kind is extremely unlikely, the comforting conclusion is that the Great Depression cannot occur again and should be of interest only to historians, and perhaps also to economists interested in a curiosity cabinet of extreme disequilibria.

The three types of interpretation outlined above (self-destruction, backlash, and weaknesses in institutional regulation) may all be applied to the analysis of the end of globalization in the interwar years with the onset of the Great Depression. The vision of a system collapsing through its own contradictions of course underlay the Marxist interpretation of the experience, which proved exceptionally compelling (especially to intellectuals) and made the brutal doctrines of Communism and its approach to economic management appealing for a generation. But plenty of non-Communists saw international capital movements as a major culprit, and indeed this interpretation, brilliantly formulated by John Maynard Keynes and by Ragnar Nurkse, provided the basis of the post-1945 economic order, the so-called Bretton Woods regime, which aimed at a restoration of trade relations but saw capital movements as destabilizing and undesirable.

O'Rourke and Williamson, though not dealing directly with the Great Depression, see it not as evidence of a systemic flaw but instead as the logical outcome of the pre-1914 "globalization backlash." They formulate the case very strikingly: "History shows that globalization can plant the seeds of its own destruction. Those seeds were planted in the 1870s, sprouted in the 1880s, grew vigorously around the turn of the century, and then came to full flower in the dark years between the two world wars."[8] They are quite emphatic that it did not require a Great War to produce a Great Depression. This line of analysis had already been pursued by Joseph Schumpeter. In an article on "The Instability of Capitalism," published in 1928, at the height of the decade's prosperity, he referred to "the tendency towards self-destruction from inherent economic causes, or towards outgrowing its own frame." At a moment when there appeared to be no immediate danger of financial turbulence, he argued, "Capitalism, whilst economically stable, and even gaining in stability, creates, by rationalizing the human mind, a mentality and a style of life incompatible with it sown fundamental conditions, motives and social institutions."[9]

This book also supports such an analysis: that the pre-1914 international economy, prosperous and integrated as it was, contained severe flaws. Such flaws include those identified by O'Rourke and Williamson, in particular the increased demand for trade protection and the growing hostility in recipient countries to emigration. But the problems went wider, and encompassed a set of expectations about what states and societies should do to limit the impact of globalization that put on the political process an increasingly insupportable burden of expectations.

The Universal Age

Before we begin to consider the nineteenth-century wave of globalization, we might contemplate some of the lessons from an earlier age of internationalism: the period of the great explorations, and the creation of large new state forms that prompted analysts to think for the first time in terms of the new concept of sovereignty. The sixteenth century could offer a parable of the perils of globalization.

Interpretations that emphasize the way a mechanism can destroy itself (collapse through its own contradictions) might have a field day with the sixteenth-century experience. The discoveries brought new wealth, but the growth of commerce helped new political centers that subverted the older political units. Spain colonized the New World, but the Netherlands revolted and built a powerful and prosperous new state on the basis of trade. Whether or not the story of Columbus' sailors bringing back syphilis from the West Indies is correct, new diseases from the New World made Europe unhealthier. Monetary inflation, the product of the large inflows first of gold and then of silver, made prices uncertain and destabilized society. The new moneys paid for larger armies, which then set about their brutal and destructive work.

The conservative Spanish philosopher José Ortega y Gasset, in 1933, at just the moment when the Great Depression was breaking civilization down, reinterpreted the cosmopolitanism of the early modern Renaissance as an age of cultural crisis and rebarbarization. The search of the Renaissance for men of action, for the Cesare Borgias, was a sign of profound malaise. "As the albatross is the harbinger of storms," he wrote, "the man of action always appears on the horizon when a new crisis is breaking."[10]

But the sixteenth-century interpretation of the experience of a large world society looked very different from modern accounts of how a mechanism creates strains and backlashes. Contemporaries responded to their new environment with a heightened sense of human imperfection and fragility. "Sin" was the way in which global challenges might be comprehended.

One of the driving forces of both the great religious movements of the sixteenth century in Europe, the Protestant Reformation and the Catholic Counter-Reformation, was a search for a less sinful life. Such reform movements are a highly characteristic response to the features of a universal age, whose characteristics were expressed in a world shaped by religion. Martin Luther, who had a peculiarly heightened sensibility of sin, found the words that allowed the new world to be comprehended. That was the secret of his success. One of his most important early social tracts addressed the problem of commercial life. *Trade and Usury*, published in 1524, begins with a straightforward declaration of the sinfulness of much commercial activity. "It is to be feared that the words of Ecclesiasticus apply here, namely, that merchants can hardly be without sin. Indeed, I think St. Paul's saying in the last chapter of the first epistle to Timothy fits the case, 'The love of money is the root of all evils.'" Where did the sin lie? Not in the buying and selling of commodities that "serve a necessary and honorable purpose," such as cattle, wool, grain, butter, or milk. It was long-distance commerce, involving the exchange or loss of precious metals, that was pernicious:

> But foreign trade, which brings from Calcutta and India and such places wares like costly silks, articles of gold, and spices—which minister only to ostentation but serve no useful purpose, and which drain away the money of land and people—would not be permitted if we had proper government and princes . . . God has cast us Germans off to such an extent that we have to fling our gold and silver into foreign lands and make the whole world rich, while we ourselves remain beggars.[11]

The universalism that made many people feel deeply uncomfortable during the Reformation had at least six features:

1. There was constant change. In humanist literature, the spirit of the age was portrayed as Fortuna (rather than as a Christian providence), whose wheel made and broke fortunes. The cult of Fortuna reached a high point in the writings of Machiavelli, who also elaborated the view that the virtuous man had the mission of taming Fortuna. Shakespeare's plays, in particular the tragedies, can be read as extended meditations on Fortuna.

2. There was contact, mostly commercial, between peoples across large distances. In the sixteenth century this contact most commonly took the form of trading that linked the Europes of the

Mediterranean, the Atlantic, and the Baltic. But the most spectacular contacts and conflicts with remote societies were a consequence of the transoceanic explorations and the penetration of European adventurers into completely alien worlds. Cortes and Pizarro confronted non-European civilization.

3. The changeability and the new physical geography produced feelings that the wealth of many other people was illegitimate and could not be justified by the traditional criteria given in the moral universe of that age. The great Augsburg merchant Jakob Fugger, who built up his position by lending money to the Habsburg imperial dynasty, liked to explain that he was "rich by the grace of God"; but in fact he was attacked by clerics as a "sore on the body politic" or as someone who stood "alone in the trough like an old sow and won't let the other hogs in."[12]

4. The changeability and the new physical geography produced feelings that one's own wealth was illegitimate. Not everyone was as secure as a Jakob Fugger, but even he (and his descendants) gave generously in order to demonstrate the legitimacy of their wealth. Charitable giving generally increased: there were new hospitals, schools, colleges.

5. The changeability and the new physical geography produced feelings that the poverty of many other people was illegitimate. New charities, new poor laws, and new institutions (the hospitalization of the poor) tried to deal with the consequences.

6. The changeability and the new physical geography produced feelings that one's own poverty was illegitimate. Brigands such as Marco Sciarra built up powerful legends on the basis of robbery ostensibly to help the poor. So-called peasants' wars swept early modern Europe—with dramatic conflagrations in central Europe in 1525, in France in 1636, 1639, and 1675, in England in 1536 and 1649 (the revolt of the Levellers). These movements usually combined political radicalism with a profound social conservatism: they wanted to restore a lost but legitimate world.

Such dramatic fluctuations produced the widespread belief that traditional values were under threat. Two responses might be formulated: the humanist one, in which *virtù* tamed Fortuna; or the message of "sin," in which—as in Luther's formulation—the existing world was condemned.

Nevertheless, it was easier to live with the psychological consequences of dramatic changes, because everyone was quite familiar from the drama of individual existence—the likelihood of sudden catastrophic illnesses or other disasters—with a world that was mutable. The practical outcomes actually resembled each other: the statesman of *virtù* was supposed to impose his vision on the anarchy of Fortuna, and Luther appealed for a strong state to deal with an amoral world. "Christians are rare people on earth. This is why the world needs a strict, harsh temporal government which will compel and constrain the wicked to refrain from theft and robbery, and to return what they borrow (although a Christian ought to neither demand nor expect it). This is necessary in order that the world may not become a desert, peace vanish, and men's trade and society be utterly destroyed."[13] The awareness of sin conjured up the state as a way of institutionalizing an adequate response to human error and fallibility.

The Universal Age in the Nineteenth Century

In economic history, the late nineteenth century is a universal age, in which integration and progress went hand in hand.[14] At the beginning of his great novel of the last turn of the century, *Der Stechlin,* Theodor Fontane describes the remote Lake Stechlin: "Everything is quiet here. And yet, from time to time, just this place comes alive. That is when out there in the world, in Iceland or Java, the earth trembles and roars, or when the ash from a Hawaiian volcano rains down on the Pacific. Then the water here stirs, and a fountain shoots up and falls again."[15] Fontane regarded the changes of his age with an elegiac, sometimes nostalgic pathos. Most of his contemporaries were much more optimistic. But this dynamic and self-confident world was soon to break apart. The breakup destroyed the optimistic belief in cooperation across national boundaries, and indeed in human progress.

At the end of the nineteenth century, the world was highly integrated economically, through mobility of capital, information, goods, and people. Capital moved freely between states and continents. The movement of capital would not have been possible without improved mechanisms for spreading news and ideas. An integration of capital markets presupposed a means of knowing with at least some degree of certainty what was happening to that capital. Markets became interconnected as a result of improved communication. The first transatlantic cable was laid in 1866. The railroad opened up the interiors of continents and created national markets, while the steamship connected the shores of the world's great oceans. Already from 1838 there was a regular transatlantic service by steamship, although mass goods did not move in this way until the 1860s. In the subsequent decades, refrigeration made the transport of a wider range of foods possible.

Trade was largely unhindered, even in apparently protectionist states such as the German empire. Above all, people moved. They did not need passports. There were hardly any debates about citizenship. In a search for freedom, security, and prosperity—three values that are closely related— the peoples of Europe and Asia left their homes and took often uncomfortable journeys by rail and by ship, often as part of gigantic human treks. Between 1871 and 1915, 36 million people left Europe.[16] In the countries of immigration, the inflows brought substantial economic growth. At the same time, the countries left behind experienced large productivity gains as surplus (low-productivity) populations were eliminated. Such flows eased the desperate poverty of, among others, Ireland and Norway. The great streams of capital, trade, and migration were linked. Without the capital flows, it would have been impossible to construct the infrastructure—the railways, the cities—for the new migrants. The new developments created large markets for European engineering products as well as for consumer goods, textiles, clothing, musical instruments.

These interrelated flows helped to ensure a measure of global economic stability. Nearly fifty years ago the economist Brinley Thomas brilliantly demonstrated an inverse correlation between business cycles in Britain and the United States: slower economic growth in Britain helped to make the Atlantic passage more attractive. The new immigrants stimulated the American economy, and hence also British exports, and the British economy could revive.[17] Flows of labor and capital, as well as trade in goods, created a general market in which factor prices (the return on capital, land, and labor) were equalized. According to O'Rourke and Williamson, most (70 percent) of real-wage convergence in this period was explained by the integration of labor markets through migration, and the rest by international trade.[18]

This integrated world bears a close resemblance to our own. In our world also, the returns on capital are increasingly equalized. In rich industrial countries, labor is deeply troubled by the prospect of a globalization-induced lowering of real wages (especially for the unskilled).

Economists who have tried to find a statistical basis for a comparison of this first era of globalization with our own era are usually struck by the degree of similarity. How can we measure international integration? One way is to look at the size of net capital movements. Measured in relation to gross national product (GNP), both the imports and the exports of capital were much greater than today: between 1870 and 1890 Argentina imported capital equivalent to 18.7 percent of national income, and Australia 8.2 percent. Compare these figures with the 1990s, when the respective figures of these large capital importers were a meager 2.2 and 4 percent.[19] The story with exports of capital is even more dramatic. On the eve of the First World War, Great Britain was exporting 7 percent of its national income. No country in the post-1945 world has even approached such a level, not even Japan or the pre-1989 Federal Republic of Germany.

The trade comparison is only slightly less dramatic. For most countries, despite all the intervening improvements in the means of transportation, the levels of trade of the prewar world were not reached again until the 1980s. For Britain in 1913, the share of exports in GNP was around 30 percent. The rather lower German figure in 1913 of 20 percent was reached only in the early 1970s.[20]

But we do not need to look only at figures as an indicator of integration. We may also think of the standardization of the world, whereby railways in civilized countries ran on a track with a gauge of 4 feet 8.5 inches (the Russian empire's choice of a wider gauge was an early indication that Russia did not wish to follow a Western course). But there was also a standardization of products that anticipated the rise of the McDonald's hamburger as the icon of globalism. A whole world clothed itself in the cheap (and hygienic) cotton textiles of the type developed originally in Manchester. Women wanted to sew at home with machines made by the Singer Company.

Another approach to globalization is even more impressionistic, and relies on an examination of attitudes to internationalism. The optimism of the age can be used as a testimony to its internationalism or cosmopolitanism. Some analysts believed that the dynamic of integration was so great that it could not be halted by anything—indeed, that it made war between highly developed industrial states impossible. This attractive but eventually illusory proposition was formulated with great brilliance by the British writer Norman Angell in a book published in 1911, and immediately available (such was the extent of global intellectual integration) in fourteen countries and eighteen languages. Capitalists thought that their version of internationalism had made states so dependent on the bond market that they could not afford to give any shocks to business confidence. Socialists believed that the existence of a self-consciously international proletariat could frustrate the plans of the militarists.

The great drive to free trade treaties in the 1860s, which was launched by the Anglo-French treaty (often known as the Cobden-Chevalier treaty), was motivated in large part by commercial considerations, by a contemplation of the gains from trade. But Richard Cobden was a great liberal idealist, and in his belief enhanced commerce would bring peace. The sentiment seems to have been general, for on the conclusion of the Cobden-Chevalier treaty on 23 January 1860, the Prussian ambassador in London immediately reported that the treaty made war between the two countries "impossible."[21]

As the integrated, international world evolved it produced a response or reaction—at first an idea, and then the institutional embodiment of that idea. The realization of the implications of a global economy and an international society provoked a strong nationalism. Nationalism means at least two distinct processes. One is the formulation of identities and commonalities in response to an external threat or the perception of a threat. This sort of response can easily tip over into xenophobia. Second, there is a process of institution-building, justified in terms of the first response, in which the nation-state, the typical political construct of the nineteenth century, evolved as a defensive mechanism against threats to stability coming from the outside.

Backlashes and Reactions

In almost every country globalization almost immediately produced demands for protection from the effects of changes and crises coming from the outside. The nation-state, as we know it, is a response to the challenges of the first wave of globalization. The technical and economic change that came with globalization, and especially with improved communications, made possible the infrastructure of the modern nation-state.[22] Telegraphs, improved roads, railways, cheaper and more readily available printed material linked the new form of political unit. The technical changes also created the potential for more military power, and one of the functions of the nation-state was to act as a military protector against the enhanced power of other political units. But the nation-state began to have a new function.

The decades in which the world economy became interconnected were also the period of a gigantic change in political and social assumptions about what the state should do. States in the premodern era had as a primary goal military defense. Modern states were supposed to offer social defense as well. It was in 1863 that Adolph Wagner formulated his "law" of the rising activity of the public sector and the state.[23] Expectations about what the state should do rose at the same time as states opened themselves to international trade.[24] The new protection may even be regarded as a prerequisite for the process of economic opening, for without it there would have been a harsher and more destructive reaction against the new economic forces. In particular, the state should—it was believed—protect those who were threatened by foreign goods.

The nineteenth-century roots of the later reaction in the interwar period against the international economy can be demonstrated in precisely those three areas that were central to global interconnectivity: trade, migration, and capital movements. The purpose of the new tariffs in the later nineteenth century was often expressed in traditional terms, as not so much social as national defense. In public discussion, most attention focused on grain tariffs. Higher food prices for the consumer might be justified if the result of food protection was to increase the cultivated area, and thus raise the capacity of the state to defend itself in longer struggles against others in the competition of nations. But this argument then shaded into a social variant. Only an army based on a rural population, it was argued, could be effective; and so the farmer had to be preserved as a mainstay of military as well as of social order.

The adoption of protective tariffs in continental Europe was a direct response to the lower freight rates and falling grain prices of the 1870s. The price changes directly affected land prices, and thus the basis of political power in a feudal-agrarian world. Where agrarians were politically influential, they used every possible means of applying pressure and building coalitions for the protection of their interests. In making these coalitions, they reinterpreted the function of the nation-state, in terms of offering security for the victims of global events.

The most obvious response was trade protection, because goods were seen increasingly in national terms. In Britain in the 1880s, an almost hysterical reaction against the allegedly illegitimate competition of German producers focused on highly visible consumer goods, from picture postcards and Christmas cards to toys and musical instruments. The legislative response was a law, the 1887 Merchandise Marks Acts, which required products to be stamped with their country of origin. Similar legislation was soon adopted in many countries. But the protests went on—indeed they were fueled by the labeling. The author of a furious British polemic of 1896, E. E. Williams, who titled his diatribe *Made in Germany*, complained that when he started to write, he looked at his pencil and saw, to his horror, that it was "Made in Germany."[25] But Germany had an equally nationalistic response, which complained about the British trade envy ("Handelsneid").[26]

States also engaged in increased redistribution through the budget in response to greater social expectations of "protection." In France, social services accounted for 4.3 percent of central government expenditure in 1912, but 21.7 percent in 1928; the comparable figures for Germany are 5.0 percent and 34.2 percent. Correspondingly, total figures for government expenditure rose.[27]

Exports were often viewed as an alternative to the loss of population. Population policy constituted a key part of politics. It was the foundation for military power, and states with inadequate reproductive capacity, such as Third Republic France, feared that they were losing a military race. An adequate rate of demographic growth was required for economic growth—as the material basis for power—but also simply in order to provide a pool of recruits for armies. But how could this increasing human potential be productively employed? In the 1890s the German chancellor Leo von Caprivi had defended his attempts to liberalize trade policy by saying that the alternative would be pauperization and increased emigration. "We must export. Either we export goods or we export people."[28]

In this period, one response to trade crises and financial crises, both in the countries of mass immigration and in some industrial countries, was to restrict the movement of people. Citizenship and nationality, and the entitlements they brought with them, now became central elements in political discussions.

In Australia and the United States lower growth and the financial crises of the 1890s provoked mass protests against immigration. Australia began its strict "white Australia" policy. Americans complained that the new immigrants were replacing skilled native workers.[29] In 1897 the U.S. Congress debated a reading test for immigrants. Ten years later, a commission was established to find a way of restricting the "new immigrants" who were allegedly coming only for economic reasons and for a short time. In Canada, farmers protested against "the scum of Continental Europe; we do not want men and women who have behind them a thousand years of ignorance, superstition, anarchy, filth and immorality."[30]

Such resentment against foreign migrant workers also gripped some European countries. Germany in particular had become a country of immigration, with over a million foreign workers, especially in mining and in eastern agriculture. There was a clear demand: the Prussian Agricultural Ministry had indeed in 1890 commissioned a study on the feasibility of employing Chinese farm laborers in Germany.[31] But simultaneously the efforts to stop such inflows intensified. In 1885 the Prussian interior minister Robert von Puttkamer had ordered the exclusion of Polish temporary migrants, and immigration was rigorously controlled after 1887. The provincial governor of Westphalia ordered "suitable measures" to secure a "drastic" reduction in the number of Poles in the Westphalian industrial area.[32] Perhaps the most famous critic of the labor-policy implications of globalization was Max Weber. The arguments that he presented about the distributional consequences of admitting low-skill immigrants have a distinctly modern tone.

The integrated world, he argued, would necessarily produce a general lowering of economic and also of cultural standards. He explained his objections to immigration on the basis of different propensities to consume: since Polish workers were satisfied with poorer nutrition, their employment would be a danger to living standards in richer countries. "There is a certain situation of capitalistically disorganized economies, in which the higher culture is not victorious but rather loses in the existential fight with lower cultures."[33] This type of analysis of the dangers of globalization came to be a feature of the new left-liberal coalition that was forming at the beginning of the century.

What, then, of the third pillar of nineteenth-century globalization, the capital markets? The beginning of globalization in the last half of the century was also the beginning of attempts to regulate and control capital movements, especially when their volatility produced regular and massive financial crises. Capital did not flow in a smooth stream; rather, waves of exuberant overconfidence were followed by speculative collapses. In the 1820s large amounts of British capital went to the new South American republics, but in 1825 there was a default.[34] For the next decade, British money went to North America instead. A new wave of lending to South America in the 1850s and 1860s and then to the post–Civil War United

States was followed by collapse in 1873. Lending resumed, mostly for infrastructure investments in the 1880s, but there was a new and very severe crisis in 1890. The financial panics produced dramatic effects on the real economies, with output collapses comparable in scale to those that took place in crisis countries (mostly in East Asia) in the 1990s.[35]

Long-term capital movements were largely unregulated, with the exception of occasional efforts to promote or to block particular bond issues for political reasons. But from the beginning there were attempts to limit or offset the effects of short-term flows on monetary behavior and hence on price levels. The modern view, often forcefully expressed in the 1990s, that long-term movements are beneficial and short-term ones destabilizing, was widely held at the beginning of the age of globalization.

There were two central elements in the new approach to monetary policy: the linkage to the gold standard, and the creation of central banks or the extension of their powers. Before the 1870s, the gold standard as a monetary rule was followed only in Britain and Portugal: the adherence of the new German empire after passage of the currency laws of 1871 and 1873 created a momentum that made this a universal standard. In order to create confidence in their economic management, and thus to attract foreign funds, one country after another subsequently adopted the gold standard rule. It is worth noting that currency and money were more international before the adoption of a common international standard. Silver and gold coins circulated regardless of national frontiers. For instance, in Germany as late as the early 1870s, after national unification, almost a tenth of the coins in circulation were foreign.[36] The new currency order was a way of establishing a relationship between a new order of national moneys.

National central banks suddenly appeared to be necessary in order to manage these moneys. Thereafter central banks came to play a decisive part in the management of the monetary consequences of internationalization. The earliest central banks were essentially private creations, responding to a market need for clearing transactions.[37] But in the 1870s a new wave of central bank creation began, with a completely different purpose. The gold standard system is often treated in the literature as the high point of political and economic liberalism; in fact the debates about the gold standard and the institutions (notably central banks) that were believed necessary for its operation were about guiding and channeling capital to uses that were felt to be politically, militarily, diplomatically, and otherwise desirable. Russian loans, for instance, were given preferential access to French markets: the Foreign Ministry pleaded for special favoring of France's strategic ally, the press was bribed (in what a later analyst depicted as "l'abominable vénalité de la presse française"), and investors concluded that Russian government finances had been reconstructed on so sound a basis that default was unlikely. The gold standard was adopted in many countries in order to create international confidence—to be a "seal of approval" for good housekeeping, by limiting the scope for autonomous money creation and fiscal irresponsibility.[38] The new policy regime was intended to encourage international inflows of capital. At the same time central banks were established to use monetary instruments to regulate short-term flows and prevent disturbances.

Central banks had an important role to fill precisely because they could guide flows that would otherwise have been automatic. They were a response to financial panics and crises. The crisis brought home the lesson that the world marketplace was dangerous, with the potential to produce sudden and unexpected shifts in income and wealth. Wealthy private individuals or firms might play a part in stabilizing expectations and preventing panics. For much of the nineteenth century, the house of Rothschild took this function. In the United States at the end of the century, J. P. Morgan acted in a similar way; for instance, he put up enough gold to stop the panic of 1896–97. But such—fundamentally beneficial—activity in providing a public good (stability) came under increasing criticism as democratic politics came to be more dominant. Few people were prepared to say that they welcomed the accretion of massive personal fortune, even though such wealth was clearly required if the Rothschilds or Morgans were to play their helpful role. During the U.S. Civil War the Rothschilds and their American agent were subject to bitter attacks from the Republican party.[39] After the crisis of 1907, a campaign against J. P. Morgan began, based on the belief that Morgan had taken an illegitimate advantage of the crisis to augment his personal fortune, buying up shares of the Tennessee Coal and Iron company at a fraction of their real value. (Many nevertheless saw this deal as a key to breaking the financial panic of 1907, including President Theodore Roosevelt, who explained with reference to the Morgans that it was "to their interest, as to the interest of every responsible businessman, to try to prevent a panic and general industrial smashup at this time.")[40]

In Germany serious debate about a Reichsbank began after the major crash of 1873, in which bank failures destabilized the German economy. But they were also supposed to regulate the inflow and outflow of precious metals. The immediate impetus for the creation of the Reichsbank was the dramatic outflow of gold coinage in 1874. It was at this time that the concept of "guardian of the currency" ("Hüterin der Währung") began to be used. The international linkages created by gold required a new approach to monetary management.

The older central banks, and especially the venerable Bank of England, began to be much more concerned with their international activities, and with the protection of the British economy from the effects of external flows.

Like its German equivalent, the U.S. Federal Reserve System was born out of financial panic and international crisis. A speculative bubble collapsed in 1907. As New York banks faced demands for the payment of deposits, they restricted payments. In retrospect, most commentators felt that the banks neither needed to nor should have resorted to the suspension of payments that rapidly hit business conditions across the country. The consequence was that the function of lender of last resort needed to be a public responsibility, which could not be left to the presumed benevolence of the large New York private banks. In the past the United States had depended on a foreign liquidity provider of last resort, in complete conformity with the logic of the gold standard regime. In 1907, the crisis in New York and the resulting U.S. demand for gold led to gold outflows and increased discount rates in Europe, especially from London. The British financial system was in effect acting as a pool of liquidity for the United States, providing the functions normally associated with a central bank. When, in response to the 1907 crisis, the Federal Reserve Act came into force in 1914, the United States at last had a national monetary manager.

Other countries drew similar lessons from 1907: that the experience of crisis showed the limits of international cooperation and the need for more effective national intervention and control. In Germany the dangers of overconfidence were already evident in 1907. The atmosphere of panic in the City of London made bankers unwilling to lend, so that it was hard for German bankers to finance themselves in the usual way, and they turned instead to the Reichsbank.[41] But the German central bank also felt constrained in its actions in the international panic. On 77 out of 156 days in 1907 on which there was a stock-exchange notation, the Berlin quotation of the Mark exceeded the upper gold point, when gold exports became profitable for arbitrageurs. The reserves of the Reichsbank consequently fell, and the Reichsbank raised its discount rate repeatedly in October and November.[42]

One result of the 1907 panic in Germany was a new debate about what international action could be undertaken to prevent such worldwide crises of confidence—now made more nearly simultaneous because of the transfer of news through the transatlantic telegraph cable. Some past crises had been overcome cooperatively. In 1890, after a financial breakdown in Argentina and a threat to the London bank of Barings, the Bank of England had mastered the crisis by drawing on support organized by Rothschilds and the Banque de France.[43] Again in 1901, France had assisted Britain during the financial turmoils associated with the Boer War; and in 1907 the Banque de France had given an advance to the Bank of England and agreed to discount first-class American bills in order to help the New York market.[44] After 1907 Germans saw no possibility of similar actions, in part because of the magnitude and simultaneity of financial crises, but also in part because the deteriorating international political situation made foreign help look increasingly problematic. The 1911 crisis associated with Morocco was a telling example. In any case, Germany had played little part in the central bank cooperation of 1907, while at an early stage of the crisis even the Austrian National Bank had stepped in to supply the Bank of England and the Banque de France with gold.[45]

For not just goods were now interpreted in a national way, with demands for protection of the national economy. This discussion about national capital had been an important part of the debate about the working of a national institution such as the Reichsbank. The parties of the right feared that an international deflation, the consequence of the general adoption of gold as a monetary standard, would destroy the basis of their economic and political power. They now demanded a "silver wall around our golden treasure." Money should be national. One Reichstag deputy cited an old song: "What good to me is a beautiful girl, when other men go out promenading with her?"[46] When the agrarian leader Count Kanitz demanded interest-rate reductions in the Reichstag, he stressed the necessity of defending against an international danger: "the present crisis is so dangerous precisely because of its international character."[47]

With the spread of ideas about protection of goods and labor markets, but also of capital markets, the stage was set for the drama of a Great Depression. The perspectives of 1907 resembled those of 1929 in many ways: the search for more security, more welfare state in Europe and the United States, and more of a defense against predatory capital. But there was no dramatic drop in consumption—as occurred in the later crisis—which might have led to an even more dramatic institutional reordering. For the moment, the nation-state and the national central bank (the newest of which was the U.S. Federal Reserve System) appeared secure as the only possible defense against the harmful or destabilizing consequences of global technical change.

The Nineteenth Century and Its Sins

The great critical accounts of the economic transformations of the nineteenth century emphasize not only the tendency to autodestruction inherent in the transformative process of modern economic development, but also the problematical origins of the process. Karl Marx and his followers believed that he was uncovering the laws of motion of economic society. The falling rate of profit and the increased immiseration of the working population would eventually produce a final crisis. The final stage in this crisis was constituted by internationalization. To the extent to which this development played a central role in Marx's argument, Marx became the first systemic critic of globalism.

In a famous passage at the end of the first volume of *Capital*, Marx explained his principle of the increasing centralization of control and production. "This expropriation [of the capitalist] is accomplished by the action of the immanent laws of capitalistic production itself, by the centralization of capital. One capitalist kills many." The result was "the entanglement of all peoples in the net of the world market, and with this, the international character of the capitalistic regime. Along with the constantly diminishing number of the magnates of capital, who usurp and monopolize all advantages of this process of transformation, grows the mass of misery, oppression, slavery, degradation, exploitation."[48]

That final crisis also corresponds to a moral crisis, in that the spectacular successes of capitalism were based on previous theft and violence. Marx in his account of the origins of the modern economy gave enormous attention—far more than these episodes really warrant—to the English enclosures, the settlement of Ulster, and the Scottish highland clearances. These are the original sins of capitalism, which will always haunt the system: the economic term for original sin that Marx liked to use was "primitive capitalist accumulation." Without that accumulation, the product of violence, there would be no dynamism and growth. (In building a socialist society, the Soviet Union took something of this story as a model, and viewed the brutally violent expropriation of the kulaks as "primitive socialist accumulation.") The products of such brutality were transferred across national frontiers. "A great deal of capital, which appears today in the United States without any certificate of birth, was yesterday, in England, the capitalized blood of children."[49]

In the final stages of capitalism, financial speculation would become ever more prominent and controlling over the real economy. By the third volume of *Capital*, Marx was exploding with rage about finance capital:

> Talk about centralization! The credit system, which has its focus in the so-called national banks and the big money-lenders and usurers surrounding them, constitutes enormous centralization, and gives to this class of parasites the fabulous power, not only to periodically despoil industrial capitalists, but also to interfere in actual production in a most dangerous manner—and this gang knows nothing about production and has nothing to do with it. The [English Bank] Acts of 1844 and 1845 are proof of the growing power of these bandits, who are augmented by financiers and stock-jobbers.[50]

So far, it might be thought that Marx's account reads just like many of the countless tracts of the 1990s on the evils of uncontrolled global integration. A standard feature of many of the complaints is the power of financial speculators. Even Paul Krugman notes: "No individuals or small groups could really affect the currency value of even a middle-sized economy, could they? Well, maybe they could. One of the most bizarre aspects of the economic crisis of the last few years has been the prominent part played by 'hedge funds' . . . in at least a few cases, the evil speculator has staged a comeback."[51]

The evil speculator is a standard figure of all dramas of financial crisis. In the nineteenth century he became almost a stock literary figure, across national frontiers, from August Melmotte in Anthony Trollope's *The Way We Live Now* (1874–75), to Friedrich Spielhagen's Philipp Schmidt in *Storm Flood* (1877) (both creatures of the panic of 1873), and Frank Algernon Cowperwood in Theodore Dreiser's *The Financier* (1912). Politicians eagerly took up the stereotypes. In 1907 President Roosevelt complained that "certain malefactors of great wealth" were attempting to use the panic to destroy his administration's policies "so that they may enjoy unmolested the fruits of their evil-doing."[52] In introducing one of the score of biographies of the most famous of interwar speculators, the Swedish "Match King" Ivar Kreuger, John Kenneth Galbraith explained of the weaknesses that led to vulnerability in the face of financial crime: "no one should imagine that they were confined in time and place to New York of the twenties."[53] Much of the initial commentary on the depression, even from serious economists such as Lionel Robbins, laid a great deal of the blame on the "proliferation of fashionable fraud" and "speculation."[54] When British prime minister Harold Wilson felt his government's policies were being undermined in the 1960s, he blamed the "gnomes of Zurich."

But there is substantially more nuance to Marx's argument. He was very explicit in developing the religious analogy underlying his analogy:

> Primitive accumulation plays in Political Economy about the same part as original sin in theology. Adam bit the apple, and thereupon sin fell on the human race . . . The capitalist system presupposes the complete separation of the laborers from all property in the means by which they can realize their labor. As soon as capitalist production is once on its own legs, it not only maintains this separation, but reproduces it on a continually extending scale. The process, therefore, that clears the way for the capitalist system, can be none other than the process which takes away from the laborer the possession of his means of production; a process that transforms, on the one hand, the social means of subsistence and of production into capital, on the other, the immediate producers into wage-laborers.[55]

Richard Wagner's operatic Tetralogy, the *Ring of the Nibelungs,* has—as George Bernard Shaw pointed out—considerable parallels to the mental world of Marx. The system is bound to destroy itself, because it was constructed by the gods—chiefly by Wotan—on the basis of laws, which the gods cannot break without undermining the reason for their own existence. Hence the best the gods can do is to reconcile themselves to the inevitability of a collapse. In the critical second act of the *Valkyrie,* Wotan explodes in frustrated rage and calls for a final cataclysm, "Das Ende." At the same time, Wotan is obliged to recognize that the world he created is based on theft, even if originally it was someone else's theft: the dwarf Alberich steals the gold of the Rhine from the Rhine maidens (that is, the state of nature), and then Wotan conspires to steal the gold from Alberich. This was a similar sort of parable to that offered in Marx's *Capital,* in which both creativity and crime begin when a dwarf seizes gold from the Rhine maidens and endowed it with a curse. The gold is supposed to bring absolute power; but the dwarf loses the gold to Wotan, who uses it to pay two giants, one of whom then kills the other to steal the gold. The giant, trans-formed into a huge dragon, is killed by the hero, who gives the ring to a woman, but then seizes it back again when he wants to give the woman to someone else, and is himself killed for the gold ring. Only at this stage do the waters of the Rhine rise up, fill the stage, and allow the Rhine maidens to reclaim the ring from the last murderer. In total, the operas involve seven thefts, one dubious purchase, and one gift (in order to purchase love, which the curse tells us is the one feat that the gold cannot perform). Wag-ner creates a model of the economy as a flow of goods and services, medi-ated by gold that is stolen as much as it is traded.

The late-nineteenth-century British conservative politician and thinker Robert Cecil, third marquis of Salisbury, wrote from the standpoint of a reactionary about how the increase of industry and commerce—the strik-ing feature of the globalized world at whose center Britain then was—gen-erated more and more protests about inequality. The new inequalities were particularly hard to bear because, unlike those of a traditional and aristo-cratic age, they could never appear simply irrational, the product of time, and thus quite independent of the personal merits and endeavors of an in-dividual. In the modern age, Salisbury believed, "the flood of evils wells up ceaselessly." By the 1880s, he had become bitterly pessimistic:

> Vast multitudes have not had a chance of accumulating, or have ne-glected it; and whenever the stream of prosperity slackens for a time, pri-vation overtakes the huge crowds who have no reserve, and produces widespread suffering. At such times the contrasted comfort or luxury of a comparatively small number becomes irritating and even maddening to look upon, and its sting is sharpened by the modern discoveries which have brought home to the knowledge of every class the doings of its neighbours. That organizer of decay, the Radical agitator, soon makes his appearance under these conditions.

Jealousy on a class basis was, in this semi-Marxist analysis, the inevitable consequence of development and led to "political debility" and "disinte-gration"—in short, to an end of the world that had permitted the indus-trial and commercial riches in the first place.[56]

The stories that the nineteenth century told about the global world built on a secular concept of original sin. The remedy that many thinkers then provided to the illegitimacy of the system echoed Luther's quite precisely (in a secular manner). Strong public authority was needed to overcome the legacy of that sin. There was a natural community that had been broken apart by creative greed, but the state could create its own order and community, and thus channel the destructive forces of dynamic capitalism. This strategy would offer the only way of avoiding the apocalyptic crises prophesied by a Marx or a Wagner or a Lord Salisbury. A powerful national and political bulwark alone could contain the evils of an unstable world.

Did the guns of August 1914 explode belief in the desirability of international society? It was certainly harder to be optimistic. But after the horrors of the war it was also hard not to have a nostalgic yearning for the internationalism and the security of the prewar world. The hope of the peacemakers was a "return to normalcy": the old certainties should be restored. But at the same time they should be secured and institutionalized through international institutions, such as the Covenant and the League of Nations, and through treaties, such as the permanent pact of peace concluded at the initiative of U.S. secretary of state Frank Kellogg and French foreign minister Aristide Briand. Such a framework would allow the markets to operate; and indeed international capital resumed its flow. George Grosz in a memorable caricature saw the dollar as the sun that warmed the European continent. Migrations resumed. And markets, it was assumed, would make peace: every observer of the 1920s was struck, for instance, by how dependence on foreign capital imports made eccentric, destructive, and belligerent figures such as the Italian leader Benito Mussolini into responsible and even pacific statesmen.

Rarely had there been so much enthusiasm for internationalism and international institutions as in the 1920s. The standard British textbook on European history of the interwar years concluded, after a long comparison of the virtues of the League of Nations with the flaws of the post-1815 Congress system: "As we balance hopes against fears we may derive some comfort from the study of history which shows that some such organisation as is given by the League is at once necessary, reasonable, and possible."[57]

The new League of Nations oversaw financial stabilizations, combining rigorous policy reform imposed from without with economic assistance in a way that anticipated the post-1945 International Monetary Fund. The Bank for International Settlements coordinated the actions of central banks. Trade negotiations were no longer bilateral, as they had been in the case of such famous landmarks of liberalization as the Cobden-Chevalier treaty, but were conducted within a framework of large international conferences, usually organized by the League.

None of these attempts was really successful. Given the catastrophes of the late 1920s, it is tempting to think that an excessive idealism about internationalism may have played a role in the collapse. All the beliefs—part hopes, part illusions—in the restoration of one market-driven world by means of international institutional engineering were destroyed by the experience of the Great Depression. In the 1930s the world descended into economic nationalism and protectionism. There were competitive devaluations. Autarky and war economy became national goals.

The devastation of that depression still exercises a colossal fascination. In the second half of the century, whenever there was an interruption to growth or a threat to prosperity, many people asked themselves whether we were not once more back in the grips of the Great Depression. In the mid-1970s, the recession that followed from the sudden quadrupling of oil prices was taken as a new world crisis, combining a threat to the economy with a threat to political democracy. The lessons learned from the Great Depression at that time involved the desirability of a Keynesian demand stimulus. At the beginning of the 1980s, a recession in the industrial world and the Latin American debt crisis led to a new wave of pessimistic forecasts, and a new interest in the history of depression. Then the lesson was lower interest rates. In October 1987 in analyzing the stock-exchange collapse, almost every major newspaper printed charts juxtaposing the developments of 1929 and 1987. Again, after the outbreak of an Asian crisis in 1997, and the contagion effects in Russia and then in Brazil, the parallels to 1929 recurred. Helmut Schmidt, who as chancellor in the 1970s had been terrified of the possibility of a replication of the Great Depression, for instance now wrote: "The main parallel lies in the helplessness of many governments, which had not noticed in time that they had been locked in a financial trap, and now have no idea of how they might escape."[58] Academic analysts have loved these parallels too. A chart showing the number of academic articles on the depression reveals a striking parallelism to the economic development of Western economies. We are constantly concerned with the possibility of a repetition of the breakdown of globalization.

In the 1920s previously successful remedies were applied once more. There was a dangerous interplay between monetary policy and trade policy

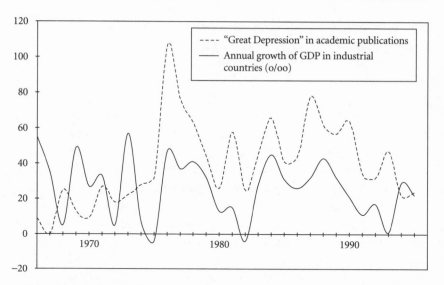

GREAT
GRAPH!

Figure 1.1 Correlation of journal articles on the Great Depression and general economic conditions
(Sources: calculated from Social Science Citation Index and IMF, *International Financial Statistics* (Washington, D.C.), various issues)

and migration law. In each area, the state needed to respond to raised demands and expectations for state activism; but policy in one area often had to grapple with the consequences of other policies. Monetary policy on an international level was destabilizing. With prices fluctuating more dramatically, the results of tariff protection and other trade policy measures were much more harmful than in the relatively stable prewar world. As monetary policy and trade policy produced suboptimal outcomes, the pressure for restrictions on migration increased.

How and why did the interwar depression turn back the push of globalization? There were high hopes of what the state and the economy might deliver: a wish for prosperity on command.[59] The search for new means of securing integration ended in the late 1920s with a series of shocks.

First, since the middle of the 1920s, raw material prices had been falling, in part as a consequence of the extension of the area of production during the world war, in part as a result of inept schemes for price manipulation, such as the Stevenson scheme, which aimed to keep an artificially high rubber price. This price decline made the situation for many capital-importing countries more difficult. But from the perspective of the industrial countries, the results appeared beneficial, since raw materials and foods—at that time a much larger component of household budgets than currently—were cheaper. With additional available income, consumers might buy new products. Such calculations sustained the giddy glitter of the jazz age.

Second, the international political situation in Europe was burdened by an impossible conflict over war debts and reparations. Impossible, because the more credits flowed, the more inextricable the situation became. Germany was supposed to pay a substantial part of the burden of the war through the reparations imposed under the Versailles Treaty. France needed reparations not only to reconstruct, but also to pay the wartime debt to Britain and the United States. Germany—that is, German corporations and the German public sector—borrowed substantial sums largely on the American market; this borrowing financed at least indirectly the reparations payments. But as the payments were made through the second half of the 1920s, it became increasingly apparent that this was not a game that could be played forever: that at one moment, there would come a choice when either the United States could continue to receive reparation payments or U.S. creditors could have their private loans serviced. At least some German policymakers, notably Hjalmar Schacht, president of the Reichsbank, made this calculation in all cynicism, in the belief that the resulting debacle would demonstrate the folly of reparations. The reassessment of the reparations burden in 1929, in which at last a final term was set for the payment of reparation (payments were to continue until 1988), made clear to more investors the impossible nature of their bet, and Germany's chances of external credit deteriorated dramatically.[60]

Third, there was a tendency to react to economic problems in the 1920s by trade measures. The model for this was the U.S. Fordney-McCumber tariff act of 1922. It was not that the level of protection was especially high (most analysts now see that the overall level of protection was actually lower than before the First World War). But the possibility that such measures might be applied in response to other, financial problems, and the increased popularity of nontariff protection (quotas) made for a greater restriction of trade. Governments were more responsive to popular pressures because of the extension of the suffrage and the increased level of political mobilization that followed the First World War.

There were plenty of economic problems in the world before the dramatic collapse of Wall Street in October 1929. Australia, with its dependence on exported wool, and Brazil, almost exclusively reliant on coffee exports, were deeply depressed. In Germany cyclical production indicators had already turned down in the autumn of 1927 (the stock market weakness appeared even earlier). What produced the crash of 1929 in the United States is still mysterious, at least for believers in the rationality of markets. What did stock market investors know on "Black Thursday," 24 October 1929, that they had not known on Tuesday or Wednesday? There had been "bad news" since early September, and the weight of evidence had accumulated to such an extent that there was a panic in the face of the likelihood of the decline of stock prices. The only plausible answer for those who wish a rational account of the stock market collapse is that American investors were contemplating the likelihood of the implementation of a new piece of legislation, which went under the names of Hawley and Smoot. This tariff bill had begun as a promise by Herbert Hoover in the presidential campaign of 1929 to improve the situation of the American farmer (with the agricultural price collapse, the farmer was the major loser of jazz-age prosperity). In the course of congressional debate, however, each representative tried to add new items (there were 1,253 Senate amendments alone). The result—a tariff with 21,000 tariff positions—was extreme protectionism; but worse, until the final narrow vote in June 1930, there was constant uncertainty about the future of trade policy.

But if the story of the depression does not begin with the stock market crash and Hawley-Smoot, neither does it end there. There were some signs of recovery in 1930: stock prices in the United States rebounded, and the lower level of the market made foreign issues appear attractive again.

What made the depression the *Great* Depression rather than a short-lived stock market problem or a depression for commodity producers was a chain of linkages that operated through the financial markets. The desperate state of the commodity producers along with the reparations-induced problems of Germany set off a domino reaction. In this sense the depression was directly a product of disorderly financial markets.

Is the fragility of the financial mechanism enough to explain the extent of the subsequent economic crisis? The financial catastrophe brought back all the resentments and reactions of the nineteenth century, but in a much more militant and violent form. Instead of a harmonious liberal vision of an integrated and prosperous world, beliefs about the inevitability of conflict and importance of national priorities gripped populations and politicians. They now talked about enrichment at the expense of others—what critics then termed "beggar thy neighbor" or now call a zero-sum approach. The domestic and international tensions that followed destroyed the mechanisms and institutions that had kept the world together, and precluded any effective institutional reform. The reaction against the international economy put an end to globalization.

2

◆

Monetary Policy
and Banking Instability

This chapter examines the financial links between an international economic system and domestic economies. The world depression of the late 1920s and early 1930s was an era of budgetary orthodoxy. In most countries, governments reacted to declining prices and economic activity with attempts to balance budgets, with a deflationary result: the reduction in aggregate demand intensified the process of decline, and in this way the public economy played a major role in the transmission of deflation (and thus depression) across nations.

Governments felt powerless in stabilizing expectations because of three circumstances. First, financial and banking systems were volatile and vulnerable to panic. The less stable the banking system, the greater the implicit fiscal liability, as governments were expected to tackle the damage inflicted on the economy by failed banks, but also the greater the helplessness of the government. Second, there existed no agreement or consensus about what governments should do domestically. What consensus might have existed previously evaporated during the depression. Third, there was an increasing consensus that the true function of government was an international one, to externalize adjustment costs (less politely, to make the foreigner pay).

At the outset of the story, countries looked very different from one another in terms of economic potentials and problems. But after the financial panic had set in, each country looked unhappy in a pretty standard way. Fiscal and financial crises reinforced each other: fiscal difficulties led to capital flight, and the withdrawal of capital weakened banks and created a potential or actual fiscal burden. Banking problems thus led to fiscal problems, because the cost of taking over bad banks strained the budget.

But budget imbalances were interpreted by investors, foreign and domestic, as meaning that there were limits to the government's ability realistically to offer support for banks, and that it was therefore time to get out.

The story of differing national origins of a crisis that would eventually become a regional and then a global one is familiar from analyses of the crises of the 1990s, in which "twin crises"—banking and financial—reinforced each other but developed along particular paths.[1] Thus Thailand in 1997 had a problem primarily because of the unsoundness of its banking system. Malaysia had experienced an asset boom (or bubble), along with a surge of public-sector investment, and although the bubble had burst in 1993, the banks camouflaged their bad loans. Korea had a very high foreign currency debt and insolvent conglomerates (chaebols), with a wave of corporate bankruptcies beginning in January 1997; but the foreign debt crisis occurred nearly twelve months later, when the threat that foreign short-term bank debt could not be rolled over set off a general flight. These different experiences of crisis and the threat of crisis rested on two common bases: a surge in foreign lending in the first half of the 1990s, including loans to banks that had a weak capital structure; and an approach to exchange-rate policy in which a fixed rate encouraged capital inflows taking advantage of interest-rate differentials. In these modern crises, the monetary authorities—like their interwar predecessors—faced impossible choices. They could attempt to defend their currency by interest-rate increases, but this course risked damaging the domestic credit structure, as borrowing would become impossibly expensive and lead to a wave of domestic bankruptcies. Alternately, they could abandon foreign-exchange pegs and let their currencies slide. This approach would damage the banks and corporations that had borrowed cheaply in foreign currency and then lent in domestic currency. A devaluation would be likely to lead to further currency declines as the effect on the corporate sector became apparent, and massive capital flight would follow. These modern policy dilemmas have precise analogues in the unpleasant character of policy choices available at the beginning of the 1930s.

The hopelessness of the situation in the interwar period not surprisingly led to a way of thinking about depressions that emphasized irrational or psychological factors. Such interpretations, which have been popular at regular intervals (often coinciding with depressions), depend on a belief that markets are driven by psychological and nonrational calculations.

The mechanism of financial panic played a crucial role in linking the depressions in the capital-importing world (the "emerging markets" of the 1920s) and the capital exporters (the advanced industrial countries, in particular Britain, the United States, and France). Modern writing on the transmission of crises and on early-warning signals of potential banking problems emphasizes that an important and reliable sign of an imminent financial problem is the extent of banks' overseas short-term liabilities. Banks are especially vulnerable in the aftermath of inflations, hyperinflations, and financial liberalizations that may attract large sums of foreign capital. In their function as capital exporters, the large industrial countries also received extensive short-term deposits from the countries to which they lent. This exposure to risk played a major role in the development of a second stage of the crisis.

The following sections examine why international action and coordination of policy responses against the forces of depression and deflation were so ineffective, why crises converged in the emerging markets, and how panic spread to the industrial world and the dominoes began to topple, one by one.

The Weakness of the International System

The international financial system of the interwar period was more ordered and regulated than the nostalgically celebrated prewar gold standard. Whereas the nineteenth-century gold standard had evolved by accident, because in the 1870s Germany and the United States chose a gold-based currency, and thus created a bandwagon effect,[2] the restoration of gold in the 1920s corresponded to a plan. This plan, elaborated most clearly in 1922 at the Genoa international monetary conference, involved: gold convertibility, the establishment of independent central banks, the disciplining of fiscal policy, conditional financial assistance for countries on the margins of the system, and the continued cooperation of central banks in the management of the system.

Gold Convertibility

Peter Temin's survey of the depression, and Barry Eichengreen's monumental history of the "golden fetters" that limited policy, attribute the severity of the Great Depression to the policy adjustments required in the aftermath of the adoption of a restored gold (or gold-exchange) standard.[3]

The question Temin raises is a variety of the old "confidence" chestnut: the gold standard was seen as an essential part of confidence, but it also created a framework in which confidence mattered more. Would it have been more reassuring to have a system less dependent on psychology, in which flexible (or floating or free) exchange rates increased the risks for speculators playing the game of "confidence"? John Kenneth Galbraith had already identified the false pursuit of the chimera of confidence as a crucial weakness of interwar economics, "the dangerous cliché that in the financial world everything depends on confidence."[4]

Such was in fact the immediate postwar situation, from which Europe struggled painfully to emerge after the early 1920s. It proved inflationary, and unconducive to long-term international flows of productive investment.

In the early 1920s, as inflation ravaged large parts of Europe and violent revolution, civil war, and even new international conflicts seemed imminent, "experts" and politicians met in conference at Genoa. They set out to work out a way of restoring the old order: bringing domestic and international peace by the expansion of trade and the stabilization of currencies. At the heart of the new version of how to create postwar stability was the resurrection of a functioning international payments system, for without it, hopes for greater international trade would be as futile as those for domestic stability. The experts at Genoa intended the gold-exchange standard to be as little deflationary and as painlessly inflationary as possible, since in the early 1920s even the dullest analysts saw inflation as a way—though not a costless one—of reducing social tensions.

A subsequent paper produced by the Bank for International Settlements described the system devised by the Genoa experts as having an "undeniable tendency towards credit expansion," since the international stock of currency reserves was much increased by the inclusion of key currencies (sterling and the dollar) as well as metallic money.[5] In fact some countries, notably Japan, had already maintained an exchange standard before the war. This step had represented a considerable economy, in that reserves could be held in the form of commercial or treasury bills, normally in London, rather than as unproductive and non-interest-bearing gold.

The experts who devised schemes such as that of Genoa were supposed to offer neutral, apolitical, or at best depoliticized advice and solutions. A decade later the Swedish economist Per Jacobsson gave a fine but disenchanted definition of what this expertise involved: an expert was "a man who can express the opinion of his Government in technical terms."[6] The postwar inflations that they were expected to solve had a technical and immediate cause—unbalanced budgets—but also a much broader political and social background. The experts realized this well. One of the most intelligent observers, the director of the League of Nations Economic and Financial Section, Sir Arthur Salter, told the U.S. Senate's Commission of Gold and Silver Enquiry: "There is still sometimes too great a disposition to regard inflation as merely a financial vice, a sort of post war Finance Minister's drug habit. It is too little recognized that it was in many cases the only practicable method of avoiding social collapse in the conditions left immediately after the War. Inflation is, in my view, the practically inevitable complement of war and post war [domestic] loans after these passed a certain proportion of the national income or annual taxable capacity of a country."[7]

The experts' solutions aimed at creating an automatic mechanism that could control the instincts of political parties and pressure groups to push for the continual expansion of state expenditure even while demanding reduced taxation. Budget balancing, imposed through external constraints, meant a limitation on the political process and on national sovereignty. It was in the latter sense that fiscal orthodoxy formed a part of the creation of the new international order of the 1920s.

The pleasing ambiguity of the gold-exchange standard, which helped to secure its political acceptability, was that it provided at the same time a restraint and an element of international order, and also that no one could tell quite how restraining it would turn out to be. Its charm lay precisely in that it seemed to offer a dry path between the two ditches of inflation and deflation.

Independent Central Banks

The doctrine of central banking held that monetary authorities should be independent of governments so that they would not need to respond to political pressures. They should run monetary policy in accordance, not with domestic priorities, but rather with the requirements of the international system.

The most forthright exponent of this theory, the long-serving governor of the Bank of England, Montagu Norman, made quite explicit the political role that the central bank needed to play:

Central Banking is young and experimental and has no tradition: it may last and may develop, or its usefulness, to fill a short post-war need and no more, may soon come to an end. On the one hand its sphere is limited by the qualification that no Central Bank can be greater than its own State—the creature greater than the creator. On the other hand, a Central Bank should acquire by external help (as in some ex-enemy countries) or by internal recognition (as in France) a certain freedom or independence within, and perhaps without, its own State. By such means alone can real co-operation be made possible. I cannot define the position thus acquired but it should surely permit a Bank to "nag" its own Government even in public and to decide on questions on other than political grounds.[8]

Central banks were to be established before a country stabilized on gold in order to prepare the institutional ground. The Brussels Conference made the same point as Norman when it concluded in 1920, "Banks and especially Banks of Issue should be free from political pressure and should be conducted only on lines of prudent finance."[9] The constitutions of the new banks were thus framed with clear political objectives. Norman made the point quite explicit: "It seems evident that the limitations imposed on new or reorganised [Central] banks during the last few years arise more from the fear and mistrust of political interference than from the needs of Central Banking as such."[10]

But it was not just vis-à-vis their governments that central banks needed independence: they were also threatened by the claims of their commercial banking systems. As continental central banks fueled inflation by cheap rediscounting of bills (the German Reichsbank raised its rate only in 1922, long after the inflation had become hyperinflation), Norman declared: "A Central Bank should protect its own traders from the rapacity of other banks in his own country."[11]

The new central banks of the interwar years included those associated with currency stabilization schemes in Austria, Hungary, and Germany; but the principle was extended throughout the world. Chile had a new bank in 1926, Argentina in 1936, and in Brazil commission after commission staffed with British or American advisers recommended the introduction of this institution. Canada established its bank in 1935.

The central bank governors saw themselves as members of a club, engaging in friendly and intimate relationship with one another. "You are a dear queer old duck and one of my duties seems to be to lecture you now and then," wrote Benjamin Strong of the Federal Reserve Bank of New York to Montagu Norman.[12] In particular Strong, Norman, and their German colleague Hjalmar Horace Greeley Schacht shared a similarity of outlook and behavior. After Strong's death in 1928 from complications following from tuberculosis, his successor, George Harrison, never recaptured the imagination or loyalty of his European colleagues. Five years after Strong's departure, Schacht wrote to Norman: "I feel most strongly that, after the death of our American friend, you and I are the only two men who understood what had to be achieved."[13] France, which stabilized relatively late, remained on the edge of the charmed circle of bankers.

The Disciplining of Fiscal Policy

The immediate purpose of the adoption of the gold-exchange standard and the strengthening of central banks was control of fiscal policy. It was an ambitious effort, because the whole foundation of nineteenth-century prudent public finance had been destroyed by the Great War. No country could finance a total twentieth-century war through taxation. In every state, the major source of war finance had been borrowing—either through bond issues or, as governments became increasingly desperate, through short-term issuing of treasury bills. As a consequence, every state emerged with a high public debt: the Russian empire's increased by a factor of four, Italy's and France's by five, Germany's by eight, Britain's by eleven, and that of the United States (where there had been only a very small public debt before the war) by nineteen.[14] In addition to the cost of servicing this debt, the legacy of war inevitably brought new expenditures. The most obvious were the pensions for war widows and for those crippled in battle.

After the war there appeared to be a stark choice: either to revert to fiscal rigor or to wipe out the national debt with inflation. The first required a conviction that sacrifice could be imposed without provoking revolution. Measures such as the British "Geddes Axe," the report of 1922 by a committee on public expenditure under Sir Eric Geddes, recommended military cuts, reductions in educational spending, and the abolition of five government departments. Continental Europe, with stronger left wing and revolutionary movements, largely felt unable or unwilling to take such action, and opted for inflation instead. But this too had an immense—and rising—social and political cost. Alone in central Europe, the Czechoslovak finance minister Alois Rašin tried to found his new state on the basis of a sound currency. As surrounding states collapsed in inflationary disasters, capital flooded into Czechoslovakia and drove up the exchange rate. The Czech crown rose in value against the stable Swiss franc from 5 centimes to 20 centimes in September 1922. Such a real appreciation did great damage, and Rašin became massively unpopular. In January 1923 he was assassinated.[15]

Given such political constraints, an externally imposed stabilization—with the gold standard as a nominal anchor—looked like the only way of explaining to a domestic audience why fiscal expansion had to stop.

Conditional Financial Assistance

The first stabilizations that reflected this new "expert" and "apolitical" order occurred in Austria and Hungary after the initial breakdown of the Paris peace treaties.[16] Both countries were in a hopeless position, and it soon became apparent that they could not pay war reparations. In May 1921 the Allied governments had wound up the Austrian section of the Reparations Commission. The next year the League of Nations devised a stabilization scheme for Austria involving the floating of a foreign loan, the issue of a new currency (schilling), the creation of an independent central bank, and above all the imposition of financial control by a League commissioner, the Dutchman Dr. Alfred Zimmermann, who would control the distribution of League funds. Many public revenues would go directly to the commissioner rather than to the Austrian government. The immediate price to be paid—to show that austerity was being implemented—involved the dismissal of 100,000 Austrian civil servants.

Hungary had a similar scheme, devised in December 1923, again with a bank of issue, a new pengö currency, a 7.5 percent League loan of 250 million gold crowns ($50 million), a League commissioner (Jeremiah Smith), a British adviser to the national bank, and an austerity program agreed in consultation with the League. By 1925, 25,000 Hungarian government jobs had been suppressed.[17]

The economic situation of Hungary was slightly better than that of Austria, but the political position was worse, with a revolutionary Communist dictatorship in 1919 whose rule had been ended only by an invasion of the Rumanian army. In its place came a right-wing authoritarian regime, which the League's spokesman termed "strong, stable, and drastic." The international politics of the Hungarian stabilization were also more difficult. Before the package was complete, the League needed to consult not only with the great powers but also with Hungary's angry and in part unstable neighbors, Rumania, Yugoslavia, and Czechoslovakia. Clause VI of the scheme devised by the League Financial Committee stipulated "satisfactory political relations between Hungary and her neighbors."[18]

These schemes for Austria and Hungary, which indeed halted inflation and transferred the blame for this costly operation from the national government to the international organization, provided a model for later stabilizations.[19] But so great was the political humiliation that no other government was willing to go to the League. Subsequent stabilizations, such as that of Germany, were worked out by the great powers or—increasingly—by the private capital markets. The League complained bitterly that the availability of bank money was undermining its attempt to restore general principles of fiscal rectitude. "If American money is going to be made available in this way," the senior League financial official wrote, "we must either expect to have come pretty well to the end of our financial reconstruction or we must have some effective way of bringing American banking into our organisation."[20] The whole process was similar to that of modern developing countries running away from the allegedly harsh terms of the IMF and finding private-sector lenders more complaisant.

The most controversial stabilization, as well as the most significant in terms of its international implications, occurred in Germany after the creeping inflation of the war and immediate postwar period and then the hyperinflation of 1922–23. In stabilizing Germany, international politics loomed large. In 1923 France tried to detach the Rhineland from Germany by making overtures to German businessmen and drawing up a plan for a separate Rhineland currency. The French government hoped thus to use the might of finance to answer its security concerns. The German government responded to the French move by treating currency stabilization, for the first time, as an issue of pressing importance and by begging for British assistance. It approached the London capital market and set up a new central banking institution with a capital base in pounds sterling, at a time when the pound had not yet returned to a fixed gold parity.

The superior financial power of the United States and the evident German need for external capital inflows destroyed the prospect of a Mark stabilized on a sterling base. The eventual scheme adopted on the recommendation of the Dawes Committee of 1924 envisaged a return to a gold currency and assistance in the form of an international dollar loan.[21] This marked the beginning of an era of dollar hegemony. The American financier Paul Warburg, one of the founders of the Federal Reserve System, wrote to Owen Young, a member of the Dawes Committee: "The opportunity that the present emergency in Europe offers is unique, and I don't believe that it will ever again be within as easy a grasp of the United States as it is today. It is the question of whether the Dollar shall permanently retain a dominant position, or whether we are willing to surrender financial mastery to the Pound Sterling for good and all."[22]

The German stabilization with a new currency, the Reichsmark, on a dollar base, together with an announcement that South Africa, then the world's major gold producer, would return to a gold standard by May 1925, forced Britain's hand. On 25 May 1925 the pound returned to the prewar parity against the dollar of $4.86. Sterling stabilization meant the effective end of a period of financial chaos in which only a few currencies—those of Mexico and the United States—had been linked to gold. The Belgian franc returned to gold in October 1925, the Danish crown and the Italian lira in 1926. In August 1926 the French franc was pegged, and a legal stabilization followed in June 1928. By the end of 1928 the gold-exchange standard had spread to thirty-one countries.

The gold-exchange standard represented the best way of providing such guarantees of stability as might allow large international capital flows to occur. Debates about whether the gold standard was an optimal system of management of international payments often miss the point that investors demanded such a system, with its stability and its constraints on the operation of sovereign monetary and financial policies. Its attractions lay precisely in the limitations it imposed on policy options.

International Central Bank Cooperation

Norman and Strong engineered first a system of informal cooperation among central banks. Later that cooperation was criticized for obliging countries and central banks to act against their own national interest for the sake of a vaguely conceived good of the international order, which would be soon undermined by specific national problems. In particular, in 1927, at a private meeting at the house of the U.S. Treasury secretary in Long Island, the European central banks persuaded Strong that Europe desperately needed an interest-rate reduction. Strong's acceptance of this argument was later criticized as a cause of the asset bubble of the Wall Street boom.

Such cooperation rested on the precarious footing of the personal sympathies of Norman and Strong. When Strong died, in October 1928, Norman was frightened of financial destabilization. He tried to reach out to Strong beyond the grave, and invented the Bank for International Settlements as a way of achieving this economic spiritualism.

The Bank for International Settlements (BIS) had two purposes, which its founders may have intended to be complementary, but which proved instead to be quite contradictory. On the one hand, the Bank was supposed to end the politicization of the reparations issue, which had plagued the international financial system of the 1920s, and to provide a neutral, "market" solution. On the other hand, the Bank would act as an instrument of central bank cooperation, making the international capital markets less volatile. In effect, as a central bankers' central bank, it was intended as a sort of world central bank.

The fact that this was in practice a "reparations bank" ensured that France and Britain would be locked in conflict about its role and function. Norman, more than the British Foreign Office, regarded reparations as pernicious and saw the Bank as a valuable instrument in demonstrating the absurdity of the entire concept. France—and the Banque de France shared this sentiment—saw the Bank as a means to guarantee the continuation of German payments for French reconstruction until the date (1988) established in the Young Plan adopted by the international conferences in The Hague. This conflict poisoned Franco-British discussions of monetary policy, and more generally—and with very long-lasting effects—brought about an intellectual bankruptcy in discussions of monetary policy. For a long time, central banks and central bank cooperation were associated with the terrible failures of the depression era. This "lesson" of the depression influenced the design of the Bretton Woods order; and it was only in the 1980s and especially in the 1990s that an assertion of the value of independent central banks reappeared generally (Germany and the Bundesbank served as a model in this discussion).

The Young Plan for settling German reparations in 1929 replaced the previous mechanism for the transfer of reparation payments through an agent-general, who was responsible for converting the Marks paid by the German government into foreign exchange and for making a judgment as to whether the foreign-exchange market would allow such a large transaction. Instead, Germany was to pay her reparations Marks to a new institution, the Bank for International Settlements. The BIS replaced the transfer-protection mechanism of the Dawes Plan through its discretionary power to reinvest reparation payments in German securities, and thus to remove pressure from the exchange rate. The Bank also acted as the fiscal agent for the Dawes and Young loans, as well as other international loans (the 1930 International Loan of Austria).

The BIS, however, was intended as rather more than a reparations bank. Its founders saw it as a way of mending the international order: stabilizing money, and providing depoliticized solutions to economic problems. Sir Charles Addis, a member of the Organization Committee established at The Hague conference to design the new bank, wrote: "it was hoped by this plan to fulfill the dream of Genoa by the gradual development of the BIS into a cooperative society of Central Banks, the governors of which would regularly meet together in concert in order to exchange information, and to devise means for promoting economy in the use of gold and for preventing by a common policy undue fluctuations in its value."[23] Later the objectives of the Bank were described as collaboration to "evolve a common body of monetary doctrine," to "smooth out the business cycle, and to contribute toward a greater equilibrium in the general level of economic activity."[24]

Montagu Norman formulated a very ambitious program as a way of implementing these objectives. He saw the prime tasks of the bank as lying in the "centralization of international monetary relations. It would act to prevent excessive credit leading to "overproduction when prices are artificially maintained (rubber etc.)." (Norman was thinking of the abortive Stevenson scheme, which had made rubber exports dependent on the price, had briefly raised rubber prices, and then led to overplanting and a catastrophic price collapse during the depression years.) The Bank would thus attempt to restrict the excessive amount of short-term capital moving internationally. One common diagnosis of the ills of the 1920s contrasted the long-term nature of prewar international capital movements with the volatile short-term flows of the 1920s (a debate reminiscent of some analyses of the ills of the 1990s). "To attract short-term capital to long-term markets is another task which can only be accomplished by identifying the policies of the Central banks, by coordinating the movements of their discount rates, by increasing the control of each in its own market."[25]

France agreed about some of these goals. The French expert Pierre

Quesnay saw the desirability of centralizing the statistical work of the various central banks in order to know more about the problems raised by international capital flows. But French thinking went much further and proposed that the BIS adopt a new gold currency ("grammor") as a unit of account. The idea, characteristically French, goes back intellectually to the proposals of Emperor Napoleon III for a world monetary standard at the 1867 International Monetary Conference. Stripped of the gold element, however, it also looks forward to Keynes's discussion of an artificial international currency ("bancor") in the negotiations preceding Bretton Woods. The result would be that the defense of a currency in the case of a speculative attack would not require the sales of another currency (and hence the likelihood of transmitting the attack elsewhere).[26] There were enormous hopes. The BIS in fact was the last great attempt to establish international economic cooperation before the Second World War.

The Bank's statutes stipulated its responsibility "to promote the cooperation of Central Banks and to provide additional facilities for international financial operations." It began operations on 17 May 1930 with an initial capital of 500 million gold Swiss francs, subscribed by central banks or (in the case of Japan and United States) banking groups.[27] (To give some idea of the contrast in size with more recent institutions: the capitalization of the BIS amounted to 0.107 percent of 1930 U.S. GNP; the capital of the IMF was 4.019 percent of U.S. GNP in 1945.)

Its constitution, however, represented a rather political sort of compromise. The Paris experts, the Hague conferences, and the Organization Committee left the BIS, in the words of one of its directors, "vague, obscure, badly arranged and sometimes inconsistent."[28] In the first place, its membership betrayed clearly its origins as a reparations bank: it excluded all of South and Central America, Africa, the British overseas dominions, and Asia, with the exception of Japan, which owed its inclusion to its status as a (very small) reparations creditor. In Europe, Spain was left out. The United States, however, was brought in, though the representation was inevitably unofficial since the Federal Reserve System was forbidden to participate (because of the risk of involving the United States officially in the reparations quagmire). As a consequence, the BIS held its dollar deposits at two leading private New York banks.

The Bank was not located in any major financial center. The choice of site initially lay among the small countries of Europe, Belgium, the Netherlands, and Switzerland, with France strongly advocating a Belgian location and Britain and Germany equally militantly opposed. In Switzerland, the eventual choice, Zurich was rejected because although it was a major financial center, it was too German; Geneva involved too much of an entanglement with the League; and thus the choice fell on Basle. Norman had actually urged an even more peculiar Swiss choice, Bern, which had "the advantage of being a diplomatic, university and scientific centre and less of a money-making atmosphere": the intention of maintaining the clublike atmosphere of 1920s in a rarified air was clear.[29] Basle also had the advantage in the railway age of being at the intersection of the major European routes, London–Hoek van Holland–Rome, Paris–Vienna, and Berlin–Madrid.

The staffing took place in accordance with the principle of national representation. The first president of the Bank, Gates McGarrah, was an American; but the general manager in charge of the actual operation of policy was an extremely talented young Banque de France official, Pierre Quesnay, entirely dedicated to French national interests. German protests (especially from the Reichsbank president, Hjalmar Schacht) that he had been the figure responsible for organizing a speculative attack on the Mark in the spring of 1929 were ignored. Quesnay in fact had a powerful claim to his new position. Owen Young, the architect of the new reparations plan, hailed the thirty-six-year-old economist as the principal author of both the Young Plan and the Bank.[30] As a means of conciliating Germany, Quesnay's deputy was a German, Ernst Hülse from the Berlin Reichsbank. He proved a blinkered and unimaginative bureaucrat, more intent on warding off invasions of his administrative turf than on rescuing the international financial system.[31] The result would have been a complete deadlock or a descent into routine and trivial business had Quesnay not possessed rather more imagination and initiative than Hülse.

It was difficult after the deliberations of the Organization Committee to avoid the conclusion drawn by a later British director of the Bank, Sir Otto Niemeyer: "No one who started out to construct a Super Bank for world cooperative purposes could conceivably have hit on the constitution proposed for the BIS."[32] The capital of the Bank came from the participating banks of issue. When the BIS began operations, its resources were so limited that the banking policy soon ran into a dead end: within months, by August 1930, the BIS approached complete illiquidity at the very time that the signs of world deflation and depression had become quite obvious.[33] In the first year of its activity, the BIS had 1.8 billion Swiss francs in deposits, of which 300 million were reinvested in Germany, 650 million were short-term deposits by the reparations creditors who had not yet transferred their annuities, and 800 million represented other central bank deposits. Its only business that coincided with Norman's vision was a stabilization credit for the Spanish peseta of £3 million in April 1931, which was designed to allow Spain to return to the gold standard (in fact the world financial crisis intervened).

The Bank was not permitted to make medium- or long-term investments (outside Germany) of the kind that might have been needed in drawing up stabilization packages. One of its staff now came to the conclusion that "if things continue to take their present course, the Bank will be in a completely frozen position within a month and unable to meet its liabilities without borrowing."[34]

The urgent need for middle-term credits arose out of the world depression, which immobilized many bank loans: this was an instance in which a well-capitalized de facto lender of last resort might have played a powerful role in freeing the world from the incubus of frozen debt and illiquid banks. A subcommittee of the BIS in the autumn of 1930 started an inquiry into how the Bank might make up the shortfall caused by the growing bank problems of central Europe:

> The [commercial] banks . . . are no longer prepared to continue this custom [the central European tradition of making long-term credits to commercial and above all industrial borrowers], which, from the point of view of rigid banking principles might be called an abuse, as, owing to the post-war economic depression these credits have become frozen almost everywhere, with the result that the banks are no longer prepared to invest money in companies with which they have already invested large sums not to mention the further fact that this freezing of credits has transformed a considerable portion of the liquid funds of the banks into fixed investments.[35]

The subcommittee recommended that a sum equivalent to the BIS's capital, in addition to some permanent deposits, be placed in medium-term bills bought from banks in order to thaw central European credit. A more ambitious variant of the scheme appeared in February 1931 from the Bank of England and became known as the Kindersley scheme (Sir Robert Kindersley was a director of the Bank of England and of the BIS). It aimed to overcome the failure of international bond markets, in which—because of the collapse in security prices—new issues had become practically impossible. Kindersley and Norman recommended the creation of an international corporation with a capital of £25–50 million, which might issue bonds up to three times its capital to "foreign governments, municipalities, mortgage banks, harbor boards, railways and public utility companies." "At a period like the present, when the capitalist system is largely under the microscope and is being attacked from many sides, it is of the greatest importance that capitalists as a whole should thus make an effort to find a remedy for at least one important difficulty which faces the money markets of the world today."[36]

In fact the scheme, which attracted German support—since there the danger of financial collapse became ever more acute—found the French hostile and suspicious that this was an attempt to chip away at France's political advantage arising out of the strength of the French capital market. The governor of the Banque de France, Clément Moret, argued that BIS participation in the Kindersley scheme would be contrary to the Bank's statutes. Moreover, it was French banks that were supposed to subscribe most of the bonds under the scheme, "without being given the means of controlling the use of the funds furnished." The debtor countries had only themselves to blame for the current weakness of international capital markets: "If a number of borrowers at the present time do not possess all the desirable facilities for procuring the capital of which they are reasonably in need, this is mainly because in the course of previous years too large a number of them have not strictly kept the engagements which they had undertaken with respect to their creditors." There could be no point in relying on guarantees given by a borrowing state, since "in practice the creditor is powerless before a defaulting State; he comes into conflict with the 'sovereignty' of his debtor, and the political evolution of the last few years seems to have strengthened the force of this conception. The security given has only a very relative value and generally no value at all (for example Mexico, Turkey . . .)."[37] The perils of sovereign lending became obvious to all during the depression.

Moret's view seems plausible in retrospect. The first defaults came in Latin America. Bolivia had let its currency slip against gold in October 1930, and in January 1931 defaulted on its debt. Peru followed in March, Chile in July, and Brazil and Colombia in October. There then came the central European defaults: exchange control in Austria, Hungary, and Germany in 1931, and defaults by Hungary, Yugoslavia, and Greece in 1932 and by Austria and Germany in 1933.[38] There was growing skepticism about sovereign loans. By the mid-1930s the liberal Swedish economist Per Jacobsson, chief economist at the BIS, was writing: "Political influence in lending is, as a rule, very costly; when a government has to put its influence behind a loan, the likelihood is that there is something wrong with the security of the loan."[39] But Moret's pessimistic analysis does not take into account the possibility that early action might have limited the extent of financial contagion.

It was not, however, merely French opposition that brought down the Norman-Kindersley scheme. The American financiers were not sympathetic to a large-scale rescue operation. BIS president McGarrah cabled to Morgan partners Thomas W. Lamont and Seymour Parker Gilbert that the proposal was impractical and that it would have been much better to organize an investment trust through private banking channels. The Morgan bankers agreed with this assessment.[40] Thus the proposal disintegrated, and Governor Norman noted sadly: "The fact is that the BIS is already slipping to the bottom of a ditch and in that position seems likely to do no more than helpfully perform a number of routine and Central Banking operations."[41]

A more modest, but in some ways more interesting, proposal made by the middle-term credit subcommittee under the chairmanship of the influential Belgian commercial (not central) banker Emile Francqui, for the rediscounting by the BIS of commercial paper up to £10 million in order to prepare the way for a semiprivate corporation to be built up by the speculative Swedish financier Ivar Kreuger, fared little better. The idea was that rescue efforts involving central banks and official institutions alone would be doomed to failure. It was essential to "bail in" (to use more modern terminology) the private sector. But Francqui's initiative was not at all well received by the two hostile camps in BIS policymaking. On the one hand, the British and Germans at the BIS regarded the idea as inadequate and limited; on the other, Moret described it as "utopian," since "an issue of bonds at the present moment would, to say the least of it, be difficult."[42]

Governor Moret's pessimism was not unjustified, since the BIS Board meeting at which he delivered the death blow to the Francqui as well as Kindersley plans took place one week after the collapse of the Vienna Creditanstalt. The central European credit crisis now set in: the Viennese panic brought down banks in Amsterdam and Warsaw. In June and July the scare spread to Germany, and from there immediately to Latvia, Turkey, and Egypt (and within a few months to England and the United States). Less than one year after he was supposed to devise a scheme that might rescue the central bankers and the central European banks, Ivar Kreuger killed himself in a Paris apartment.

Capital Flows Resume

The second half of the 1920s looked as if they justified the hopes in the gold-exchange standard. From 1924 to 1930 $9 billion (and possibly as much as $11 billion) flowed, 60 percent of this sum coming from the United States. The United Kingdom lent some $1.3 billion and France $1.34 billion over the same period.[43]

Most of the flows from Britain and—more significantly in quantitative terms—the United States took the form of long-term capital bonds (see Table 2.1).

The overall capital flows in the interwar period were considerably lower than those of the prewar period and do not really justify the frequent description as an orgy of overlending. This fact becomes apparent once we consider the direction of lending and the flows from industrial to developing countries. For 1911–1913, the average annual capital export of Britain, France, Germany, and the United States to the rest of the world was $1.4 billion. In 1924–1928 this flow of capital to the developing world dropped to $860 million, or in price-deflated terms $550 million. In other words, if Germany—as a major recipient of the capital flows of the 1920s—is removed from Table 2.1, the stream of international lending looks rather modest.[44] And the reasons for German borrowing were highly peculiar.

The shape of international capital flows in the 1920s and 1930s, however, looks similar to the boom-bust episodes that were characteristic of

Table 2.1 Average annual long-term capital exports, United States and Britain, 1919–1938 (millions of $U.S.)

Country	1919–1923	1924–1928	1929–1931	1932–1938
United States	531	1,142	595	28
Britain	416	587	399	143

Source: United Nations, Department of Economic Affairs, International Capital Movements during the Inter-War Period (Lake Success, N.Y., 1949), p. 25.

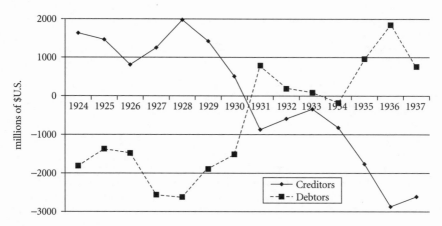

Figure 2.1 Capital flows, 1924–1937
(Source: Charles H. Feinstein and Catherine Watson, "Private International Capital Flows in the Inter-War Period," in *Banking, Currency, and Finance in Europe between the Wars,* ed. Charles H. Feinstein [Oxford: Oxford University Press, 1995], p. 108.)

the nineteenth century or the restored capital markets after the 1970s. A flow of capital to debtor countries was followed by a collapse of confidence and then by a period in which the direction of the capital flow was reversed. Capital in the second phase returned to the creditor countries, and debtor countries were forced into adjustment (see Figure 2.1). For both Britain and the United States, the peak year of capital outflow was 1927. After that the U.S. collapse was much more dramatic, and after 1931 capital long-term outflows practically ceased. Britain still exported capital, but mostly to the empire and dominions.

Britain, however, was also a major short-term debtor (as it had probably been already before 1914). So, in the 1920s, were Germany (then the world's biggest debtor) and the United States. The BIS estimated total world short-term indebtedness in 1930 at 70 billion Swiss francs or $13.5 billion, of which only $4.3 billion related to commercial transactions. Germany accounted for $3.9 billion, the United States for $2.7 billion, and Britain for $1.9 billion.[45] Figures solely for banking liabilities, however, show a higher British than U.S. net liability in 1930 (see Table 2.2). Both Britain and the United States played a similar role: they converted short-term deposits into long-term lending.

The origins of the relatively high short-term indebtedness of Britain and

Table 2.2 Short-term banking liabilities, United States and Britain, 1927–1930
(billions of $U.S.)

Year	United States		Britain	
	Gross	Net	Gross	Net
1927	3.096	—	2.037	1.359
1928	2.892	—	2.444	1.470
1929	3.078	1.512	2.192	1.338
1930	2.794	1.069	2.112	1.330

Note: Liabilities = total short-term funds due to foreigners on banking account.
Source: League of Nations, *Balances of Payments, 1930* (Geneva, 1932), pp. 165, 181.

the United States lay not so much in any domestic problems as in foreign inflows that followed political uncertainty in Europe and Latin America. It would be wrong to see in British indebtedness a sign of economic vulnerability or an early symptom of industrial decline. The deposits originated in the turbulent circumstances of the postwar European continent. In the social explosions and inflations, large amounts of capital fled—out of central Europe, but also out of France.

As an example, the McKenna Committee in 1924, which set out to examine the extent of German capital abroad, produced the figure, almost certainly too low, of 6.75 billion Gold Marks (GM) ($1.6 billion). Germans bought foreign exchange, while foreigners in turn used the Marks they received in order to buy nominal assets, which frequently depreciated rapidly as a consequence of inflation. Foreigners' deposits in the Berlin great banks, which were estimated at 31.3 billion Marks (1.8 million GM, or $429 million), were worth only 140 million GM by the end of 1922 and 30 million GM in 1923.[46]

Short-term inflows to Britain continued during the great credit boom of the second half of the 1920s. After the great crisis of 1931, however, the general direction of the flows shifted; a massive wave of capital flight—estimated by Charles Feinstein and Catherine Watson at $3.5 billion—went to the United States and Britain.[47] At first the motivation was fear of economic crisis and renewed currency instability; but as economic crisis had its poisonous and corrosive effects on political stability, there came an increasing political fear, of the likelihood of European war.

The Crisis in the Emerging Markets

The experience of central Europe in 1931 demonstrated to what an extent financial shocks could aggravate the business depression, and how much the behavior of money mattered in the course of depression. In central Europe, banking crises brought more general economic and also political collapses. Two sets of problems came together: the instability of banking and the political impossibility of balancing budgets.

The League of Nations Economic Committee described the "new phase" of the world depression that began after the spring of 1931. "The crisis thereupon took on a more specifically financial character. The disturbance, however, extends to all spheres of activity. The operation of the world's economic organization rests on confidence; as soon as this disappears it undergoes profound disturbances and the evil spreads rapidly."[48]

The peculiarity of central European banks was their close relationship to industry. Traditionally the *Universalbanken* had taken short-term deposits but given long-term loans (so-called *Kontokorrentkredit*) to business; they also held shares while waiting for a favorable moment for flotation on the Bourse. This style of banking predominated in the Habsburg empire and its successor states, in Italy after the 1890s, and also in Germany and Belgium (where the oldest universal bank, the Société Générale, had begun operating in the 1830s). Elsewhere, in Scandinavia or the Netherlands or Switzerland, banks also held substantial long-term industrial assets, but usually through intermediaries, subsidiaries, or trust companies.

The central European pattern was in the 1920s and even later often considered to hold advantages for long-term industrial development, in that banks were much better supplied with information not only about companies but also about business conditions in general than investors operating in a system built around a stock exchange. The better information allowed a more rational basis for investment decisions, and this in the long run stimulated and promoted economic growth.

However, the financial situation of all these countries with universal banking practices was severely disturbed by the postwar hyperinflations. In the case of the former Habsburg empire, territorial changes and the splitting up of the big Viennese banks added to the dislocation. When banks reopened after currency stabilizations, their balance sheets were usually reduced to between a third and a fifteenth of prewar levels. This initial opening was usually followed by a period in which deposits and credits grew quickly: a catch-up phase. Above all, the banks expanded on the basis of foreign loans, usually short-term, which they converted in the quite traditional manner into long-term credits or equity participations.

Companies financed their recoveries after stabilization through credits from banks. The disproportion here between developments in the capital-exporting countries and in the capital-importing countries of central Europe is striking. Whereas from 1926 to 1930 the indebtedness of business corporations as a proportion of owned capital remained steady or fell in the United States (from 65.9 to 60.9 percent) and Britain (from 58.0 to 50.3 percent), these ratios in central Europe increased dramatically. Hungary went from 69.3 percent to a dangerous 80.3 percent; Germany from 65.1 to 88.9 percent. In Italy, which had universal banks but no substantial capital inflows, the indebtedness ratio declined, from 98.6 percent to 83.2 percent, in the absence of imported capital. On the other hand, as the figures indicated, there was a substantial degree of borrowing that made the industrial and business credit structure highly vulnerable to debt deflation should prices fall.[49]

Such credit structures were vulnerable in two eventualities: if the external inflow of capital, with which expansion had been financed, were to cease; and if a price decline led to a collapse of the value of the banks' equity investments and endangered their loans by reducing the value of the collateral.

The worldwide application of the doctrine of independent central banking as expounded by the Bank of England and the Federal Reserve Bank of New York increased the vulnerability of central European credit structures. In order to demonstrate the "independence" that constituted the prerequisite for the maintenance of a continuing inflow of capital, central banks had to show that they were restraining monetary developments. Yet this was difficult in economies in which commercial banks had so much leeway in granting credits. Reserve requirements at the central bank were rare: indeed in Hungary it was considered unusual and dishonorable for banks to keep deposits at the central bank or to discount bills there. In these cases the central banks could generate international confidence and approval only by staging little crises. The peculiar agony of central Europe followed from the combination of strong national banking traditions with new Anglo-Saxon principles of central banking.

The banking systems became even more vulnerable because of the intensity of competition in banking in the 1920s, and because of the effects of a merger wave. In Germany, the most significant merger was that of the Deutsche Bank with the Disconto-Gesellschaft in 1929.

In the spring and summer of 1931 three different central European crises converged. The Austrian crisis started as a banking crisis, which then became a foreign-exchange and fiscal crisis. In Hungary a fiscal crisis set off a foreign-exchange panic and then a banking crisis. In Germany a fiscal and banking crisis coincided and set off the foreign-exchange crisis. These were not "twin" but "triplet" crises.

Austria suffered doubly in the 1920s: it was overbanked because of the legacy of Vienna as the financial capital of the Habsburg empire, and because of the large number of speculative institutions set up in the inflation. After the split-up of the empire, the Vienna banks were often left with the poorest assets in the successor states, while newly created national banks there took the investment plums. The stabilization of the Austrian currency was followed by bank collapses and mergers. In 1926 the Vienna Creditanstalt took over the Austrian business of the Anglo-Austrian Bank, and the Bodenkreditanstalt took over the Allgemeine Verkehrsbank und Unionsbank. In 1929 the Bodenkreditanstalt, which could survive only by rediscounting its bill portfolio at the national bank, was merged, at the instance of the government, with the Creditanstalt. This merger set up an Austrian colossus: according to a recent estimate, 60 percent of Austrian industry was dependent on the Creditanstalt.[50]

A crisis could have arisen at any time after the merger with the Bodenkreditanstalt. The moment came by chance, when one of the Creditanstalt's directors, Zoltan Hajdu, suddenly, indeed inexplicably, in 1931 indicated that he would not sign the balance sheet "until the usual method of drawing it up was changed." In the spring of 1931 the publication of accounts was delayed while Hajdu insisted that there be a comprehensive examination and revaluation of the bank's assets. In the course of this reexamination it became clear that a revaluation would mean insolvency.[51]

Thus the first difficulties in central Europe appeared as early as 1929, in reaction to the lower capital inflows of 1928 and falling prices. In Italy the first bank problems began in the summer of 1930, and the affected banks depended on advances for the central bank (the Bank of Italy) to survive. From December 1930, deposits in the largest three Italian banks fell, and the movement became a near panic in April 1931.

Austria was remarkably and surprisingly calm until the spring of 1931. There had been a few small failures in 1929, but the general consensus was that these had not been enough to purge Austrian credit. "In spite of recent failures," *The Banker* noted, "there are still too many banks in Vienna, expectations of whose development as an international financial centre have failed to materialize."[52] The announcement of a customs union between Germany and Austria, followed by the French protest against this démarche, increased nervousness; but there do not appear to have been any significant withdrawals of foreign short-term credits. The shock came suddenly: the Creditanstalt announced a delay in the publication of its accounts, and then, in the night of 11–12 May, revealed losses of 140 million schillings, which it attributed to the costly aftermath of the absorption of the Bodenkreditanstalt. Before 11 May, most foreign creditors had not realized what was occurring: but thereafter the affair became highly political. Depositors lost confidence in the Creditanstalt. By the end of May the bank had lost 200 million schillings in deposits. But only a quarter of this sum was deposited with other banks; the rest moved out over the exchange.[53] As a run on the schilling started, the Austrian exchange was threatened, and Austria appealed for international help.

Governor Norman staged a rescue operation that was specifically intended to prevent the French from using the Austrian position for foreign-policy advantages. But Norman was also aware from the first of the dangerous international financial repercussions of the Creditanstalt case (what we now call contagion). "Nor must we forget," he cabled to the New York Federal Reserve, "that a monetary breakdown in Austria might quickly produce a similar result in several other countries."[54] It took two weeks of tense negotiations to provide what was in the end a token amount, and which did nothing to restore confidence in Austria or in any other country.

The problem lay in the French response to Norman. The governor of the Banque de France, Clément Moret, knew, on the basis of information supplied from Basle by Pierre Quesnay, in this matter quite assiduous in the pursuit of France's national interest, that the London market was too weak to help Austria. The London Rothschilds could not afford to support the Creditanstalt: "It can thus be foreseen that the Austrian government will sooner or later be obliged to sell its shares to a private group. In this respect it appears that the London Rothschild house will not be capable of acting. M. Quesnay announces the possibility that this offers to interested French banks."[55]

Norman's initiative resulted in two central bank loans organized by the BIS, though in July Moret tried to block the second Austrian loan because he could now argue that the international capital market had been so destroyed that it would be impossible to float a bond issue to pay off the loan.[56] But these loans were a classic case of too little, too late: the initial 100 million schilling ($14 million) loan did not even correspond to the first, grotesquely minimal, estimate of the Creditanstalt's losses. Charles Kindleberger's verdict is on the mark: "The niggardliness and the delay proved disastrous."[57]

The Creditanstalt was also an enormous domestic Austrian problem. The government rescued the bank through the purchase of bills by the national bank. On 16 June, as panic conditions spread through central Europe, the Creditanstalt's creditors reached an agreement to keep the bank going, as otherwise the whole Austrian economy would collapse. At this stage the losses were calculated at around 500 million schillings, and the national bank had 690 million schillings' worth of Creditanstalt paper. But even these figures underestimated the extent of the losses, which became apparent only in the course of an audit: at the end of 1931 the losses were reckoned to be 923 million schillings, or 725 million schillings more than the nominal capital and reserves after the government-inspired May 1931 reorganization of the bank. The assets included frozen loans to Austrian and central European industry. For 31 May 1931, the audited accounts produced by the London firm of Binder Hamlyn showed a total engagement of the bank of 1.339 billion schillings; the largest elements consisted of loans to the textile industry (11.9 percent of the total), petroleum (10.3 percent), automobiles (9.6 percent), state and local government (4.2 percent), and above all other banks (16.7 percent).[58]

By the spring of 1932 it became apparent that the Creditanstalt was by no means the only problem in Austrian banking, and that the other two large banks—the Niederösterreichische Escompte-Gesellschaft (NEG) and the Wiener Bankverein—had their own and equally grave problems. The representative of Austria's foreign creditors complained about the "culpable frivolity" of the management of the NEG;[59] and in the end he pushed through a merger of the Creditanstalt and the two other banks on 25 May 1934, with the frozen (and mostly worthless) industrial assets of the NEG separated out into a state-owned holding company, Österreichische Industriekredit AG.

The Creditanstalt catastrophe turned into a national emergency because of the immediate effect of the bank losses on the national budget. From the beginning, there had been a close association between the views of foreign bankers on Austria and the state of public finance. The cost of the Creditanstalt rescue alone amounted to 9 percent of Austria's annual GNP. When this is added to the cost of other bank rescues, including that of the vulnerable system of publicly owned postal banks, the cost was comparable to that of bank bailouts in 1990s crises. (For Mexico in the 1990s, for instance, the rescue of the banking system cost 14.5 percent of GDP.)[60]

The Austrian budget had already been swollen by the rapid expansion of state initiatives in the later 1920s. Partly the new expenditure simply followed from the emergency program of the stabilization: the burden of pensions for the dismissed officials mounted continually. But the budget deficits were also driven by increased spending on welfare and on capital investment projects. Funds for these outlays seemed to be available because of the high tax levels established at the time of the stabilization in 1922–23. From 1923 to 1929 federal spending rose by 88 percent (from 6.3 to 9.1 percent of GNP), and local government spending by 169 percent (from 3.1 to 6.5 percent of GNP).[61] Since the political dynamic to increase spending could not easily be reversed, short of massive external pressure on Austria, falling production and prices during the depression led directly to large deficits. The severity of the Austrian slump was also, however, a product of the high levels of government spending: the combination of high benefit levels and a high degree of unionization kept wages high, despite poor productivity growth in the late 1920s and falling productivity in the depression.[62] Thus the development of large deficits during the depression functioned as an alarm signal for the whole of the Austrian economy (see Table 2.3).

In early May 1931, *before* the Creditanstalt difficulties were publicized, opinionmakers such as the Morgans in New York were alarmed by predic-

Table 2.3 Austrian budgets, 1928–1934 (millions of schillings)

	1928	1929	1930	1931	1932	1933	1934
Budget expenditure	1,341.6	1,307.9	1,592.6	1,630.5	1,289.7	1,493.6	1,574.1
Cash balance	−80.9	19.7	−261.2	−322.7	−9.2	−235.9	−231.0

Source: League of Nations, *Public Finance, 1935: Austria* (Geneva, 1935).

tions of a large budget deficit for 1931.[63] In France, even socialist newspapers were outraged by the size of the "hypertrophied" Austrian state.[64] The bank rescue obviously widened the deficit, and threatened the capacity of Austria to service the League of Nations 1923 loan. In consequence, in January 1932 another Dutchman, Rost van Tonningen, was appointed by the League Financial Committee to supervise the Austrian budget. He devised schemes to raise taxes, cut civil service and railway staffs, salaries and wages, and pensions; but despite the imposed austerity on 1 July 1932 Austria halted the service of the League loan, and the foreign creditors were obliged to accept a new agreement (the Lausanne Protocol), which included a conversion loan secured on the gross receipts of Austrian customs and the tobacco monopoly, as well as a new domestic austerity program that narrowly passed the Austrian parliament, the Bundesrat, with a majority of one vote.

Hungary had been weakened by the collapse of raw material prices, since foodstuffs and raw materials constituted 59.9 percent of Hungary's exports in 1929. Wheat alone represented 10.8 percent of the value of Hungary's exports, and animals another 10.5 percent.[65] Instead of bringing higher export returns, the superabundant harvest of 1929 simply depressed prices and contributed to the growth in stocks, with the result that in 1930, with a much poorer harvest, the price still fell. The average wheat price in 1927 had been 31.87 pengö/quintal, in 1930 19.11, and in 1931 12.78.[66] Hungary had also borrowed extensively, and by the early 1930s the external debt service amounted to an impossibly high 16 percent of national income, or 48 percent of the value of exports.[67]

In the story of the Hungarian collapse, the mix of banking failure, crisis in public finance, external (exchange) problems, and foreign policy entanglement was very similar to Austria's; but these problems were resolved in a rather different way.

Agricultural support by the government formed part of the problem, since it was the cash situation of the Hungarian treasury that precipitated the crisis in the summer of 1931. As early as 1930, Hungarian money started to move abroad nervously: the total losses for the year amounted to 70–80 million pengös. "Though all the facts are known only to a very few individuals, there are signs that public confidence is not to be relied on," the National Bank governor Sándor Popovics confided to a Bank of England official in February 1931.[68]

As in Austria, uncertainty over the public budget was a critical element in the collapse of confidence. Here, however, the fiscal problem played a key part at the beginning of the crisis. The National Bank described the Hungarian difficulties in the following way:

> the fact that such a situation could remain undisclosed until so late a stage argued a lack of financial control and administrative organization which could not be denied. Individual departments had got out of hand; they had misled the Treasury and incurred liabilities on their own authority. The Government as a whole had also been too liberal, for example in affording various kinds of relief. But the chief source of trouble was the failure of revenue on account of the agricultural depression.[69]

One major problem lay in the extent of the losses incurred by the government in the operation of the *boletta*, a wheat price-support scheme that suffered as the wheat price plummeted, and of the *futura*, a buffer stock of wheat.[70]

The difficulties in public authority budgets were, however, less significant than the problems of publicly owned enterprises. An extensive nationalization, coupled with the attempt to build up strategic industries and reduce dependence on imports, transferred the problems of industry in the world depression into difficulties in the state budget, and by this route straight to the attention of the international financial community.

From 11 May 1931, the date of the open Creditanstalt crisis, Hungary's National Bank lost foreign exchange at a rate of 150,000 pengös a day. The National Bank attributed the losses to a combination of American withdrawals and Hungarian capital flight: Hungarians were buying Hungarian shares domiciled abroad after the failure of the Austrian bank and security house Auspitz Leben & Co. in the wake of the Creditanstalt crisis.[71] In order to finance these purchases, Hungarians withdrew deposits from banks, and then the general panic set in. Current accounts in the twelve largest Budapest banks and in the postal savings banks fell from 757.6 million pengös in May to 637.1 million pengös in October; and as banks withdrew credits to meet these demands, the number of bankruptcies jumped. This was the Hungarian version of debt deflation.

The National Bank kept the banks alive by generous rediscounting *before* a public collapse of the credit institutes, unlike in the Austrian case. This generosity allowed the outflow of funds across the exchange to swell, so that the strain fell on the external exchange rather than directly on the Hungarian banks. Initially, this strain was managed with the help of the

BIS: on 6 June the BIS gave a $5 million credit, and on 11 June a further £1 million (approximately $5 million) followed; a third $5 million loan went out on 22 June. But this did not look like solving very much, since the BIS, and the foreign creditors, could calculate that over the next three months, even without a banking panic, £5 million in credits were due (of which £3 million was owed by the government).

A substantial part of the problem lay in foreign indebtedness. The total obligations of the Hungarian banks amounted to 483.21 million pengös, of which 232.26 (48 percent) was owed to U.S. creditors and 104.95 (22 percent) to British creditors.[72] The foreign creditors negotiated a standstill agreement that became a model for subsequent similar accords with Austria and Germany. It was a general framework, and it took longer to elaborate the particular details, with the British banks reaching a settlement on 14 March 1932 and the U.S. banks on 21 June. At the outset of the crisis, the Hungarian government complained that "the United States had not yet gone through the school which a leading nation had to pass through before it could count on the confidence of all its customers."[73] The United States, in short, was not acting as a beneficent hegemon.

As in Austria, the foreign credit situation appeared in Hungary to require the imposition of austerity. In the autumn of 1931 Hungary drew up an eleven-point program for the League of Nations, which included the predictable list: civil service pay and pension cuts, tax increases, the ending of state subsidies, and in particular the abolition of the *boletta* and *futura*. Civil servants indeed had their pay docked, but the agricultural support schemes continued. The cutbacks are clearly discernible in the public administration budgets of 1932–33; but it is also clear that public undertakings were affected less severely. The *boletta* operated until July 1934, by which time wheat prices had substantially recovered. Under agrarian pressure, the government in 1932 and 1933 introduced extensive legislation to make farm bankruptcy impossible.

The most dramatic and extensive central European banking crisis occurred in Germany, where on 13 July 1931 the Darmstädter und Nationalbank (usually called the Danat Bank) shut its doors, the government declared a bank holiday, and the entire financial system required reconstruction with costly government assistance. The origins of the crisis were very similar to those in Austria and Hungary: the vulnerability of banks because of recent hyperinflation, the flight of domestic capital, the reaction to political uncertainty (both domestic and international), pressure by

farmers for more effective protection against bankruptcy, and the trigger-
ing effects of relatively small cash deficits in the public accounts.

German capital flight predated the world depression. The origins lay in
the war, and above all in the immediate postwar period, when a large number of German corporations founded and used subsidiaries in Switzerland
and the Netherlands to move capital out of Germany. Another wave came
in the late 1920s, partly in order to escape taxation but also in response to
continued insecurity about German developments. *Before* the onset of the
depression and the disintegration of the German polity, from 1927 to 1930,
the capital accounts reveal an outflow of 3.9 billion Reichsmarks (RM)
in short-term capital and 4.9 billion RM in long-term capital, while the
short-term liabilities of the United States rose.

In 1929 a large number of small German banks failed: Richard Harte,
Berlin; Julius Cunow & Co., Berlin; Fritz Kienstedt, Lübeck; Kieler Bank
and Bankhaus Horst Fritzsche, Dresden; Paul-Schlesinger-Trier & Co.,
Frankfurt. Most significantly in August there was a major collapse of an insurance firm, the Frankfurter Allgemeine Versicherungs AG, followed by
runs on municipal savings banks in Berlin and Frankfurt. A foreign peri-
odical commented in April 1930 on the aftermath of these little crises:
"The crisis which caused the failure of innumerable commercial firms and
a large number of small banks seems to have passed its climax, and it is believed that those banking and commercial firms which have survived the
crisis may be regarded as safe and sound."[74] Unfortunately this prediction
did not come true.

From May 1930, German banks lost deposits, and by June 1931 the
money supply had in consequence fallen by 17 percent. The banks had
substantial foreign short-term liabilities. In July 1931, after a substantial
part of the foreign loans had already been called, the German banks still
owed 5.9 billion RM, and total German short-term indebtedness
amounted to 13.1 billion RM. The total foreign indebtedness one year earlier is estimated at 15.5–16.5 billion RM. Foreigners had treated Germany
with greater suspicion since the government crises of December 1929,
when the finance minister was forced to resign; March 1930, when the so-
cialist-liberal Great Coalition collapsed; and September 1930, when the
Nazi party achieved an unexpectedly high vote in the Reichstag election.

On the other hand, the problem for Germany lay less in the absolute
quantity of foreign investment than in the double danger posed by the vulnerability of the German banks and the weakness of public finances. The
banking system had expanded rapidly after the currency stabilization.

After the Creditanstalt crisis, German banks began to lose funds more rapidly. In May, the Berlin great banks lost 337 million RM (or 2.6 percent of their deposits); and in June the bank with the weakest reputation, the Danat, lost 40.9 percent, while the more solid Deutsche Bank lost 8.2 percent. Most of the initial withdrawals were not foreign, but were made by Germans; and it was also Germans who moved money across the exchange into the Netherlands and Switzerland. By the middle of June, however, the foreign banks had become highly concerned. On 23 June the Bankers Trust cut its credit line to the Deutsche Bank. On 3 July the governor of the New York Federal Reserve Bank called in leading New York bankers, representatives of J. P. Morgan, Lee Higginson, Chase, National City Bank, Blair & Co., New York Trust Co., and Central Hanover Bank and Trust Co. After some persuasion they agreed to "at least maintain their present position and in some cases indicated that they would even reopen unused credit lines."[75] But on 6 July the Guaranty Company of New York started to withdraw from Germany. It was, nevertheless, rather late in the day: a great deal of capital had moved before the Americans started to feel nervous.

Because the withdrawals and the capital flight took place across the exchange, the Reichsbank lost reserves. On 30 May the gold reserve stood at 2.39 billion RM; by 23 June it was only 1.421 billion RM. This was close to the minimum reserve of 40 percent of note issue laid down by the Reichsbank law, and the president of the Reichsbank, Hans Luther, appealed for foreign help, and in particular for central bank credits. The BIS arranged a $100 million credit from the Bank of England, the Banque de France, and the Federal Reserve Bank of New York. On 20 June U.S. president Herbert Hoover announced a one-year "holiday" on reparations and inter-Allied debt payments.

But the price for this help was an insistence that the Reichsbank restrict its discounts in order to make capital flight out of Germany more difficult. This is what Luther did on 22 June, but the measure completely failed to stop the movement out. Partly politics were to blame: the French refused to agree to the Hoover moratorium until early July, and thus international tension grew. But Governor Harrison of the FRBNY, as well as Norman, blamed Luther for not taking more effective steps to stop capital flight, which he believed to be at the heart of the German problem. Harrison cabled to Norman: "I felt that the chief difficulty was a flight from the Reichsmark by German nationals and that the Reichsbank should resort to much more drastic credit control than apparently was the case." And again: "Rationing of credit is of course a drastic and disagreeable procedure but it has been applied effectively in Germany in the past without proving to be fatal. On the contrary, in each instance it has been most helpful in repatriating German capital and in checking further outflows of funds and I cannot see why it might not be equally effective at this time if applied with equal force."[76]

The Germans were vulnerable because of the character of their financial structure. The shock to German confidence lay partly in the vulnerability of German banks: in their overcommitment to specific firms such as Nordwolle (the immediate apparent cause of the Danat's difficulties) and the brewery Schultheiss-Patzenhofer. But there existed also a fear of public bankruptcy. This is where the political element—which played a major role in the German crisis—and the financial panic intersected.

The German Finance Ministry faced a cash problem: despite round after round of tax increases, revenues consistently fell below anticipated levels; and despite repeated economy drives, axing of capital projects, civil service pay cuts, and reductions in unemployment support, expenditures remained too high. In consequence, the German government needed to borrow money from the banks in order to make its regular payments. The reparations sums due on 15 June and 15 July looked like particularly insuperable burdens. But it became more difficult to borrow from the banks as the Reichsbank limited its discounts of bank paper; and banks, if they were to lend to the government, needed to reduce credits elsewhere. This in turn hit industrial and commercial borrowers. The large payments for mid-July hung over the increasingly frenetic debates of early July and over the desperate bid of Luther to raise another central bank credit.

On 4 July there were signs of an imminent collapse of the credit of some of the large cities of the Rhineland and Westphalia. The Danat had been particularly involved in municipal lending. On 5 July the Basle *Nationalzeitung* announced that one of the leading German banks was "in difficulties," and a discussion of the Danat's losses as a result of its involvement with Nordwolle began. After a weekend of round-the-clock talks, in which the Dresdner Bank revealed that it too was close to failure, on Monday 13 July all German banks were closed by government decree.

After this bank holiday, the state needed to intervene in order to reconstruct the German banking system. The Reichsbank and the banks founded an Acceptance and Guarantee Bank in July to provide an additional signature to make bank bills eligible for Reichsbank discounting: it was a tacit promise that the Reichsbank would introduce a more generous discount policy. This help allowed the banks to recommence operations on 5 August. But a restructuring of the banking system was still needed: enormous losses were written off with state participations in the new capitalization of banks. The Danat was merged with the Dresdner, and by 1932 91 percent of the Dresdner's capital, 70 percent of the Commerzbank's, and 35 percent of that of the Deutsche Bank was in public ownership. Other public institutions were formed to take over and write off bad assets and manage long-term industrial participations. Solving the problem of the bad banks was thus a general problem for policy in the capital-importing countries.

Contagion in Latin America

The factors that had led to the transmission of crisis in central Europe— namely a high external debt, falling export prices, government fiscal difficulties, consequent fears about debt service, panics, external drains, and internal banking crises—also produced a decade of misery in South America. But the course of subsequent events was not identical. The European countries on the whole stayed on the gold standard for as long as possible, and were "forced off" by financial and banking crises. On the other hand, Latin America and Australia quickly used depreciation as a response to commodity-price induced balance-of-payments difficulties.

Like central Europe, the region had been a major recipient of capital inflows in the 1920s, on terms very similar to those of the central European borrowers. One quarter of the new capital issues floated in New York for foreign borrowers went to Latin America, and $2 billion worth of bonds were issued in the New York bank market.[77] Such loans were marketed very aggressively in the United States. By 1932 an estimated one and a half million individuals held foreign securities, and in 1937 the Securities and Exchange Commission estimated that 600,000 to 700,000 investors held defaulted bonds. After the financial crisis, as was the case with the central European bonds, the issuing and underwriting banks were accused of carelessness in the promotion of their bonds and of grossly underestimating the risks involved. The debate contributed to a widespread feeling that a fundamental reform of banking was needed.

Charles Mitchell, the chairman of National City Bank and one of those accused of misleading the public, informed the Senate Committee on Finance that "those bonds were bought by Tom, Dick and Harry . . . without reference to the solidity or the solvency of the bonds . . . but entirely on the faith of the house issuing them in New York." Other bankers gave evidence of how American banks had used high-pressure tactics to sell loans to Latin American countries. There were twenty-nine bank representatives in Colombia. Thomas W. Lamont, a partner of one of the two banking houses that did not aggressively pursue such business, stated disapprovingly in a speech in 1927: "I have in mind the reports that I have recently heard of American bankers and firms competing on an almost violent scale for the purpose of obtaining loans in various foreign money markets overseas . . . That sort of competition tends to insecurity and unsound practice."[78]

U.S. banks also engaged in substantial short-term lending to Latin America, both to governments and to corporations. There was too a substantial British engagement both in the long- and the short-term markets. Historically, Britain had been especially involved in the financing of railroads and municipal infrastructure, and this bias remained in the 1920s. In 1931 the British-domiciled bonds outstanding of dominion and colonial governments and municipalities amounted to $5.372 billion, and the bonds of foreign governments and municipalities to $1.643 billion.[79] Vulnerable bank loans to South America played a decisive role in the critical weeks of the financial panic of 1931 in the United Kingdom.

For most of the 1920s, the loans appeared to be quite safe. There were few defaults, although the yields always lay above those of high-grade U.S. corporate bonds. The effective interest rate on long-term public-sector debt in 1927 was 6.5 percent for Germany, and 7.4 percent for Austria. The Latin American rates were exactly in this range, with the relatively prosperous and established Argentine republic paying 6.7 percent, Chile 6.9 percent, Colombia 7.0 percent, Peru 7.2 percent, and Brazil 7.5 percent.[80] Subsequent, after-the-event analysis indicated that the loans concluded in the great waves of borrowing in the 1920s were actually progressively less and less sound (in that the subsequent default rates were higher); but this was of course not apparent at the time.[81]

As the debt built up, the debt/export ration deteriorated, so that by 1930 the external debt of Bolivia was 237 percent of exports, and for Chile 121 percent, levels that were repeated in the post-1945 era only in the great debt build-up of the later 1970s. In 1930, though, Peru at 76 percent and Argentina at 46 percent looked much more manageable.[82]

In 1929–30 two related shocks occurred: export prices of many commodities fell, and the inflow of fresh funds was dramatically curtailed. Both raised questions about the ability of borrowers to continue debt service. Wheat and some metals had been falling in price steadily since 1925, but after 1928 the decline became substantially steeper. Wool prices began to decline from the middle of 1929. Coffee reached a peak in the spring of 1929, and then the price fell by almost half by the end of the year.

As prices fell, export earnings were cut. From 1929 through 1931 Argentine export values fell 32 percent (the import side was reduced even more dramatically, as the end of the flow of foreign funds led to economic contraction). In Chile over the same period, with a heavy dependence on copper, export values fell 64 percent. Since a major source of government income was collected through levies on exports, the results for public finance became quickly clear. In the event, over the same period government revenue fell a relatively modest 8 percent in Argentina, but by 20 percent in Brazil and 36 percent in Chile.[83]

Another way of measuring the severity of the Latin debt problem is to examine the debt service expressed as a share of export earnings. For Argentina in 1927 this ratio had been 7.9 percent, and for Bolivia, 6.1 percent; for 1931 the equivalent ratios were 22.5 and 24.5 percent.[84]

The combination of the difficulty of maintaining debt service as new loans dried up, and the fall in export prices, quickly led to currency depreciation. This was a different story from that in Europe, which had been more central in the history of the gold standard, and where arguments about credibility played a greater role. Latin America had been marginal in the years of the "classical," prewar, gold standard, in that there were relatively frequent suspensions of the exchange and departures from parity. A second consideration, which again diminished the weight of the credibility argument that was made so frequently and forcefully in the central European cases, was that there had been no recent experiences of extreme inflation. In consequence there was less of a need to cling to a nominal exchange anchor as a tool of stabilization policy. (To put this in terms of 1990s parallels: the situation of Latin America in the 1920s was closer to that of East Asia in the 1990s, where there was less need for an anchor, than to that of Latin American countries in the aftermath of inflations in the 1970s and 1980s.)

Currency depreciation was in many countries a fairly rapid response to falling commodity prices. Argentina and neighboring Uruguay suspended the gold standard in December 1929; at the same time the Brazilian exchange began to depreciate. In March 1930 the Bolivian exchange fell, and in September 1930 that of Venezuela. These movements were responses to trade problems, but they affected debt policy in that a consequence of depreciation was to make foreign debt service more expensive in terms of the national currency. As in central Europe, then, an attack on the exchange rate could be read as a threat to the stability of the debt structure.

Bank vulnerability constituted a final element of weakness in some of the more developed economies. The different experience of Argentine and Brazilian banking goes some way to explaining a different room for policy maneuver later in the 1930s. Argentina had experienced a large expansion of bank credit in the 1920s, and in the depression, undercapitalized banks were vulnerable to panic. In April 1931, weeks before the outbreak of the central European banking crisis, a major depositors' run set in. The government response was different from that of the central European authorities: the quasi-official Banco de Nación (there was no central bank) was allowed to discount commercial paper (including, presumably, some bills that represented purely financial transactions) at the government-owned Casa de Conversión. But the extent of the Argentine banking panic can be judged from deposit statistics: from 1928 through 1931, deposits in commercial banks contracted by 25 percent. The government program had a major fiscal cost. Already in 1930, the government deficit was 40 percent of expenditure.[85] Chile had a very similar experience (26 percent), while the Brazilian banking sector, with a contraction of only 5 percent, was barely affected.[86]

In 1930 some Latin American bonds fell sharply in price on the U.S. market, with both Brazil and Bolivia now priced below 50 percent of the nominal value. The rating agency Moody's downrated Peru to Baa, and Bolivia, Brazil, and Venezuela to Ba.[87] The first debt default came in a country with a very unfavorable debt/export ratio. In December 1930 Bolivia defaulted on the old government sinking fund, and in January 1931 on the general payment of interest. Peru, by now engulfed in civil war, defaulted in March 1931. Some countries (such as Chile), however, still even managed to raise long-term capital in 1930, as investors believed that the collapse of the copper price was only a temporary blip; but the country descended into political chaos, with a revolt in September. In March 1931 import tariffs were raised, but this measure was not sufficient to deal with the balance-of-payments deficit. In June 1931, following the Hoover moratorium on war debts, Chile suspended interest and service charges and imposed exchange controls. At the end of July the government resigned and was followed by a short-lived "Socialist Republic." At this stage, a general regional panic began. Colombia defaulted first on municipal and departmental bonds, in 1931, and on central government debt in 1933. Cuba defaulted on $170 million in U.S. debts in August.

There was little political response to the chain of Latin American defaults. It was by now a story familiar from Europe. The U.S. government refused to intervene, and in fact saw its major future task as regulating U.S. banking to prevent the abuse of the North American capital market. A U.S. Foreign Bondholders' Protective Council, created as a response to the calamity in 1933, was almost completely ineffective.[88] During the 1930s some Latin American governments, notably Chile, bought back defaulted bonds at relatively low prices. The only major country that did not default was Argentina.

Debt defaults went hand in hand with devaluations (a consequence of the default was that there was less need to worry about the effect of devaluation in increasing the internal value of external debt). What was the room for policy maneuver? In an influential essay, Carlos Díaz-Alejandro tried to differentiate between larger countries or those with "relatively autonomous public sectors," which could manipulate exchange rates, tariffs, and domestic credit. Small, mainly Central American states, on the other hand, such as Guatemala, Honduras, Nicaragua, and Panama, as well as Cuba, suffered because they had no autonomous exchange policy (they remained pegged to the U.S. dollar).[89] El Salvador had a small depreciation against the dollar, but its economic recovery remained modest.

In many of the depreciating economies the measures led to a real depreciation (i.e., prices did not follow the devaluation) and provided the basis for an export-based recovery.[90] In Argentina, Brazil, Chile, Colombia, Mexico, Peru, and Uruguay, real exchange rates were between 30 and 90 percent of their 1925–1929 levels. Wages, like prices, stayed low.[91] The result was that substituting for imported goods became a much more attractive strategy. Colombia and Brazil already showed some measure of recovery in 1932; Peruvian cotton exports picked up in 1933. But the long-term basis for a really sustained export-based recovery was threatened by the increasing trade protectionism of the industrialized countries (see Chapter 3). Where there was no default, there was a much slower recovery, and Argentina stood out as by far the poorest performer of the major South American economies in the 1930s.

The Crisis in the Industrial Countries

The central European banking crisis of 1931 had immediate repercussions throughout the world, particularly in the Middle East and Latin America, where an important part of the banking structure was in foreign ownership and thus very vulnerable to crises in Europe or North America. In Turkey in July 1931, there were runs on branches of the Deutsche Bank and the collapse of the Banque Turcque pour le Commerce et l'Industrie. In Egypt, the Cairo and Alexandria branches of the Deutsche Orientbank closed their offices. In Latvia, those banks with a German connection were hit: the Bank of Libau and the International Bank of Riga. What began in Rumania as a crisis of just the German-associated banks—particularly the Banca Generale a Tarii Romanesti—became a general panic: a run on the Banca de Credit Romana and the Banca Romaneascu. Before the end of the year, one of the leading banks, the Banca Marmarosch Blank & Co., collapsed.

In Mexico a leading bank, the Crédito Español de México, collapsed in July 1931, and the crash was followed by a run on the central bank as the confidence of foreign investors evaporated. There was the Argentine crash, and then the Chilean panic. In Italy no open panic occurred, but the intrinsic position of the banks was as weak as in central Europe. From December 1930, deposits in the three largest Italian banks fell, and in April 1931 depositors came near to panic. The state responded with a rescue operation, which transferred illiquid industrial assets to a new holding company, Istituto di Ricostruzione Industriale (IRI).[92]

These weaknesses contributed to the danger to the most international of the world's financial centers, the City of London; and then, in the *annus terribilis* of international financial relations, London produced its own shock to the world system.

Conventional wisdom has it that some sort of sterling crisis, which would inevitably lead to the abandonment of the gold standard rate of £ = $4.86, followed more or less inevitably from the choice of an overvalued parity, the prewar parity, for prestige reasons in 1925. This is the view of John Kenneth Galbraith: "In 1925 began the long series of exchange crises which, like the lions in Trafalgar Square and the streetwalkers in Piccadilly, are now an established part of the British scene."[93] This view is repeated in most recent analysis: it was most effectively argued by Donald Moggridge, but appears also in the works of Sidney Pollard and Robert Boyce (who argue that $4.86 represented a victory of a "City" financial interest over a commercial and manufacturing one), and Diane Kunz (who takes the more harmless view that it was just a mistake).[94]

This view is difficult to sustain on the basis of calculations on the value of sterling based on either purchasing power parity or real exchange rates. Milton Friedman and Anna Schwartz give a purchasing-power parity for 1929 of $5.50, indicating a substantial *under*valuation of the pound. British net exports bear out the same story, rising absolutely and in real value and relative to imports after the mid-1920s.[95] Eichengreen has used an econometric model to show that the unfavorable development in the British balance of payments in 1931 (as Britain's earnings from services and especially from shipping fell off during the world depression) cannot account for the severity of the exchange losses. Temin in consequence is obliged in his recent account to argue that the 1925 mistake was not the choice of exchange rate—the old story about the Norman mistake (the decision driven by the Bank of England's idiosyncratic governor, Montagu Norman, to return to gold at the old parity)—but rather the choice of *any* parity: it was the commitment to a fixed exchange-rate regime that tied Britain's hands. This is a much more radical objection to Norman's policy, but it is one made by hardly anyone at the time.

Instead the explanation lies in the domino effects on the banking structure of the central European events. Britain and the United States were vulnerable because of their position in the international capital markets as major short-term debtors. Britain was the first to be hit by the panic.

In memoranda produced during the 1931 crisis, the Bank of England's officials repeatedly referred to the high costs of staying on the gold standard. What did they mean? What were the high domestic costs that were being imposed as a consequence of maintaining the gold convertibility of sterling? We should refrain from adopting the anachronistic view that these costs lay in the forced reduction of public expenditure, the cuts in pay or the reduction in the dole. On the contrary, the Bank and its world were convinced that these were necessary—whatever the exchange parity—if a stable rate were to be maintained at all.

In fact the domestic costs lay in the vulnerability of the British financial system. This was already made apparent in one of the first Committee of Treasury (the critical decisionmaking body at the Bank of England during the crisis) meetings on the crisis. On 27 July 1931 the meeting was joined by a representative of the British Treasury, Sir Richard Hopkins, who had just set out a memorandum in which he formulated very clearly the British danger:

> We cannot control that we are in the midst of an unexampled slump, nor the fact that Germany is bankrupt, that great assets of ours are frozen there, and that foreign nations are drawing their credits from there over our exchanges. Nor can we control the fact that foreign nations have immense sums of money in London and will try to get them away if distrust of the pound extends . . . the first thing at which foreigners look is the budgetary position.[96]

At the same time the British clearing bank (the British term for commercial banks) representatives met to hear the Bank's view and to present their own demands.

On the twenty-seventh, Hopkins' task was to present Chancellor of the Exchequer Philip Snowden's view to the bankers: "If such credits [from France and the United States] are raised, and indeed in any present contingency, the Bank should be prepared to use its gold to the extent necessary and H. M. Government will be ready to increase the fiduciary issue to enable such gold to be released." But he also added a warning about the penalties for failure: "If credits cannot be arranged and gold continued to be withdrawn, British banks must be entirely free to withdraw credits from Germany."[97] Yet the latter could not be a realistic option. The London conference had recently recommended the maintenance of foreign short-term credit to Germany on the insistence of the world financial community, and everyone realized that it would be impossible for banks to extricate themselves from Germany without bringing the whole credit structure crashing down.

Montagu Norman and his deputy governor, Sir Ernest Harvey, left the Committee of Treasury, went to a meeting of the clearing bankers, and reported back. The clearing banks, they said, "opposed the idea of any credit," because a foreign central-bank operation to assist the Bank of England would allow the Bank to continue to make gold shipments that would be financed by the withdrawal of deposits in London banks. In short, the external drain would turn Britain into an Austria or a Germany.

It was this awareness, that the British problem lay fundamentally in the liquidity and solvency of some banks, that made the credits from France and the United States look like such a poor idea, and made the Bank unwilling to use either the Bank rate or its own reserves in the crisis. But since the problem lay in the banks and in the delicate area of confidence, it would have been entirely counterproductive for the Bank to make public this argument. Prime Minister Ramsay MacDonald also always spoke about a "flight from the pound" and a "financial panic" in the same breath: we know how the former was reflected in the exchange losses at the Bank of England, but the latter has been much more obscure.

English commercial banks had traditionally avoided long-term commitments to industry, and had indeed been taken to task for their neglect by the Macmillan committee (whose report on the weakness of the British system, published on 13 July, itself played a role in the British crisis). In fact, however, a deflationary environment, such as existed in Britain after the collapse of the postwar boom in 1920, can immobilize even short-term credits. During the 1920s British banks became ever more closely involved with the fortunes of Britain's crisis-bound staple industries, especially Lancashire textiles. There are similarities here to the continental disasters of the Austrian Bodenkreditanstalt and the German Danat, in both of which textile lending played a major role. The Bank of England, in its role as financial policeman, therefore eventually became involved in the reconstruction of Lancashire and in regional policy through the Bankers' Industrial Development Corporation.[98]

In addition to problems relating to domestic industrial commitments came in 1931 the continental situation. Foreign exposure was the Achilles' heel of the London City. The position in this regard for the large joint-stock clearing banks was much safer than that of the private bankers, Schroeders, Lazards, or Kleinworts, who had committed themselves heavily to central Europe. Since the first outbreak of the continental difficulties, rumors had swept the marketplace about the position of British banks. On 18 May 1931, Governor Harrison had thought them sufficiently grave to cable to Norman: "For your information and such comment as you care to make, persistent rumors have today run the gamut here regarding Barclays Bank in particular and also Schroeders and lastly Rothschilds."[99] In view of events in central Europe, Kleinworts appealed to the Bank of England for a guarantee of its overdraft from the Westminster Bank (one of the large commercial—in British parlance, clearing—banks), but unsuccessfully.[100] In addition to investments, the banks were threatened because of large forward positions from German, Austrian, and Hungarian persons and institutions.[101] There was some awareness of the fragility of the merchant banks even before the crisis. A rating system in the autumn of 1930 evaluated the clearing banks and the large American banks as AAA, but rated Higginson & Co. (heavily involved in central Europe) and J. H. Schroeder as A, and Kleinworts as BI.[102]

The merchant banks tried to refinance themselves with the clearers. On 15 July, for instance, the Anglo-French Banking Corporation informed the Midland Bank that it was anticipating £700,000 in withdrawals and asked to borrow that sum. There was another mechanism that touched the clearing banks: the indirect effects of the central European crisis. The Banca Commerciale Italiana had £5.5 million in credits from the Midland, some of which reflected onward lending to Germany.[103]

At the Bank of England's Currency Committee, established immediately in the wake of the devaluation, one banker argued that £100 million in deposits had been lost overall by the English system since the beginning of the year. Another banker said very candidly: "The Banks have great difficulty in making both ends meet. Their losses have been terrific."[104] For the nine clearing banks, the aggregate monthly average of deposits fell from £1.836 billion in January 1931 to £1.688 billion in October. The banks were also affected differently: in the course of 1931, Barclays lost 3.9 percent of deposits and current accounts, the Westminster 6.6 percent, Lloyds 8.5 percent, the National Provincial 10.4 percent, and the Midland (the largest English bank) 9.8 percent.

The Economist wrote that though the European standstill did not affect the joint stock banks, "several Accepting houses and especially some of the newer international banking houses founded in London during the past decade were seriously implicated, and the latter also had to face a sudden and wholesale withdrawal of their foreign deposits, which formed the bulk of their resources. With many of their assets immobilized, they had to meet the withdrawals by sales of securities at a time when the gilt-edged [government bills] market was abnormally depressed."[105]

The most energetic and persistent pressure on the Bank to devalue thus came from bankers who feared for their own position. Most striking is the position of Sir Robert Kindersley, one of the most active and vigorous directors of the Bank, and chairman of the threatened bank Lazard Bros. & Co. The bankers also turned to the politicians. On 16 September 1931, Sir William Goode, who in the 1920s had served as informal adviser to the National Bank of Hungary, wrote to Prime Minister Ramsay MacDonald, stating that the gold standard could not be kept unless long-term loans "for the other countries" of Europe started to flow again and thus reduced the strain on British banks.[106]

It was not just central Europe that presented a threat to the English banks. The final blow to sterling in the judgment of foreign markets came with the announcement of British difficulties in South America. The *Echo de Paris* reported that "the news that the Brazilian coupons would not be paid on 1 October increased the disarray. England is the largest creditor of Latin America."[107]

Concerns about the stability of English banks explain the otherwise mysterious failure to support sterling through intervention in the Paris market on 5 August: by letting the exchange slip, the Bank was warning of the possibility of an end to support, and depreciation of the speculative attack continued. It was not, however, a very skillful way of restoring confidence, and the reaction of the Banque de France made necessary the sterling pegging that continued until 20 September. On that date the cabinet prepared the legislation and the announcement abandoning the 1925 Gold Standard Act. In much greater secrecy, it also drew up a scheme for a banking holiday on the German model "in case any panic should occur."[108]

The absence of a rise in the interest rate at which the Bank of England lent (Bank Rate) is also a puzzle. Although a 6 percent level was briefly considered, the Bank did not use one of the most traditional defenses of central banks. The Bank did its best after 5 August to minimize the drama of sterling, in order to protect British banks. Raising the rate would be an acknowledgment of the strain and an encouragement to get out while it was still possible and would allow the outward flow of short-term funds to continue. Raising the rate was also rejected because higher interest levels would send up the politically sensitive unemployment rate, and that might encourage a further speculative attack on the pound.[109] Using reserves was likewise ruled out, since there was no point in doing this just to allow British banks to make payments and thus slide into illiquidity. Thus in practice the Bank of England did nothing to defend sterling.

Montagu Norman had broken down even before the pound sterling did. Faced with an apparently unstoppable speculative attack, Norman had on 28 July noted in his diary "feeling queer." He then stayed in bed in complete nervous collapse until his doctors ordered him to go on a long sea voyage abroad. The Bank's deputy governor informed him of the British devaluation in an apparently mystifying message which reached him on the ship home: "Old lady goes off on Monday." When he reached the port in Liverpool, he received the deputy governor's letter, which read: "Indeed we seem to have been afflicted with every kind of misfortune. I hope you are going to rest quietly for a bit."[110]

The British bank dilemma made officials such as Harry Siepmann, the Bank's major expert on international relations, seriously consider restrictions on capital movements as an alternative to devaluation. In addition, the more perceptive or suspicious Labour politicians became alarmed that the dispute about the dole was being made to carry the responsibility for a state of affairs that had nothing or little to do with the operation of the British labor market but arose out of financial conditions in central Europe. The secretary of state for the colonies, Sidney Webb (Lord Passfield), put the point in the following way: "If a foreign Government, which for reasons of internal politics was anxious to avoid introducing a system of national relief for the unemployed, chooses to take advantage of our exposed financial position, we can be held to ransom and compelled to make an essential change in our domestic social policy as the price of rescue for the financial interests of the City."[111]

Interpreted in this light, the devaluation of sterling in September 1931 was a wholly successful operation. It did not remove the pressure for budgetary control. On the contrary, the national government won the general election on an austerity program designed to combat inflation, and continued to pursue balanced budgets. But it did halt the deposit loss; and deposits even increased as foreigners—and in particular Indians—exchanged gold for sterling.

This strategy was so successful because of the postdevaluation behavior of sterling on the foreign-exchange markets. If sterling had fallen only slightly, with an accompanying expectation of further falls, or if sterling had fallen continuously over a sustained period (as was the case with many currencies of South American countries after devaluation), investors would have remained nervous and continued to pull short-term funds out of British banks. However, the actual course was a sharp fall and then a stabilization, with a bounce back and some belief in a future rise (see Figure 2.2). This belief induced investors to leave their funds in London. In that way, devaluation as it was practiced in the British case saved the British banks. In that way, shaking off Britain's "golden fetters" ended the British depression. It set the stage for a recovery based on a more relaxed mone-

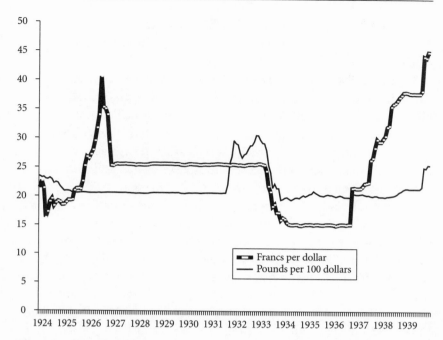

Figure 2.2 Pound and franc exchange rates relative to the U.S. dollar, 1924–1939 (Source: Global Financial Database, online at http://www/globalfindata.com, Exchange Rates)

tary policy, which encouraged credit-driven spending on housing and consumer durables.

After September 1931, financial pressure shifted to the United States. The story of the United States is clearly central to the whole story of the world depression. The United States was by far the world's largest industrial economy, and of course the world's largest capital exporter. A failure of its capital markets was a major part of the European and South American story.

The peak of American prosperity had been in 1929. But we should not assume that there was already a Great Depression with the stock market crash of October 1929. The downturn initially looked similar to—actually rather less intense than—the sharp postwar collapse of 1920–21. It took 1931, and a new sort of financial crisis, to turn the American experience into a Great Depression. The shock produced radically new, and very pessimistic, notions of the possibilities for public action in monetary and fiscal policy. Here, as elsewhere, the depression generated an intellectual paralysis.

The thesis that a contagious financial crisis had a major impact in worsening the U.S. depression may at first appear almost perverse. The mechanism for contagion seems very clear in the case of small central European or Latin American economies, dependent on the international capital market, and even in the case of Britain, where some strategically critical City banks had a major part of their assets invested in foreign undertakings. But in the United States, with its enormous internal market?

A powerful, and well-known, case has been made by Friedman and Schwartz that bank panics in the United States caused a dramatic contraction in the money supply that was not effectively countered by the Federal Reserve System. These panics, in tandem with the policy failure of the central bank, provided the monetary causes of the Great Depression. Friedman and Schwartz identified four waves of bank failures, November–December 1930, April 1931, September–October 1931, and finally February–March 1933. In the course of these, the number of banks in the United States was reduced from 24,026 at the end of 1929 to 14,440 by the end of 1933.

This analysis has stimulated a great deal of valuable research. Ben Bernanke has suggested a different, nonmonetary mechanism, whereby the failure of banks increased the cost of credit intermediation, and thus worsened general business conditions.[112]

As an explanation of the decline of the U.S. economy after 1929, the Friedman and Schwartz account is inadequate. In particular, as a recent detailed examination of the local circumstances of bank failures by Elmus Wicker has made clear, the first two of the Friedman and Schwartz waves of bank collapses have been misidentified. The first wave was not a general collapse, but rather a product of the failure of two institutions. The New York Bank of United States had $161 million in deposits. The Nashville Tennessee investment bank Caldwell & Company controlled the largest chain of banks in the South, with $200 million in assets, and its collapse in November 1930 had immediate effects in four southern states. The second wave was also a regional, rather than a national, phenomenon. In terms of Federal Reserve districts, it was limited to Chicago, Cleveland, and Philadelphia.

The most interesting, and most important, of the U.S. banking panics was the one immediately following the British departure from the gold standard. Unlike the previous localized panics, but like the European crises of 1931, this bank crisis was accompanied by an external drain. From 21 September to 8 October there was a gold outflow of $369 million from the United States, almost all to Europe, and the Federal Reserve Bank of New York (FRBNY) responded with the classic measure of an increase in its discount rate, from 1.5 to 2.5 percent.[113] The governor of the New York bank, Harrison, on 8 October expressed doubt that an increase in the New York rate would really stop the outflow: elsewhere, such a measure had undermined rather than strengthened confidence. In the next week the gold outflow doubled, and on 15 October the discount rate was increased to 3.5 percent (still low in comparison with the extraordinarily high levels that central banks in central Europe had used in the failed defense of their currencies). Friedman and Schwartz comment that this external panic "was accompanied by a spectacular increase in bank failures and runs on banks."[114] Here, as elsewhere, their argument is somewhat slippery as to causality: did the external run affect the banks, as customers withdrew deposits in order to move out of the dollar? Or did doubtful customers of weak banks simply look for stronger institutions, and believe that they existed in Europe?

New York banks, which might be thought to be the most exposed to international problems and influences, were not in fact the worst affected by the September and October panics. As in the spring of 1931, the crisis was worst in the Midwest. Another round of this sort of attack resulting from foreign withdrawals occurred in the spring of 1932. The New York banks were the most conspicuous victims, as liabilities of U.S. banks to Europeans fell by $550 million. The Europeans withdrew deposits across the exchange, with the result that the U.S. monetary gold stock fell by almost exactly the same amount ($535 million).[115]

In response to the appearance of a crisis structurally similar to that of the European trauma of 1931, policymakers believed that they had no choice except to respond to the psychology, irrational as it might be, of the market. There was no room for fiscal maneuver, not because of any economic analysis of the consequences of larger deficits, but because of the (quite reasonable) belief that nervous markets would immediately punish fiscal deviancy. The same psychology explains why the Federal Reserve was so reluctant to pursue the monetary expansion—via open-market securities purchases—that Friedman and Schwartz reasonably believe might have stabilized the monetary situation.

Up to the September crisis, President Hoover had tried to deal with the crisis by offering bold, expansionary fiscal measures (which rather belie his usual reputation as the ineffective depression-era predecessor of the more imaginative Roosevelt). On 2 June 1931 Hoover had announced that the deficit for the fiscal year 1931 would exceed $900 million. This produced some hostile comments in the press, but until the sterling crisis the federal government found no problem selling treasury bills or certificates of indebtedness (indeed they are alleged to have gone "like hot cakes").[116]

Then the impact of the sterling crisis led to a similar focus on public finance as had occurred in central Europe, and then in Britain. By the late autumn, the U.S. treasury bill situation swung round completely, and sales now affected prices in a weakened market. This in turn affected banks that held assets in securities. In December 1931 the Committee on Progress of Public Works of the President's Organization on Unemployment Relief reported the new situation. Major issues of government bonds "would cause serious declines in the market values of the present outstanding low-yield issues, and thus result in severe losses for the holders of such securities. It may well be that one result would be a considerable number of additional bank failures."[117]

By this time, maintaining—and preferably improving—bond prices became a major first step in any program to tackle depression. In part confidence could be manipulated by shifting as many items as possible off-budget: the new Reconstruction Finance Corporation of 1932, designed to support the banks, was allowed to borrow $1.5 billion in its own name, so that this would not appear as a part of the federal deficit.

Above all, a major tax increase, despite the procyclical consequences for demand, appeared the best way to reassure a nervous market. In his State of the Union message on 8 December 1931, Hoover took a sharply different line from that of only a few months earlier:

> Our first step towards recovery is to reestablish confidence and thus restore the flow of credit which is the very basis of our economic life. The first requirement of confidence and of economic recovery is financial stability of the United States Government . . . To go further than these limits in either expenditures, taxes, or borrowing will destroy confidence, de-

nude commerce and industry of their resources, jeopardize the financial system, and actually extend unemployment and demoralize agriculture rather than relieve it.[118]

The tax bill, and its success, now became the signal for success or failure in Hoover's attempt to resist inflationism.

The New York Federal Reserve Bank blamed the precarious exchange situation on conflicts in Congress, which failed to pass the tax bill because the initial version contained a highly unpopular sales tax.[119] On 3 May 1932 the U.S. Treasury announced that the deficit for the first ten months of the fiscal year had been $2.234 billion (by comparison, the previous year's figure was merely $886 million). Only at the beginning of June did the Senate pass a budget-balancing bill raising income tax, excise, and postal rates in order to yield an additional $1.121 billion, and making economies (including pay cuts for public employees) of $238 million.

Foreign investors saw in the United States the budget problems that they had witnessed the previous year in central Europe. The U.S. position, in the English view, "was very shocking . . . a lot of serious talk was going on about the dollar and our leaving the gold standard." The cause was not so much the bank failures but "politics in Congress and failure to balance the budget, which was taken by many people as evidence of a wish to get off the gold standard."[120] Governor Harrison of the New York Fed immediately used this information from London to press Secretary of the Treasury Ogden Mills and President Hoover to pass a tax bill and agree with Congress on an economy drive—in short, to perform all the deflationary routines that the U.S. bankers had forced on Europe over the previous year. Hoover's only objection to this was that he could not act out of the blue and that he needed a crisis to force Congress to accept this position: "they needed some shock, like a wide open break in the stock market or the exchanges, for instance, to prompt immediate action."[121]

The U.S. elections in November, in the campaign for which the Democratic candidate promised effective action to balance the federal budget, were accompanied by gold inflows: $16 million came in the week ending 21 November, $29 million the next week; and the movement out did not begin again until early February, when it coincided with another banking panic. From December 1932 to 15 March 1933, 447 banks were suspended, merged, or liquidated.[122] Between 1 February and 4 March the FRBNY lost 61 percent of its gold reserves, and at the beginning of March the foreign-exchange market in dollars collapsed because of heavy selling by the British Exchange Equalization Fund.[123] A recent analysis suggests that external conditions—the fear of devaluation—contributed significantly to the domestic panic.[124] (An alternative account sees the final and most destructive of the U.S. banking panics as a consequence of the disorderly declaration of bank holidays in individual states, beginning in Michigan. Depositors in other states saw what was happening and tried to withdraw their funds before the declaration of new holidays.)[125] The most plausible explanations of the two major general waves of bank failures (the only generalized panics in the United States) place the emphasis on foreign factors.

There were plenty of initiatives for dollar devaluation. Senator Thomas T. (Tom) Connally, a Texas Democrat, had tried to include this measure in the Glass-Steagall bill on reform of the monetary and banking system. There were signs that the new administration might be sympathetic. President-elect Franklin D. Roosevelt had held a meeting in December 1932 in Albany in order to discuss devaluation, and on 19 February Senator Carter Glass refused to become secretary of the Treasury because he had not been able to extract from Roosevelt a promise not to devalue. The national Banking Holiday eventually enacted in the early morning of 7 March 1933 became necessary in order to protect the Federal Reserve System from further losses, though naturally the Board wished to keep this a secret, since, as Chairman Eugene Meyer said, he "didn't want the Federal Reserve System to be blamed."[126]

The governor of the Federal Reserve Bank of New York, George Harrison, had since 1930 been an advocate of open-market purchases of government securities as a way of halting the dramatic monetary contraction. In April 1932 the program was stepped up, partly in order to forestall government legislation affecting the Federal Reserve System. By June 1932 total purchases amounted to $1 billion, but this only offset a loss of $500 million in gold and a reduction of $400 million in Federal Reserve discounts and bills bought. But given the extent of foreign nervousness, greater activity by the Federal Reserve System in this regard would have had a counterproductive effect.

Likewise, government initiatives against the crisis were effective to only a very limited extent. Hoover blamed enemies on two fronts for his dilemma. On the one hand, the bankers hemmed him in and had made the bold anticyclical schemes of the 1920s, or even of 1930, impossible to realize. Leading bankers, he said, quoting "one of the best and most influential" citizens, were "nothing less than public enemies, and all should be treated as such."[127] On the other side, Congress had damaged the government's credit by debating freely on "wild" and "vast" schemes, and had upset the market. Squeezed between politics and the market, Hoover—and indeed every other statesman of the time—was completely and hopelessly lost.

Hoover's attempts to regulate the financial markets in order to resolve the dilemma were unsuccessful. The National Credit Corporation, set up at Hoover's insistence by the bankers in October 1931, was a private corporation intended to give loans to individual banks. The Reconstruction Finance Corporation of January 1932, a government body, gave $900 million in loans through 1932. The Glass-Steagall Act (February 1932) allowed member banks to borrow on more generous terms from the Federal Reserve System.

All these innovations failed to prevent the large wave of panics and banking failures after January 1933, which led to the need to impose a nationwide banking holiday. In part, the disaster of 1933 was simply a consequence of the mishandling of two large Detroit banks. Wicker believes that "if there had been bold and effective action initially to reopen the Michigan banks, the collapse of the banking system may have been averted."[128] The only person who might have had enough political power to step in was Hoover, but he was in the last weeks of his presidency, a lame duck in the original political sense of the term. It was the new administration that thus needed to deal with a double problem of internal and external runs.

Roosevelt in his election campaign had promised fiscal orthodoxy, in line with the requirements of confidence. His program included a 25 percent reduction in federal expenditure and a balanced budget: "I regard reduction in Federal spending as one of the most important issues of this campaign. It is the most direct and effective contribution the government can make to business."[129] This was a sincere belief, and not simply a tactical move to reassure a worried electorate. Until the deep depression of 1937–38 forced a rethinking, budget balancing played an important part in the formulation of fiscal policy. The only effective measure against the financial contagion was the dollar devaluation, which Roosevelt accepted on 18 April 1933. It was made even more effective by the announcement of 3 July 1933 that the United States would not attempt to stabilize the dollar parity. The message included the claim: "The world will not long be lulled by the specious fallacy of achieving a temporary and probably an artificial stability in foreign exchange on the part of a few large countries only."[130] Roosevelt's measures made a major contribution to ending the bank runs, and with them the U.S. depression.

The effects of the contagious banking crises had included not only a direct and devastating effect on economic activity, but also a perception of the limitation on the room for fiscal maneuver by the federal government. Under Hoover, federal expenditures as a share of GNP had effectively doubled, from around 4 to 8 percent; but they could not go higher, because of the way in which the confidence limitation was perceived.

On an international level, the focus of speculation shifted elsewhere. France had received a substantial amount of international capital flight money, from central Europe in the first half of 1931, and then from Britain and especially the United States. The U.S. flows continued into 1933, so that an estimate of September 1933 gives the figure for capital flight into France as $8.3 billion, "of which a very large amount is American money," fleeing from inflation and Roosevelt; in addition the French Finance Ministry estimated that 1.5 billion treasury bills (*bons du trésor* and *bons de la défense nationale*) were held abroad.[131]

This situation made France enormously vulnerable: should confidence return elsewhere, or should the French economy show any signs of inflation, the gigantic inflows would flood out again. The capital inflows put as much pressure on governments to maintain a deflationary course as fear of capital outflows did elsewhere. The major problem facing policymakers lay in the volatility of "hot money." When did the first signs of a franc weakness become apparent? Already, it seems, before the U.S. dollar left gold.

An internal gold drain took place in late 1931 as French bankers and individuals feared inflation; and in particular those well-placed in financial circles took advantage of their information about the likely threats that followed from France's large capital imports. According to the Bank of England, when the Banque de France's gold losses were examined, "the names of two of the Regents of the Banque de France, one in his own name and one through his company, figured as purchasers of gold."[132] In December 1932 foreign banks were shipping gold out of France: the Guaranty Trust Company, the Banque Belge pour l'Etranger, and Barclays Bank.[133] In the summer of 1932 the worry was, according to part of the French financial press, that France was in "pleine inflation."[134]

But it was the U.S. gold embargo in April 1933 that sent France on a roller-coaster ride lasting for the rest of the decade. The gold exports of the

United States to France halted and were reversed: in 1934 France sent $60.5 million to the United States, in 1935 $934.2 million, and in 1936 $573.7 million. The immediate reaction to the Roosevelt declaration, according to the Banque de France's director of the Foreign Service, was that "London and most other European centers figured that France would leave the gold standard very shortly. The result was . . . that balances were being withdrawn, particularly to Switzerland."[135]

The French in consequence were from 1933 highly concerned with their vulnerability to flows, and tried to deal with it by urging an international currency stabilization. But they were frustrated in the first place by the U.S. gold purchases of 1933–34 undertaken in order to drive down the dollar; and second by British unwillingness to commit sterling to a fixed parity.

The gold standard had always made necessary a difficult balancing act between internal and external monetary policies; and France had even before the central European crisis been plagued by budget and banking problems.

France rapidly departed from the large budget surpluses that followed the franc stabilization of 1926–1928. Large initial surpluses made it appear that there were plentiful funds available for new spending projects. By the budget year 1930–31 there was a small deficit, and it grew alarmingly throughout 1931. In addition, the depression, which came relatively late in France, began to affect revenues and expenditure. Industrial output fell from June 1930, though through 1931 the decline was relatively modest. The depression, and the question of how to adjust the budget, posed more and more of a strain on French political institutions.

In the 1932 election campaign, as in the United States, both sides claimed to represent fiscal probity and anti-inflationary orthodoxy. After the narrow victory of the *cartel des gauches,* Edouard Herriot's government tried to demonstrate its concern for rectitude by appointing the technician Louis Germain-Martin as finance minister. He reduced the salaries of civil servants *(fonctionnaires),* cut expenditure, and pressed through tax increases. These measures were watered down after parliamentary debates, and the deficits remained. In December 1932 the cabinet fell over the war-debt payment due to the United States. In 1933 Edouard Daladier's Radical government attempted a more rigorous implementation of budgetary deflation. Laws of 28 February, 31 May, and 23 December aimed at reducing the scope for tax evasion; and a supplementary levy was imposed on the *fonctionnaires.* In total, in 1932 and 1933, 5.612 billion francs were saved by cuts, and 3.15 billion gained by so-called tax adjustments.[136] But the savings were canceled out by the government subsidization of agriculture required as the consequence of the imposition of a minimum grain price. As in central Europe, Germany, and also the United States, agricultural policy introduced a crucial element of destabilization into fiscal policy.

Parliamentary politics moved in two opposed directions: on the one hand, parties were unwilling to accept responsibility for cuts in payments—particularly to the *fonctionnaires* (who the socialists feared might be driven to support the Communist party). On the other hand, all parties from right to left had a substantial rural constituency, and pressed for greater spending on agricultural support. In a memorable phrase, Herriot spoke of the French peasant as the "greatest of French philosophers" and "our silent master."[137]

At the end of 1933 the financial situation deteriorated, Daladier fell, and in February 1934 fascist demonstrations brought Paris to the edge of civil war. The public lost confidence in the government, but also lost confidence in the banks; and the latter loss made the problems of dealing with the budget more acute.

In November 1930 the first big bank failures occurred in France: the Banque Adam of Boulogne-sur-Mer and the Oustric group. The Oustric collapse raised questions about the Banque de France's policy, judgment, and political contacts: it became a characteristically French financial "affair" with a parliamentary commission of inquiry that launched an onslaught on prominent politicians and on the governor of the Banque. The Banque was blamed for its overgenerous discounting of Oustric paper in the years before the collapse. It had raised the portfolio of Oustric bills from 6.66 million francs in September 1927 to 7.7 million in December, 20.385 million in April 1929, and 128.6 million by February 1930.[138] The governor of the Banque de France, Clément Moret, tried to defend his actions in a rather high-handed way—by explaining that the Banque was a private institution whose autonomy was guaranteed by the state, and that he had no obligation to release the figures of the Oustric account.[139] But Moret in the end dismissed the officials immediately responsible for the problem.

It was not just Oustric who had been heavily committed to investments in the rest of Europe. In August 1930 the four leading French banks had, the best estimates assumed, 5–6 billion francs abroad, of which two-thirds were invested via London; but 90 percent of the sum went eventually to central Europe, and London played no more than an intermediary role.[140] In September 1930, after the German Reichstag elections, a substantial part of these French investments were repatriated.

Not only were there French investments—usually indirect—in central Europe; France also became a magnet for capital moving out of the financial trouble zones. One indication of the extent of the movement is given by the rise in private deposits at the Banque de France, which during the central European panic increased from 11.884 billion francs (27 March 1931) to 15.187 billion on 26 June 1931. The additional 3 billion represents a part of the movement of money out of central Europe.

At first the authorities tried to make light of the French difficulties. Governor Moret said that the French bank failures were "due less to intrinsically unsound positions than to a wave of exaggerated pessimism."[141] But speaking to the Regents soon after the first bank failures, Moret struck a rather gloomier note: "There is a psychological factor that entirely escapes the action of the Banque. Movements of capital are today determined less by differences in interest rates than by the greater or lesser security they offer. Now, in the troubled state of the world, in the presence of the worries that surface in many countries, the franc appears as one of the most solid currencies—as a currency of refuge."[142]

Highly volatile capital flight movements led to new problems for France. Within a few years, anyone who wanted to restore confidence in French banking and in the French economy in general had to deny that there were large sums of foreign-flight capital placed there.[143]

The legacy of the Oustric affair was that on the one hand, the Banque de France suffered criticism for the overgenerous rescue of fraudulent enterprises and, on the other, bank failures prompted demands for a more expansive central bank policy. In 1931 Chambers of Commerce protested the "excessively restrictive discount and credit policy." In 1932 the Regional Association of Chambers of Commerce in Grenoble noted a resolution of its members that "the Banque de France should demonstrate the greatest liberalism in the granting of rediscounts."[144]

In fact the Banque de France did extend new credits to numerous French banks in the wake of the banking runs. During the first crisis (October 1930–January 1931) the Banque's portfolio of bills (an indication of its lending) increased from 4.685 billion francs to 7.364 billion. It rose again in September 1931, in the aftermath of the sterling crisis and the failure of the sixth-largest French bank, the Banque Nationale de Crédit

(BNC).[145] The Banque de France tackled the panic by giving new credits to rescue the Nancéienne de Crédit, the Banque Privée, the Groupe Messine, and the Mines d'Anzin, as well as to the Société Générale.[146]

The initial crisis in France had been an affair of the second-rank banks. The Banque d'Alsace-Lorraine had been weakened by the repercussions of the German inflation of the early 1920s, and in addition had taken over a series of weak banks in the late 1920s, of which the largest was the Banque du Rhin. The BNC had been in a very shaky position in the early 1920s and had had heavy losses during the franc inflation; it had experienced only a brief recovery in 1926–1928, when it had been able to reduce its obligation to the Banque de France from 480 million francs to 3 million.[147]

From December 1932, however, all the major French banks lost deposits. As they became affected, they ran down their accounts with the Banque de France (over four months their holdings fell from 8 to 3 billion francs); and they asked for rediscounting at the Banque. They protested that they could no longer absorb the large volume of state paper issued.[148] Foreign banks (notably the Morgans and Bankers Trust) began to discount at the Banque de France too,[149] and a new series of provincial bank failures hit France: Charpentier (Cognac), Société Saint-Quentinoise de Crédit, the Banque du Centre (Limoges), Banque Renauld (Nancy).

In 1934 another major banking crisis threatened, and the big banks again looked vulnerable. There were difficulties at the Banque de l'Union Parisienne, the institution most concerned with the financing of the French armaments industry. The Crédit Lyonnais expanded its discounts with the Banque de France in February; and Paribas also needed the assistance of the central bank.[150] From the end of 1932 to the end of 1936 deposits at the four great banks fell from 21 billion francs to 15.3 billion (while savings banks retained a greater degree of public confidence, and their deposits actually rose, from 34.216 to 35.714 billion francs).[151]

The movements after 1932 are an indication of the external drain afflicting France. When bank-deposit withdrawals threatened the French credit structure, the Banque de France increased its rediscounting in order to keep the French banks liquid; but this made resources available for outward movements, and in this way the Banque while propping up the French banking structure actually nourished the flight of capital from the country.

The process can be studied quite precisely in the big franc crises of the early 1930s. From 2 December 1932 to 31 March 1933 the Banque de

France lost 3,354 million francs in gold; from 15 September to 22 December 1933, 6,774 million; from 12 January to 2 March 1934, 3.401 billion; from 29 March to 7 June 1935, 11.684 billion; and from 25 October to 6 December 1935, 6.198 billion francs. In all these crises, the Banque's portfolio increased, by 719, 1,041, 1,646, 5,430, and 3,289 million francs respectively, in line with the external capital movements; and the credit account of the great banks contracted (2,013, 835, 736, 2,206, and 657 million francs respectively).[152]

By 1935 the gold outflows had assumed such alarming proportions that internally at least some officials of the Banque de France began to doubt the Banque's official line of doing everything to resist franc devaluation. On 5 March, just before the first big panic wave of 1935 set in, the director of the Banque de France's Foreign Department, Charles Cariguel, "thought that the majority of businessmen in France were willing to make the sacrifices necessary to adjust to something like the present value of sterling but if the pound depreciated further they would probably regard adjustment as hopeless and be unwilling to make further sacrifices to that end . . . For the first time during my telephone conversations with him, Mr. Cariguel clearly implied that devaluation of the franc might be necessary to adjust their position vis-à-vis sterling."[153]

By April, Cariguel was filled with gloom about the franc, since the Belgian devaluation appeared to destroy the gold bloc; he predicted that Switzerland would follow rapidly, and then France would be exposed to the full gale. On 15 April, J. E. Crane, the deputy governor of the Federal Reserve Bank of New York, made a suggestion that sketched out the line that would eventually be followed in September 1936: he inquired about rumors of a 15–20 percent French franc devaluation: "that done, there was some possibility of a three-cornered arrangement—the dollar, the franc and sterling. He asked Cariguel how the French public would take that and Cariguel said that in his opinion the French were not ready for such a plan even if it were offered as part of an exchange stabilization all around."[154]

There were bolder spirits than Cariguel. The first major public statement in support of devaluation had come in June 1934 in a speech to the Chamber of Deputies by the conservative politician Paul Reynaud (who had in private been convinced of the need to devalue since 1933). He faced a massive onslaught from the press, who vilified him as the would-be expropriator of French small savers. Reynaud found only one major press ally, the deputy and proprietor of *Le petit journal*, Raymond Pâtenotre.

Professor Charles Rist, an influential economist and as a former deputy governor of the Banque de France something of an "insider," pleaded for devaluation from the spring of 1935. So also, most influentially, did the French financial attaché in London, Emanuel Mönick. On 1 September 1935 Mönick concluded that Britain was not likely to stabilize, and that France resembled the United States in the last days of the Hoover administration. He deduced that a "wisely measured monetary adaptation"—a circumlocution for devaluation—was needed.[155]

By early 1935 France had reached political and economic deadlock. Failure to stabilize the French budget by the familiar measures—to cut back expenditure, slash civil service pay, and raise taxes—meant movements across the exchanges, bank withdrawals, and increased borrowing from the Banque de France. Money rates in Paris soared in consequence. Some of the leading figures at the Banque de France, such as Robert Lacour-Gayet, the director of the Service d'Etudes, thought that governmental self-discipline was all that was needed: "A show of determination to put their house in order could very rapidly restore confidence and put an end to the whole of the present movement based on fear and speculation."[156] In November the business world blamed a new run on the franc on agitation in the Chamber's Commission des Finances for an end to the austerity policy.[157]

But France had reached by now the paradoxical position that the strains were so great that even deflation would undermine confidence, because of the heightened threat to the social order. Already the franc panic of early 1934 had been set off by demonstrations of the fascist Leagues in the streets of Paris on 6 February. These demonstrations had produced a mobilization on the left, and the formation of a Popular Front that included Communists. The center-right government lost support to both sides. The international market reacted by reading further deflation as a sign, not of an upgrade, but of a new menace to stability.[158]

Once France had reached this position, devaluation (which came, under a Popular Front left-coalition government, in October 1936) was the only option for breaking out of the vicious cycle of bank failures and imposed deflation.

France did not suffer alone in the 1930s. The other countries remaining on gold—the so-called gold bloc of Switzerland, the Netherlands, and Belgium—also suffered from chronic financial instability in which speculative movements played a major part.

These economies were vulnerable on two grounds. The ties to Germany

of Switzerland and the Netherlands presented a grave problem. Both countries attracted a great deal of capital flight that might move out again rapidly. Moreover, Swiss and Dutch money was frozen into Germany under
the standstill agreements. Short-term loans in the amount of 900 million
Swiss francs loans were subject to the German standstill; but that was not
the end of the Swiss problem. By 1934 a total of 3.39 billion in debts were
subject to compensation agreements. In 1933 Dutch credits to Germany
amounted to 1.044 billion guilders. In addition, German shares to the
nominal value of 263.8 million guilders were held by Dutchmen.[159]

Second, the maintenance of convertibility at the old parities subjected
these countries to speculative flows reacting to British, French, or American policies or anxieties. They had to pay an ever higher price for the
maintenance of an open economy.

The international exchanges reveal the extent of Swiss volatility in the
first half of the 1930s. Until the autumn of 1931 the Swiss Nationalbank
gained substantial amounts of gold: by the beginning of September it had
gained 1.158 billion Swiss francs (or 97 percent) in the year. From the sterling crisis until the devaluation of the dollar, its gold holdings remained
steady. After this, there were crises that corresponded with problems in
France. From March to July 1933 the Nationalbank lost 716 million Swiss
francs in gold; from January to April 1934, 364 million; and from March to
June 1935 517 million.

These flows in and out also affected the liquidity position of the Swiss
banks. The big inflows of 1931 resulted in enormously bloated cash reserves in the commercial banks (these rose from 467 million Swiss francs
in 1930 to 1.29 billion in 1931—in other words, they account for almost all
of the gold inflow).

In Switzerland a major political debate centered upon the consequences.
"Capital export," its critics said, had brought few gains and benefited only a
small urban financial elite, while exposing the country to external risks and
random shocks from international politics. The peasant political leader
Gottfried Gnägi argued that there should be no capital export as long as
Swiss interest rates remained at crisis levels.[160] The problem lay in the way
in which external involvement undermined Swiss financial stability.

After the collapse of the summer of 1931, capital flows were regulated. A
"gentlemen's agreement" concluded by the banks in February 1932 involved a promise that they would consult the Nationalbank before em-
barking on foreign capital issues; and this regulation of long-term loan

activity intensified during the decade. On the other hand, the Nationalbank had no control, and indeed no information, about short-term movements. When, in the course of trade negotiations, the government and the
Nationalbank attempted to find out about the volume of Swiss assets in
Germany, the Swiss banks simply refused to reply.[161] In late 1934 a banking
commission had been formed in order to investigate Swiss banking problems, and the report warned that the Swiss exposure to Germany presented
great risks, and that even a partial guarantee of the German assets could
not remove the likelihood of financial panics.

The banks' obstinacy appeared self-defeating in view of their vulnerability and their dependence on government support; but it was also in reality
a way of protecting themselves from revelations about just how weak they
really were. In order to mask their difficulties the Swiss banks insisted that
bank secrecy (Article 9 of the interwar Bank Law) formed an essential element of the Swiss way of life.[162]

In fact by 1934 a substantial amount of damage had already occurred.
One of the eight great banks, the Geneva Banque de l'Escompte, had already been in trouble in 1931. In 1932 it reported that of its total assets
of 392 million Swiss francs, 200 million were frozen in foreign investments (mostly in Hungary and Germany), and that it would be forced
to declare bankruptcy if Germany imposed a moratorium.[163] The state
supported the ailing bank, lending 55 million Swiss francs through a
newly created government-owned loan institute (the Schweizerische
Eidgenössische Darlehnskasse), and participated to the extent of 20 million Swiss francs in a recapitalization of the bank.[164] But even this reconstruction involved an optimistic valuation of the assets and a willful ignor-
ing of the severity of the central European crisis and its impact on the
Swiss. At the government discussions about assistance to the Banque de
l'Escompte, one banker explained: "In valuing the assets we can't use the
principle of a *bon père de famille*. That is possible only in normal times."
But there existed little doubt about the urgency of the task. In the view of
Federal Councillor Jean-Marie Musy, "A sudden closure of the Banque de
l'Escompte would have an influence on the stability of our currency. The
higher interests of our country demand that we intervene to save the
bank."[165]

In November 1933 another of the great banks, the Banque Populaire
Suisse (Schweizerische Volksbank), also needed reorganization after 150
million Swiss franc credits were written off. And in the wake of this 1933

crisis, the Swiss commercial banks lost deposits, and there was a movement toward the cantonal banks (which were less exposed to foreign risks).

The German and central European connection did not represent the only source of instability in Swiss financial life. The bank commission echoed the complaints made in other countries about the existence of unbalanced public budgets; in the Swiss case, the cantons suffered especially from increased social obligations during the depression even as their revenues were collapsing. But—as in other countries—it proved convenient to blame outsiders and foreigners.

The persistent deflationary pressure on public spending—since even small deficits could provoke dramatic flights of money in and out—combined with a tradition of populist democracy, eventually provoked a revolt. On the one side, the peasant party argued against Swiss financial dependence on other countries; on the other, the socialists organized a legislative initiative calling for a program to combat the depression. It included a detailed set of work-creation measures. At the same time, government funds would provide debt relief, promote tourism, and stimulate exports. The program would be accompanied by the imposition of control over financial markets and the prohibition of capital export. The total cost of this ambitious scheme amounted to around a third of national income. Its opponents argued that it would bring at worst panic and best devaluation of the Swiss franc, and on the strength of this objection the initiative was narrowly defeated in June 1935. It was a very bitter debate that deeply split Swiss politics. Here was a case in which it might be convenient to blame the foreigner for the destabilization of Swiss affairs.

International banking provided a convenient scapegoat. The Swiss foreign ministry rightly believed that it was English merchant banks (not the clearing banks) that had suffered in 1931. The diplomats argued that the City of London hoped that international confidence in sterling might return if other countries plunged over the abyss, and as a result spread rumors about the instability of the gold-bloc countries. The maverick British *Financial News* correspondent Paul Einzig had indeed given wide publicity to stories about a massive Swiss and Dutch capital flight. But this was not the fundamental cause of Swiss difficulties. Given the international position, the only way of safeguarding Switzerland from dramatic exchange movements lay in an alteration of parity.

The first country of the gold bloc to succumb to the strains of being a small and relatively open economy on gold was Belgium. Once again the immediate impetus for devaluation was not a theoretical plan or the convincing arguments of economists, but rather a banking crisis.[166] Belgian banks stood firmly in the continental tradition of universal banking, and in consequence faced heavy losses on their industrial lending and participations. The bank losses prompted an external drain in August 1934, and by March 1935 all the Belgian banks except the largest (the Société Générale) were close to collapse. Industry protested against attempts to rescue the banks and prevent further capital outflows by raising Belgian interest rates, since this, it claimed, would only intensify the business depression.[167] Devaluation was thus the only option (March), and the pressure on the Netherlands and Switzerland increased.

In the Netherlands, with less of a tradition of universal banking and no threat of a major banking collapse, the government of Hendrik Colijn followed a course analogous to that of Heinrich Brüning in Germany or Pierre Laval in France. Systematic deflation, in which government spending, wages, and prices were all cut, offered a way of spreading the costs that seemed equitable. Some of Colijn's supporters even cited the "success" of Brüning's policy as evidence for the desirability of a consistent deflation,[168] and Colijn himself had built his political reputation on his successful battle against inflation in the early 1920s. He thus resisted devaluation strenuously.

In the September 1936 crisis, French developments affected the smaller gold-bloc states. In addition, the Swiss market had been disturbed by the flotation on 21 September of a very large defense loan. The Swiss now lost gold at a fast rate—$9.5 million on 26 September alone—and quickly followed the French franc by devaluing in the range of 25.94–34.55 percent. Unlike in France, the devaluation was an unambiguous success. It offered above all a way of establishing social peace in Switzerland. The 1937 labor agreement, which set a highly managed and corporatist framework for the resolution of conflicts about wages and conditions, would have been impossible without the greater confidence that followed the ending of the large capital movements.[169]

Once Switzerland had left, Colijn was persuaded by the governor of the central bank that the Netherlands could not stand the strain of being the world's only country on gold at the old parity. The Dutch followed France's example and devalued to a new range of gold values, between 20 and 25 percent below the previous level. Escaping from the gold bloc proved yet again to be the only way of avoiding banking instability.

An Alternative Course: Protection from Contagion

The gold standard had provided a transmission mechanism that made economies with weak banking systems vulnerable to shock. Central banks, which had originally been conceived as an institutional mechanism for alleviating the domestic consequences of external monetary shocks, had increased the instability because of the prevalence of a concern for preserving confidence. The central European weakness was especially acute because of the destruction of capital in postwar hyperinflations, and the weakened banks provided a poor basis for subsequent borrowing.

In order to find counterexamples, in which banks could withstand the strains imposed by the international financial system, it is necessary to move a long way from the world of the Genoa conference and the Geneva ideology of internationalism. Both Canada and Japan proved financially quite robust; and such robustness shortened the depression and provided a potential for successful recovery policies.

The order of events in Japan's commitment to the international economy was quite different from the European picture of stabilization on the basis of a gold-standard parity (nominal anchor), capital inflows, loss of confidence, and banking and fiscal crisis. Japan experienced capital inflows, and then a banking crisis in 1927, prior to a commitment to the gold standard. The major capital inflows occurred before 1927. In April 1927 domestic bank runs set in.

Before the 1927 crisis, the governor of the Bank of Japan, Inoue Junnosoke, who fully supported the new international vision of the responsibilities of central banks in a fixed-parity world, had been a major advocate of a return to gold, which he saw as the answer to Japan's high inflation and interest rates. But this course had been opposed by many major figures in the banking establishment (Yashiro Norihiko, of Sumitomo Bank; Kusihida Manzo, of Mitsubishi Bank; Ikeda Kenzo, of Daihyakyu Bank; Kodama Kenji, of the Yokohama Specie Bank).[170] The Tokyo earthquake of 1923 further hindered the idea of a return to fixed parity. After the bank crisis of 1927, a wave of bank mergers strengthened the banking system, and some former opponents of the gold standard began to be sympathetic to the idea of stabilization. Inoue's power increased, and in July 1929 he became finance minister. Just six months later, at the beginning of 1930, he announced Japan's return to a gold parity.

Japan went off the gold standard again quite quickly, at the end of 1931, not because of the kind of banking and financial panic that afflicted central Europe and then Britain, the United States, and finally the gold bloc, but because of the trade effects of the British devaluation in September 1931. At the same time, a political change brought in a party opposed to gold (again, a novelty in comparison with other countries, in which the attachment to gold was generally part of the accoutrement of political respectability as surely as was the wearing of a hat). The Seiyukai party came to power in a disreputable way in December 1931, as the result of military pressure (the new government is sometimes described as the product of a coup). Only one day after his appointment, the new prime minister, Inukai Tsuyoshi, took Japan off the gold standard, and within two months won a major election victory.

The basis for a sustained recovery was laid by a foreign-exchange policy that let the yen depreciate and generated a revival in exports, especially of cotton textiles. Average annual growth for the recovery years 1931–1936 was 4.3 percent—an impressive contrast with the depression-ridden world elsewhere. The export offensive was accompanied by increased militarization, with larger public spending, raising overall demand in the Japanese economy. From 1932 to 1935 government expenditure on both emergency relief and military expansion following the 1931 Manchuria Incident was financed largely through bond issues, of which four-fifths were refinanced through the Bank of Japan. Deficits amounted to about 30 percent of government expenditure. Only in 1935 did the expansionary finance minister Takahashi Korekiyo attempt to rein in the inflationary deficits and adopt a policy known as "the gradual rationing of government bond issues." But this application of economic brakes quickly produced a military mutiny, and Takahashi was assassinated in February 1936. Military expenditure subsequently increased even more rapidly.[171]

Canada had an equally happy economic (if less politically turbulent) experience, although it remained on the gold standard for a substantial time. The Canadian strength lay in a more robust banking system than that of the southern neighbor. Branch banking was less vulnerable than single banks or statewide banks to regional weaknesses, and there were—surprisingly—no Canadian bank failures despite the massive vulnerability of the economy (including the financial sector) to problems caused by the fall in the price of wheat, Canada's major export. Nevertheless, the decline in Canadian real GDP and the rise in unemployment were similar to the U.S. experience: the depression was transmitted not through the financial system but through trade.[172]

A second strength lay in the fact that Canada, which then had no central bank, was consequently not vulnerable to the kind of institutional shock that had affected other countries as a result of the restrictive actions of central banks.[173]

Lessons for the 1990s

An initial response to the economic turmoil of the 1930s involved the abandonment of all the elements of the Genoa-Geneva consensus. The gold standard was discredited. Orthodox fiscal policy, which was required in order to generate gold-standard credibility, was discredited. The heroes of the 1930s were expansionists, who managed to find new ways of financing state deficits: Finance Minister Takahashi in Japan or Economics Minister Hjalmar Schacht in Germany.

Also discredited were independent or autonomous central banks, which had been so crucial to the vision of how to restore economic order in the 1920s. And so too were capital movements.

Central banks engaged in a curious rearguard action, which may be responsible for much continued intellectual confusion, when they defended themselves by insisting that monetary policy had no great impact on economic activity.

The organ of central bank cooperation, the BIS, transformed itself into an institution for economic analysis, in brilliantly conceived annual reports from the distinguished pen of the Swedish economist Per Jacobsson, and for the collection of statistics about the world economy. None of this impressed Montagu Norman, who had a quite different concept of what was involved in central bank cooperation. In December 1932 he told a meeting of central bank governors at the BIS that he was "against statistics: he thought the figures were misleading and he believed that if central banks or currency Authorities worked on statistics, even the best statistics, they were more likely to be misled than anything else."[174]

This collapse of the BIS into a center for merely routine operations was part of a broader breakdown of the theory of central bank action. As the depression deepened, and as criticism mounted on all sides, central bankers more and more believed that their only mission lay in announcing loudly that they could do nothing, that monetary policy could not influence the development of the real economy. This was a complete break with the central bank activism of the mid-1920s. It was also of course theoretical nonsense, which arose out of the (forgivable) feeling that politicians' rather than central bankers' blunders had made the financial mess. If this was what was meant by a "common body of monetary doctrine," it was one that led away from giving central banks great room for maneuver in international financial matters.

In dealing with the League of Nations' inquiry into the gold problem, the central bankers adopted the position that monetary policy was ineffective, and their view informed the majority report of June 1932 (a more far-ranging minority report, signed by Sir Henry Strakosch as well as Sir Reginald Mant and Albert Janssen, recommended concerted international action to raise commodity prices).

The modest recommendations centered upon the restoration of freedom of exchange. Central banks should allow the automatism of the gold standard to operate: "gold movements must not be prevented from making their influence felt both in the country losing gold and in the country receiving gold." Governments were to take the burden of adjustment, accumulating budget surpluses and repaying debt in the deficit countries:

> in each individual country the necessary steps shall be taken to restore and to maintain equilibrium in the national economy. This means that the budgets of the State and other public bodies must be balanced on sound principles, and also that the national economic system as a whole, and especially costs of production and costs of living, should be adjusted to the international economic and financial position, so as to enable the country to restore or to maintain the equilibrium of its balance of international payments.[175]

In private, the central bank consensus was stated even more explicitly:

> We are quite unwilling to lend our authority to those who would exonerate politicians and businessmen from responsibility by explaining the terrible tragedy of the present world crisis as being due solely to a scarcity of gold . . . But it was evident to the Delegation, as is clearly expressed in the Second Report, that the causes responsible for this maldistribution were mainly of a general economic, financial and political nature. As

these causes were not primarily monetary, monetary policies could not be expected to cure the world of the resulting ills.

The Italian finance minister Guido Jung explained that "it would be disastrous to the reconstruction of the world if in a report of ours we were to give to people the impression that there exists a monetary witchcraft, which can, by its own force, work miracles and avoid the necessity of . . . solving the political and economic problems, which have brought the world to its present conditions."[176]

Part of the task of the 1933 World Economic Conference in London lay in discussing the contribution of central banking policy to crisis, but the central bankers themselves resented the interference. The preliminary meeting of American economic experts held at the Federal Reserve Bank of New York was quite characteristic. In the presence of Hoover's secretary of state (Henry Stimson) and secretary of the Treasury (Ogden Mills), Governor Harrison and Chairman of the Board Eugene Meyer "emphasized the necessity of keeping off the agenda of a governmental conference purely central bank questions such as for example central bank credit and gold policies. They also pointed out that most of the monetary questions which could be placed on the agenda were of interest to central banks and that they thought it was of the utmost importance for the World Conference to avoid invading the central bank field or making any suggestions or giving any instructions to central banks which might prove embarrassing."[177]

At an unofficial meeting of the BIS governors in February 1933, the president of the Belgian national bank urged against any central bank agreement before London, because this "would give a catastrophic reinforcement to the erroneous idea that the monetary factor is a primary factor which plays a preponderant role in the world crisis." Norman agreed wholeheartedly. Eventually the BIS governors did produce a document to preempt London, titled "Rules of the Gold Standard." It contained, perhaps it is needless to say, nothing but platitudes.

Central banks, orthodox finance, and international capital movements were such obvious villains in the drama of the depression that few commentators at the time bothered to devote attention to the problems of financial-sector instability. Indeed this aspect of the problems of the interwar order received more attention only with the rapid globalization of financial markets since the 1970s, in the course of which some of the problems of the older order began to reemerge.

Recent literature suggests that in many cases since the 1970s, banking difficulties preceded currency or foreign-exchange crises. It is easy to see some of the mechanisms: central banks or governments try to deal with actual or even incipient banking difficulties by monetary expansion or by fiscal actions (socializing bank debt, as in Mexico in the 1990s). The result is a real overvaluation, which creates the potential for speculative attack on the currency. This literature also frequently suggests that the banking crises are preceded by financial liberalization and deregulation, which encourages potentially destabilizing capital inflows. If these arguments were already being formulated as a response to the problems of the European Monetary System and Mexican crises of the early 1990s, the effect of the Asian crisis after 1997 strengthened this line of interpretation.[178]

The experience of the first stage of the Great Depression offers an analogy with this very contemporary problem. Banking instability played a critical part in creating the potential for currency crises. In the interwar period, the problem lay in central Europe in the tradition of universal banking, reconstructed in the wake of an inflationary shock on an undercapitalized base, and in the United States in the poor development of branch banking. In the 1990s, in East Asia, many Latin American countries, and Russia, the vulnerability lies in poorly developed accounting systems, corruption, and the intrusion of politics. In both periods thin markets, which dried up in a panic, made the weaknesses worse. The critical question for today is the extent to which the financial exposure of industrial countries may lead to a repetition of the story of the second half of the Great Depression experience.

One way of presenting the case for alarm about the transfer of crisis from the periphery to the core of the international financial system is in the form of a table. It shows, for various years and countries, banks' gross foreign liabilities as a share of international reserves (see Table 2.4). A brief inspection will confirm some of the themes discussed above: countries are vulnerable when their banks have a high share of foreign liabilities relative to reserves, and the precursors of the outbreak of the crisis are dramatic changes in the preceding year or years. The G-7 figures may give an indication of a potential vulnerability, at least in the economies in which the financial sector plays a large part. The United Kingdom, as in 1931, is the most vulnerable to this kind of problem.

Ultimately, however, schematic overviews are not very useful as accurate predictors of likely sources of financial and banking weakness. There were

Table 2.4 Banks' gross foreign liabilities as a share of international reserves, various countries and years (%)

Country	Share	% annual change
Germany (July 1931)	3.7	−25
Mexico (3d quarter 1994)	0.6	33.7
East Asia (mid-1997)		
South Korea	1.3	15.1
Indonesia	0.7	−10.1
Thailand	1.7	17.8
Singapore	0.8	5.9
Hong Kong	9.4	−13.5
Philippines	1.7	39.1
China	0.5	−21.3
G-7 (1st quarter 1999)		
Germany	7.2	−5.3
United Kingdom	64.7	12.3

Sources: Harold James, *The German Slump: Politics and Economics, 1924–1936* (Oxford: Oxford University Press, 1986), p. 294; and IMF, *International Financial Statistics*, various issues.

few anticipatory exposés of the problems of Korean and Thai banks before 1997, just as in the United Kingdom an official report (by the Macmillan Committee on Trade and Industry) celebrating the superiority of the German banking system over the British was by chance published on precisely the day, 13 July 1931, on which Germany's most famous risk-taking industrial bank failed and brought down with it the entire German banking system.

Boom-bust cycles of international credit had of course been a characteristic feature of the nineteenth-century globalized economy, with many failures in the periphery. Was 1930–31 different in that it was a systemic crisis of the gold-standard system? In the nineteenth century the gold standard had been robust enough that the countries at the core of the system in western Europe never contemplated a departure from gold, even though the United states in the mid-1890s came close to being pushed off. The 1920s at first apparently followed the course of a typically nineteenth-century credit boom, but the bust in 1930–31 then assumed a systemic character that destroyed the gold-exchange standard. The international financial system in the 1990s proved more robust than some commentators suggested and feared. But there are vulnerabilities, which resemble the interwar weaknesses. Fixed exchange-rate commitments represent an easy transmission mechanism for crisis, and although they are now unpopular with economists, they continue to be widely regarded as the only realistic solution to obtaining capital in many mid-income emerging markets.

The preceding survey of banks and financial panics in the depression era and any reflection on the contrasts with 1997–98 also make clear the centrality of appropriate monetary policy in the major economies. The response in October 1998 to the threat of global financial contagion was a monetary easing, notably in the United States, combined with a dedication of additional resources to international financial institutions. Under the impact of the Brazil crisis and its consequences for the rest of Latin America, the U.S. Congress finally accepted a quota increase for the IMF, which previously it had resisted.

But the major lesson of both the 1920s and the 1990s experiences is that financial-sector stability is a key element in preventing self-destructive panics in a world of globalized capital.

3

◆

Tariffs, Trade Policy, and the Collapse of International Trade

In the unstable world of the 1920s, previously successful trade remedies were applied once more. There was a dangerous interplay between monetary policy, trade policy, and migration law. In each area the state needed to respond to raised demands and expectations for state activism, but policymakers in one area often had to grapple with the consequences of other policies. Monetary policy on an international level was destabilizing. With prices fluctuating more dramatically, the results of tariff protection and other trade policy measures were much more harmful than in the relatively stable prewar world.

Again, as in the case of the financial and banking discussions, at a high political level governments began the 1920s with apparently the best of intentions. Nowhere was trade high-mindedness formulated more clearly than in the third of President Wilson's Fourteen Points, which called for the "removal, as far as possible, of economic barriers and the establishment of an equality of trade conditions among all nations consenting to the peace and associating itself with its maintenance." The doctrine of the linkage between an open international economy and international peace, which also underlay U.S. thinking during and after the Second World War, was here explicitly laid out as the basis for a new international order.

The high-mindedness did not in practice survive the monetary chaos of the early 1920s. Thus in 1925, once the limits placed by the Versailles Treaty on German tariff autonomy came to an end, Germany immediately reapplied the rates of the Bülow tariff of 1902. But with the decline in agricultural prices, these rates rapidly proved inadequate against pressures from the farm lobby, for prices continued to fall. By the 1920s, many states built into their tariff measures a flexibility that allowed them to raise rates in the light of changing circumstances. The model for this legislation was the U.S. Fordney-McCumber Tariff Act of 1920, which envisaged rapid decisions by an expert and apolitical Tariff Commission. Flexibility, however, in practice meant an upward ratchet effect.

After 1928 world trade contracted in an ever-collapsing spiral. No economic measure has produced such a unanimous outburst of condemnation from economists as the Hawley-Smoot Tariff Act of 1930. These facts are sometimes taken to be an explanation of the depression. In this view, both tariff and then increasingly nontariff protective measures (quotas, hygiene measures) played the leading part in bringing about the world depression. Exchange control, imposed in the wake of the financial crises, was instrumentalized in the regulation of trade.

In the same way as modern monetary policymakers often make rhetorical use of the great deflation as a justification for stabilizing or reflationary monetary measures (such as in October 1987, or again in the fall of 1998), trade experts see new Hawley-Smoots lurking behind the special interests pushing commercial policy decisions.

Was trade history exceptional and abnormal in the 1920s or in the 1930s? Much of our analysis of the cause of the international depression rests on the answer to this question. If the trade problems of the 1920s were unique, then they might provide an important part of the explanation for the collapse of the world economy at the end of the decade. If, on the other hand, it is only in the 1930s that the peculiarity lies, then trade will explain not so much the origins of depression, but rather the peculiar shape of the recovery.

The collapse of trade in quantitative terms was preceded by a price decline in almost all internationally traded items after 1925: a gentle downward movement in the case of food and manufactured products until 1929 (when the fall became much steeper), but an already quite sharp decline in the prices of raw materials. The overall movement indicated the steady deflationary weakness in the world economy, a weakness to which protectionism may have been the most logical response.

Nobody would suggest that the restrictive trade regimes of the 1930s adopted in country after country represented an optimal path. But there is a powerful argument that they represented a viable, and indeed perhaps the only viable, second-best option. When other countries were imposing monetary deflation and restricting their trade, an attempt to preserve in-

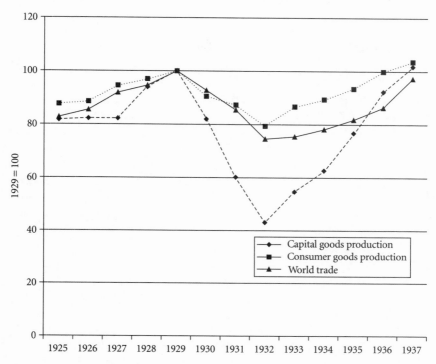

Figure 3.1 World production and trade, 1925–1937
(Sources: calculated from League of Nations, *World Production and Prices*
[Geneva], various years)

comes by means of protective legislation represented a logical strategy against externally imposed misery.

The analysis of financial flows in the previous chapter suggests one answer, that the 1920s were less abnormal than the succeeding decade, because of the availability of capital flows. It is difficult to imagine all countries in a world economy running more or less balanced trade and invisible accounts; and if they tried to do this—to buy only when they sold—the result would have been to restrict the overall growth of trade. The imbalances that occur naturally in the course of development are met by capital movements. The capital flows of the 1920s were required in order to finance imbalances arising from the recovery of world trade after the First World War; in the 1930s, when such capital was no longer available because of changes in the world's financial markets, the growth rates of trade

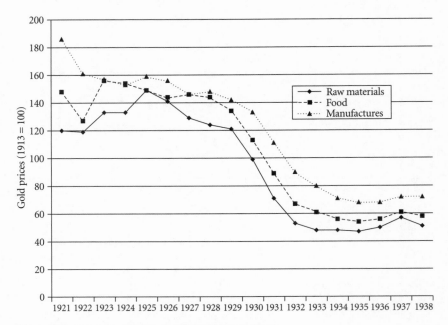

Figure 3.2 Prices in international trade, 1921–1938
(Sources: calculated from League of Nations, *World Production and Prices*
[Geneva], various years)

collapsed. The halt followed from the increasing uncertainty and from the
loss of "confidence" during the depression. But there is a two-way relationship between finance and trade. It could be argued that the nervousness of
the financial markets represented a reaction to new barriers obstructing
commerce.

The most powerful case for 1920s normality and 1930s abnormality has
been made by W. Arthur Lewis. He examined the global pattern of commerce by placing the relationship between world manufacturing production and trade in primary products at the core of the analysis. Lewis
showed that this relationship in the 1920s still fitted into the prewar pattern, but that in the 1930s the ratio was quite new, with a much lower proportion of primary products traded.[1]

But an imbalance between manufacture and primary product trade is
not the only possible source of commercial disturbance. In fact, though
trade recovered in the 1920s from the impact of the First World War, by

1929 the recovery was less complete than it "should" have been if prewar trends had continued. If there had been a full catching up, and if 1929 had lain on the trend of the growth of trade between 1900 and 1914, the exports of the major industrial countries should have been 20 percent higher.[2] Indeed, this calculation underestimates the degree of the shortfall. Since the peace settlement divided up old empires and increased the number of states, the volume of trade should have grown still faster in order to be on line with the trend. As a result of the war, Europe had nine new economic territories, thirteen new currencies, and 20,000 kilometers in additional customs frontiers.

The recoveries of the 1920s and 1930s in fact have something in common, and something that distinguishes them from pre-1914 upswings. In the recovery of the 1930s, world production once more considerably outpaced the growth of international commerce. Primary production in 1937, the next cyclical high point, was 10 percent higher than in 1929, and manufacturing output was 19 percent higher (these figures include the USSR, which accounts for a great deal of the increase in the 1930s). But world trade was 3 percent lower.[3]

In addition, price behavior also shows peculiarities in the 1920s as well as in the 1930s. Trade in the 1920s bore the marks of a lopsided deflation. From 1925 through 1929 the quantity of trade grew at an annual rate of 4.8 percent, but the value of international trade grew much less dramatically, at a rate of 1.6 percent.[4] This development reflected the postwar recovery in agricultural production, but also the price decline that followed from increased supply with low demand elasticities.

Finally, tariffs and tariff policy constitute another area where opinions about the respective peculiarities of the two decades are divided. Lewis makes the point that both the international negotiating system, depending on most-favored-nation (MFN) clauses, and the actual level of tariffs changed little from the prewar period. Under these arrangements, a rational course of action lay in initially establishing legislation with very high levels of protection (sometimes known as "fighting tariffs") and then negotiating them down with the most important trade partner, in return for concessions that would subsequently be extended through the MFN principle. However, Lewis's view of the substantial continuity from pre- to postwar eras is tenable only on a very high level of abstraction. Analysis of the development of individual countries and individual commodities produces a rather different picture: the overall balance of the 1920s came about because tariffs on primary products and on manufactured goods were adjusted in different directions.

The peculiarities of the 1920s may be explained in the following complementary ways:

- as a consequence of the spread of industrialization: as the result of a long-term development of the production of primary products and the relative demand schedules of primary products and manufactured goods
- as the product of trade policy: political developments altered the incentives in calculations about restricting or expanding the degree of international openness in the major economies

The Consequence of Industrialization Strategies

Many contemporary commentators expected the share of international trade in industrial production to enter a secular decline as more countries industrialized. As states moved away from dependence on agricultural production, the international division of labor would decrease. This is an argument that had been put forward as early as 1821 by Robert Torrens ("An Essay on the Production of Wealth") and by Werner Sombart in 1909, but it was revived in the 1930s by Keynes and Robertson.[5]

These views were not confined to academic circles: on the contrary, they were popularized and taken up by very diverse political leaders. Adolf Hitler, for instance, thought precisely in these terms: "If this export of the means of production were continued indefinitely, it would simply be the end of the vital prerequisite for European industry. Therefore international agreements on limiting the export of the means of production are necessary."[6]

The loss of comparative advantage of the first industrializers was augmented by policy choices elsewhere: states would try to build up their industries. As the economist Dennis Robertson put it: "We can therefore affirm as a fact, so to speak, of natural history, that a relative shrinking of world trade due to a narrowing of the gap of Comparative Advantage is likely to be associated with a further shrinkage due to policy, since it tends both to make more prominent the evils of instability and insecurity and to lower the real cost to the community of attempting to mitigate them."[7]

Britain, as an exporter of staple goods, especially cottons and woolens, suffered especially from the development of textile manufacture in Japan, India, and also Latin America. In 1913 Britain had accounted for 42.9 percent of world export of textiles and clothing, and in 1929 the share was still 33.0 percent; but the volume had declined. Britain's total share of manufacture exports over this time fell from 30.2 to 22.4 percent. Meanwhile the Japanese share of world textile exports rose from 4.3 to 9.5 percent, and it reached 3.9 percent of all manufacturing exports.[8] There was thus a particular British problem about the orientation and character of its exports. The Balfour Committee (Committee on Industry and Trade) concluded: "The most obvious and immediate effect is, of course, a restrictive one. Goods that formerly found a ready sale in a particular market are now wholly or partially excluded by the competition of the locally produced article under the protection of an import tariff."[9]

On the other hand, the process of industrialization through import substitution still required substantial imports, particularly of equipment and raw materials; and after 1945 substantial industrialization drove, rather than braked, an expansion of world trade. There were signs of such new demand in the interwar years. Japan may have imported fewer staples from Britain, but it bought more machinery from the United States. India, which had taken 85 percent of its imports of manufactures from Britain in 1913, by 1937 bought only one-seventh of the prewar figure, but it bought large quantities of goods from Japan. In other words, the propensity for trade in manufactures to decline turned out to be an especially British, rather than a world, phenomenon. Britain suffered far more than any other exporter in the 1920s from the consequences of import substitution.[10]

Countries following a clearly-worked-out strategy of import substitution in the 1920s in central Europe imposed high tariff levels on manufactured goods, but low rates on raw materials and machine tools. The European country with the most explicit development strategy through high tariffs was Czechoslovakia. Machinery imports were entirely free. Hungary hoped to build a new industrial center on the Danube. Along with government building programs and subsidies, there were trade political measures: as in Czechoslovakia, a new tariff in 1924 attempted to concentrate production in finished goods, and gave quota exemptions for unfinished goods from its generally high levels of tariffs. From 1924 to 1927 the proportion of imported textile goods fell as a proportion of total imports from 25.1 percent to 19.7 percent, and Hungarian steel output rose by 50 percent.[11]

Such necessary imports could be financed either through capital inflows, corresponding to trade surpluses in the economies of the major industrialized countries, or through expansion of raw material or foodstuff exports. But in the mid-1920s European agriculture had again reached prewar productivity. As the production of goods with low price elasticities of demand increased, stocks rose, and prices fell from the middle of the decade. Exporting in order to industrialize now became highly precarious, since even big increases in exports brought reduced returns because of the price situation.

Some commodities were regulated by international agreement: the Stevenson rubber scheme of 1924 attempted to do this for a commodity with extremely inelastic supply, and failed to include the individual small-scale producers of the Dutch East Indies.[12] The scheme held up prices for a time, but then the buffer stocks became too great. Their existence, and the difficulty of financing it, then depressed prices.

One other way of shielding producers from price collapses was trade protection, and in particular tariffs.

Trade Policy in the 1920s

The turn to protection on a massive scale was the most obvious feature of the interwar collapse of globalism. It is notoriously difficult to measure, especially in the most common approach, which uses some sort of a tariff index to measure protection on the basis of the value of customs collected as a proportion of the total value of imports. For major industrial countries, this tariff index rose through the interwar years as follows: in 1923–1926, 11 percent; in 1927–1931, 13 percent; and in 1932–1939, 18 percent.[13]

Such an approach is open to the objection that when tariffs succeed in stopping imports (which was often their purpose in the interwar period), they are not reflected in the index. The index is therefore useful in measuring only revenue tariffs, not protective tariffs, which were the preponderant form of interwar tariff legislation. The figures above do not give a real or useful measure of the extent of the increase in trade restriction from 1927 through 1931.

Tariffs and trade agreements are highly political, and it would be surprising if their formation had not changed as a result of the great political and social upheavals that followed from the First World War. They are the products of a peculiar, and political, market: protection can be considered as a good that is exchanged. On the one hand are specific interests, calling for high tariffs in order to create or maintain flows of income which can be considered as a rent. These interests invest in politics in order to capture an additional flow of income.[14] On the other hand, political institutions can give protection in exchange for other kinds of support. There is some statistical evidence that political instability was associated with an increased propensity to use trade measures.[15]

At the same time, tariffs are an aspect of international behavior and are subject to bargaining between nations. Tariffs and their effects have been a favorite area for economists to apply game-theoretical approaches to international behavior.[16]

The world's move to protection in the 1920s and 1930s is frequently presented as a second-best outcome: although the benefits of more liberalization might have extended throughout the world, no country could afford to liberalize while others used tariffs and quotas to restrict imports. Tariffs were not simply a response to domestic protectionist pressure, but also a consequence of international interactions and a process of bargaining among nations. In the discussion of international trade, "beggar my neighbor" became a popular expression.

The degree of protection adopted correponded in part to the position of a particular country within the international economy. Whereas very small trading economies tried to remain open, large powers could use protection for domestic political reasons, unencumbered by external constraints. In between these two cases, many new countries tried to industrialize for political and social reasons, and saw trade measures as a way of promoting import substitution industrialization.

International conferences to reverse the movement to restrict international trade—notably in 1927 and 1933—and the efforts of the League of Nations Economic and Financial Committee failed. There was no rejection of the second-best alternatives, no return to an optimal solution, and no victory of common sense. Nor, after 1934, did the trade liberalization policy of the United States—the country that above all was blamed for setting a bad example with tariffs in the 1920s—produce a reverse slide into free trade. Secretary of State Cordell Hull's successes were limited to painfully slow negotiations in bilateral liberalization. It required after 1945 a complete political reordering in order to push the world back onto the course of liberalization and expanding commerce in a multilateral context. Institutions—notably the General Agreement on Tariffs and Trade (GATT)—supervised this postwar development. The GATT performed a major service initially in removing uncertainty by imposing tariff bindings—in other words, preventing unilateral and unpredictable increases. It was not very effective in reducing the overall nominal level of tariffs. The greatest push to trade liberalization in the 1950s and 1960s instead actually came as an unintended consequence of price inflation, which reduced the real level of tariffs, whose nominal levels had been fixed by agreement.

In the pure theory of international trade, a unilateral shift to free trade increases overall real income unless it provokes a significant deterioration in a country's terms of trade.[17] Conversely, a move away from free trade is likely to decrease incomes. What political calculations operated to produce such a decrease? There are several reasons that might be given, including the legacy of the war and military thinking, the consequences of democratization, reactions to interest politics, the priorities of a new nationalism, a response to harsh economic circumstances and especially to monetary disturbances, and the wish to have a bargaining weapon in trade negotiations with other countries.

THE WARTIME LEGACY.   Military planning stressed self-sufficiency, and blockades had been a major part of wartime strategy. Discussions about wartime self-sufficiency had sometimes appeared in the protectionist literature of the nineteenth century, but since most military experts had assumed that wars would be short, this remained a rather subordinate motive until 1914. The actual experience of prolonged economic warfare changed the debate, and tariffs to promote national production inevitably played a major part in policy during the First World War. At the same time, shipping capacity was scarce, so that a deliberate restriction of nonessential or luxury imports was desirable. In the United Kingdom, the 1915 McKenna tariff had placed a 33 percent rate on automobiles, musical instruments, clocks, watches, and cinema film. France raised tariff rates from 5 to 20 percent by 1918.

DEMOCRATIC POLITICS.   Democratization in Europe and elsewhere, and the overthrow of old autocracies, might have been expected to produce moves to free trade. Historically, socialist parties were heavily committed to free trade, because they associated protection primarily with agricultural interests and high consumer prices. Indeed in prewar Europe it is possible to detect a rough apparent correlation between the degree of autocracy and the height of tariffs: in descending order Russia, the Habsburg empire, and the Hohenzollern empire (72.5, 22.8, and 16.7 percent, respectively).[18]

But democracies had their own reasons to be protectionist too: France and Sweden, with very large rural populations, also had high levels of protection. Indeed, everywhere outside Britain, where agriculture, forestry, and fishing accounted for only 5.6 percent of employment, the farm population and the rural vote played a major part in political calculations. In the 1920s, 41.5 percent of the French labor force worked in farming, and 54 percent of the population lived on the land. In Germany 30.5 percent and in Sweden 40.7 percent worked in farming; and the eastern European figures are much higher, ranging from 40.3 percent in relatively industrialized Czechoslovakia, through 58.2 percent in Hungary to 76.6 percent in Poland and 77.2 percent in Rumania.[19] In the United States farm workers were 25 percent of the work force.

Farmers also sought tariffs particularly eagerly, in that the supply of land is finite: so that, unlike in other branches, where competition might destroy or erode the rent flows generated from protection, the gains of applying for protection are much more secure.

Agricultural pressure to stabilize prices against fluctuations was astonishingly effective for two reasons because, paradoxically, most farmers had a low degree of political organization and political awareness. Labor, whose interests were much more effectively represented in trade unions and in socialist parties, did much less well in large part because it was too well organized. In most countries, farmers were divided in political allegiance, because of long-standing local traditions, because of confessional differences, because they were easily susceptible to new and interesting sorts of political propaganda, or because they reacted to market changes with disenchantment about the political system. The result was that the agricultural vote might be divided and volatile. In democratic politics, this fragmentation gives an advantage, since political parties look to extend their vote outside safe interest constituencies.

Even many socialists realized that if they were to gain parliamentary majorities, they needed to extend their support beyond the urban working class. Both the French and the German Socialist parties made major efforts to appeal to farmers. But so did liberal and conservative and clerical parties. As a result, opposition to agricultural protection became very difficult.

The French prime minister André Tardieu made a claim that many French interwar cabinets felt they should echo: "We are above all an agricultural government." At a speech in Alençon he announced: "The land is our society. Inhabitants of these immobile villages in which fathers pass the torch on to sons, you will teach the grandeur of this continuity to the people of the towns."[20] A further reason agricultural pressure was so effective was that other measures could ride on the back of it, as compensation. This had already been a historical issue before 1914. The conservative turn in Bismarck's policy in the late 1870s depended on the alliance of "iron" and "rye": steel and iron producers, who had been threatened since the beginning of the decade, used the agricultural depression to convert to their cause the previously free-trading great landowners. A similar turn took place in all of continental Europe. Another characteristic example is the introduction of the French agricultural tariff by a minister of agriculture, Jules Méline, who was a textile manufacturer from the Vosges, and succeeded in establishing a compensatory industrial rate at the same time.

Thus when from the mid-1920s agricultural prices fell, there was a substantial body of opinion demanding agricultural tariffs: not always with the simplest of motives.

In the United States, the long process which led to the Hawley-Smoot Act began with falling farm prices after 1927 and the political response during Herbert Hoover's presidential campaign. Hoover made an explicit promise to farmers on 27 October 1928 that he would bring farm relief. The practice of the long negotiations—which produced a substantially different result—is another example of how business could ride on the back of agriculture. The House Ways and Means Committee added a large number of increases on nonagricultural goods, and the full House added yet more. The same operation occurred in the Senate Committee on Finance and in the Senate itself. As a result, the farmers' representatives went into open revolt against the bill, complaining rightly that they had been betrayed by the operation of the system. They were staved off by a compromise agreement worked out by Senator Joseph Grundy, a seasoned agricultural lobbyist, which increased the level of protection. The wheat tariff went up from 30 cents a bushel to 42 cents; long-staple cotton, which previously had been almost entirely imported from Egypt, was added to the list after the intervention of the Senate Committee of the Whole. The beef tariff went up from 3 to 6 cents a pound.[21]

The decline in world agricultural prices from the mid-1920s gave a new boost to agrarian protection, but here (with the exception of Germany) the new tariff regime came rather late.

Germany had had her tariff autonomy limited under the Versailles Treaty until 1925, but when this constraint disappeared, it rapidly set about reviving the old structures. By 1927 agricultural duty rates were about three-fifths higher than in 1913.[22] In December 1929, in response to pressure from farmers and their representatives in the political parties, Germany introduced a sliding scale for grain tariffs so as to keep pace with the collapse of world cereal prices. This was a clear attempt to break the link between German and world prices, and to make farming subject to national economic control alone. France started increasing agricultural tariffs only in late 1929; for most of the 1920s, they had been at levels below those of 1913. Switzerland put through significant increases only in 1931, when wheat tariffs amounted to only 5–7 percent of grain prices. Throughout the 1920s, British farmers complained that they faced ruin because of cheap imports of food.

A more common initial route to protect agriculture was the use of nontariff methods. Thus from 1929 through 1932 Belgium, France, Germany, Italy, and Sweden introduced a compulsory milling requirement of a proportion of domestic grain. In that way farmers could be protected to some extent without such an obvious effect on prices (and consequent lowering of urban living standards).

PRESSURE AND INTEREST-GROUP POLITICS.   Formulating a tariff is a very different exercise from the elaboration of the monetary and financial strategies described in Chapter 2. The characteristic of monetary policy is that it is fixed in very broad aggregates and on the basis of very generalized observations (changes in interest rates, exchange-rate movements, the volume of bank credit or currency in circulation). Tariff rates, on the other hand, are highly specified, and it is often possible to establish that only one company stands to benefit from a particular change. The eventual Hawley-Smoot Act laid down tariffs on 21,000 items. Its elaboration provided the opportunity for political fine-tuning: the bill was debated and modified over two years, and there were 1,253 Senate amendments.

The tariff in this way became a way of building political coalitions by bargaining. In the United States tariffs had long been recognized as a way of building a bridge between industry in the Northeast and midwestern farmers. The first analysis of U.S. politics in terms of interest groups began in 1908 with Arthur Fischer Bentley's *The Process of Government* as a study of tariffs.[23] At the beginning of the century, the hot slogan in Washington ran: "Young man, tariffs are the whole of politics: Study them."[24]

The 1930 tariff produced a powerful example of how the political process of making tariffs led to a result that no one had intended, and increased the overall level of protection. A contemporary analysis in terms of interests concluded: "That the political logic of protection leads to 'protection all around' is evident, for Congress has not discovered an objective ground on the basis of which it may deny protection to industries demanding it in the name of equality."[25] The participants were well aware of the process in which they had caught themselves. Senator Charles Waterman of Colorado made quite public and explicit the reciprocal nature of protection for special interests: "I have stated upon the floor of the Senate, and I have stated in the presence of Senators elsewhere, that by the Eternal, I will not vote for a tariff upon the products of another State if the Senators from that State vote against protecting the industries of any State."[26]

There was similar logrolling on the other side of the Atlantic. As a legacy of wartime experience and the co-optation of pressure groups to deal with the requirements of militarization, influence in European politics became more pronounced. Organized groups representing particular sectors of industry existed alongside "umbrella" organizations claiming to speak for the whole of the business community—such as the German Reichsverband der Deutschen Industrie (RDI), or the Federation of British Industry (FBI). In Fascist Italy, interest groupings were integrated into the framework of official corporatism.[27]

In the negotiation of the Franco-German commercial treaty of 17 August 1927, the most important international trade agreement before the depression, German and French business interests played a decisive role.[28] The treaty removed discrimination against German goods in France, and more generally involved the transition of French commercial policy to MFN basis. The provisions for its duration were complicated by the French negotiating need to keep tariff levels high in order to bargain with other countries.

Both parliaments voted enabling legislation to allow their governments to conclude agreements, but this partial abdication of parliamentary control did not remove the interests from the negotiating process. The RDI at first treated the prospective French tariff and the accompanying quota removals enthusiastically, since France would be opened to German products. The German government explicitly involved the chairman of the RDI's Speciality Group Textiles in the negotiation process, with the intention of "calling the RDI into responsibility for the agreement," especially because German textile manufacturers soon felt that not enough had been achieved.[29] But the RDI was not the only organization involved. A necessary preliminary to the treaty had been the participation of both German and French steel industries in the International Steel Cartel (ISC), although German industrialists soon felt that they were unfairly treated by the cartel's production ceilings. The German and French chemical industries concluded their own negotiations about the tariff structures in their countries. The Verein Deutscher Maschinenbau-Anstalten, the interest representative of the manufacturing industry, demanded special treatment for smaller industries (such as the Nuremberg and Pforzheim speciality and toy trades), and the liberal parties made this a condition for parliamentary support.[30] On the French side, an insistent and successful opposition to the imposition of a German wine import quota resulted from the need to obtain agricultural votes in the Chamber.[31] In other words, even extraparliamentary negotiations required a reference to pressure groups and interests, and their expressions in the political parties.

NATIONAL TARIFFS. The proliferation of states also encouraged the proliferation of tariffs. Elementary accounts of the 1920s often follow contemporary polemics in demonizing the development simply as "economic nationalism": but this is a very unsatisfactory explanation. Why should a tariff in a new state that had just come into existence, with all the possibilities for increasing factionalism—division between industry and agriculture, between exporting industry and producers oriented toward domestic consumption, between producers of "semis" and of finished products— seem the best course for binding together a new nation? The answer lies in the political process: the tariff and the negotiations surrounding it offer scope for political favors, which can strengthen the life of the new entity. People and interest groups come to the state because it has something to offer.

The extension of sovereignty to new states thus stimulated already latent protectionism. For the new successor states of the Habsburg empire, destroying the old networks of trade within the empire represented a task of national importance. The relatively less industrialized parts, notably Hungary, sought rapid industrialization. With the exception of Austria, the successor states increased the already high prewar levels of protection. Attempts to prevent this development and to preserve some of the old intra-imperial contacts were generally unsuccessful. The Danubian states never ratified the Protocol of Portarosa, which they had signed in November 1921, and which required the abolition of all import and export prohibitions.

Poland had played a major part in the tsarist economy before the First World War, sending textiles and engineering goods, as well as skilled labor, to the rest of the empire. Between the wars, its trade with the Soviet Union was virtually insignificant, accounting for less than one percent of Poland's total trade.

FLUCTUATING PRICES.   As well as political and nationalistic calculations, the violent and rapid price fluctuations immediately after the war increased the demand for protection. A traditional way of putting the protectionist case is that it presented a way of adjusting costs of production internationally. But worldwide currency and financial instability in the early 1920s made for very rapidly changing cost calculations. Japan in 1920 brought in antidumping legislation, as did Australia, Britain, and New Zealand in 1921. (There had been earlier precedents for this kind of legislation: Canada in 1908, and the United States in 1916.) The U.S. Fordney-McCumber Act of 1922 introduced a "flexible provision," which authorized the Tariff Commission, working in an "expert" and unpolitical way (and thus supposedly also independently of economic interests), to set rates so as to equalize the difference between American and foreign costs of production. This was to be the sole criterion for action by the commission. Choosing the appropriate time frame in which to make the comparison was invariably arbitrary. The wheat tariff included in the notorious Hawley-Smoot Tariff Act of 1930, for instance, was based on calculations made over a three-year period in which the rainfall pattern had been uniquely unfavorable to the United States and advantageous to Canada. And once tariffs had been raised in line with a dramatic disturbance to the structure of costs, reduction required a proportionately greater effort.

The Fordney-McCumber Act had been preceded by an Emergency Tariff Act dealing mostly with agricultural products in response to the dramatic postwar collapse in farmers' incomes. The 1922 act raised tariffs specifically on materials that had fallen in price during the recession of 1920–21 In addition, it was devised at a time when few countries outside the United States had stabilized their currencies. Fordney-McCumber quickly, however, became the major evidence produced by foreign countries when complaining about U.S. hypocrisy in failing to open American markets while insisting that the rest of the world service debt by exporting.

Outside the United States, similar criteria and similar arbitrariness applied in emergency and antidumping provisions. Countries noticed increases in costs that appeared to make them more vulnerable to increased imports. Labor costs had often risen as a result of the war; state expenditure rose and required increased taxes, which added to the augmentation of costs; in agriculture fertilizer shortages increased costs, but so also in Danubian Europe did attempts at land reform. A push on the cost side in general led to an increase in the demand for protection. The tariff was a way of redistributing internationally the costs of domestic attempts at social redistribution—of externalizing the social consequences of the war. At the same time, states were desperate to find ways of increasing revenues, and tariffs looked like a way of doing this.

Germany's high industrial tariffs of the 1920s were the product of dramatic inflation early in the decade. After they had been raised, a new reduction would present major problems. Here also the ratchet effect operated.[32] When the inflation tariff levels were taken over in the 1925 tariff, the result was a three-to-sixfold rise from prewar levels for textiles, and between four- and sixfold for automobiles. The rate for textiles now amounted to between 21 and 43 percent of the price.[33]

The aggressive approach to trade and tariffs of the 1920s was generally a legacy of a period of acute currency instability, not merely in countries that had experienced hyperinflation, or in countries with stable currencies such as the United States that felt disadvantaged in an economic war conducted through the currency.

A BARGAINING INSTRUMENT.   Finally, tariffs were a traditional means of bargaining across frontiers. High tariff levels could have a significance for power politics. One of the most plausible arguments for having them (or raising them) was that they might oblige other countries to reduce their own levels. Part of the traditional bargaining process under unconditional MFN treaties involved an initial raising of rates, which might then form the departure point for a series of individual bargaining offensives. On such a basis, even powerful and traditional arguments for free trade crumbled.

As a result, observers frequently noticed that unconditional MFN regulation involved putting *up* barriers. Yet there was a dramatic shift in the 1920s toward unconditional clauses in MFN agreements. Before the war, and until 1922, all U.S. commercial treaties (with three exceptions, for Canada, Hawaii, and Cuba) included a conditional clause: that is, concessions were granted by each party only in return for equivalent concessions (instead of being extended automatically). After the Fordney-McCumber Act of 1922, however, the Republican administrations went over to the European, unconditional form. By the end of the 1920s the United States had 29 unconditional treaties and only 14 conditional (Britain had 45 treaties, of which 4 were conditional; France, 43 and 1; and Germany, 48 and 1).

In addition, tariffs were used competitively *outside* the bargaining framework. Britain used tariffs in order to allow the development of domestic industries where there might be a threat from a powerful German industrial machine—most importantly in optical goods and chemicals. In 1923–1925 the Board of Trade established a list of British goods threatened by unfair trade practices and dumping. These protected industries, including ceramics, silk, and clothing, performed well through the interwar period (in contrast with the unprotected staple industries) and employed an estimated 500,000. Automobile producers protested that France and Italy had an advantage because of lower wages and that the vast and protected U.S. domestic market allowed Americans to dump automobiles and parts abroad.[34] There was thus a considerable vested interest in protection even before the great debate about the tariff that split British politics in the depression period.

In 1923 the British Conservative party failed miserably in the elections called by their leader, Andrew Bonar Law, to give a mandate for protection. By 1930, however, both the trade unions and employers' organizations appealed for a tariff. The Federation of British Industry in October 1930 reported that 96 percent of its members supported protection, and the Trades Union Congress also emphasized: "We must have protection of our industries," and put pressure on the free-trading Labour government. In October 1931 the general election, with an increased Conservative vote, provided increased parliamentary support for protection.

In French tariff policy, the fear of a damaging *concurrence allemande* was just as acute. After the 1926 franc stabilization, chemicals and metals were protected at rates up to 50 percent higher than in 1913, and most manufactured goods had increased levels. These new rates were built into the commercial treaties France concluded in 1927–28 with her neighbors and major trading partners: with Germany, and then with Belgium, Switzerland, and Italy. The 1927 German-French treaty was designed to bind Germany in an economic equivalent of the political pact of Locarno; but it had the curious side effect of locking France into the MFN structure.

Countries dependent on food imports such as Austria kept tariffs lower than those that had prevailed in the Habsburg empire, but even Hungary kept roughly the old tariff rates.

Thus while it is true as Lewis claims that levels of tariffs overall did not differ significantly from those before the First World War, the generalization hides important differences: that the tariff increases of the 1920s tended to be on manufactured goods, that on the whole levels of agricultural protection through tariffs were low, and that tariff increases came late in the depression.

Attempts to Stop a Protectionist Drift

The six years that saw the world slide into a dramatic and destructive protectionism were bracketed by two major international conferences aiming at trade liberalization, in 1927 and 1933. Some international negotiations produced limited successes, such as the 1925 International Convention for the Protection of Intellectual Property. But minor successes were outweighed by spectacular failures. One obvious interpretation was that goodwill was not enough, and that the nineteenth-century world had rested on something other than high-minded cooperation. Charles Kindleberger concluded that "with British hegemony lost and nothing to take its place, international relations lapsed into anarchy." He quotes a League official, J. B. Condliffe, who went on to write a textbook on the history of trade: "The pseudo-internationalism of the nineteenth century was clearly an outgrowth of British financial leadership and trading enterprise, backed by the economic supremacy of London and by the British navy."[35]

In 1927 the World Economic Conference, held in Geneva under the auspices of the League of Nations, produced a relatively optimistic report. It recommended an extension of the MFN principle, arbitration of disputed trade issues and referral to the Permanent Court of International Justice, and measures to increase the supply of industrial information throughout the world and to spread industrialization more widely. No one treated the dispersion of industry as a world economic problem. The final report restated quite boldly the principle of the international division of labor. "Nations may determine, for political and other reasons, that it is essential to their safety to develop increased self-sufficiencies, but it is appropriate for the Conference to point out that this has in most cases involved a sacrifice of material prosperity." It also called for a radical reversal of the prevailing trade policies of the 1920s: "Governments should immediately prepare plans for removing or diminishing by successive stages those barriers that gravely hamper trade, starting with those duties which have been imposed to counteract the effect of disturbances that are now past."[36] Trade barriers were too high, and should be reduced.

The prevailing negotiating structure militated against the success of the Geneva principles. The conference had assumed a world liberalizing through the application of unconditional MFN agreements (under which all concessions in a bilateral treaty were granted to a third party linked with an MFN clause). Such accords meant that in a protectionist climate it became virtually impossible to negotiate bilateral tariff reductions, since the benefits would automatically be passed on to countries that had made no concessions, and a valuable bargaining lever would be thrown away. In the late 1920s the process of trade bargaining grew ever slower, as countries feared that concluding an agreement, or even being near to conclusion, would destroy the chances of other settlements. If reductions were difficult, there arose at the same time powerful incentives to raise the general level of the tariff accorded to the most favored partner.

Traditional tariff theory emphasizes the welfare losses involved in the imposition of tariffs, since more expensive domestic production is substituted for cheaper foreign articles. Viewed purely in welfare terms, protection is justified only where a monopoly position allows the tariff-imposing country to alter the terms of trade in its favor. However, independently of the welfare consequences, countries might wish for a greater degree of industrialization[37]—as a good in itself, in order to increase military potential, or (for instance, in the case of southern and eastern Europe) to mop up additional supplies of labor that could no longer emigrate. In the interwar period, all these considerations played a role and altered the economic calculation of costs and benefits in imposing protection. They frustrated the attempts of international organizations and institutions to demonstrate the folly, irrationality, and absurdity of tariff increases and trade restriction.

In 1929 the League Assembly sought to become more specific and push along the process of negotiation for reducing tariffs by international coordination. It called on governments to meet in order to draw up a program for negotiations to cut trade barriers. In the meantime there should be a customs truce. The Council of the League appointed a committee to supervise the preparations. "We are now nearing the end of 1929 and are obliged to admit that in spite of a few sporadic efforts no decisive movement has occurred in this direction." In March 1930 a Commercial Convention provided for the prolongation for one year of expiring bilateral commercial treaties, but by the end of that year there had been only ten ratifications of the convention. In January 1931 the Dutch politician Hendrik Colijn, surveying the results of the League's efforts, concluded realistically that "to be quite frank, [they] have been extremely poor."[38]

The recognition of the international impasse came after the U.S. Hawley-Smoot tariff became effective (17 June 1930): the tariff was followed by a precipitate decline in U.S. imports, though a great part of the decline can be explained in terms of the income effects of the depression, rather than as a consequence of the tariff itself. From a total of $4.4 billion in 1929, U.S. imports fell in 1930 by more than $1.3 billion; but this is a proportion less than the simultaneous drop in industrial production, and no very good correlation existed between duty increases for particular goods and falls in imports, with perhaps a few notorious and well-publicized exceptions. The sales of Japanese raw silk and of Swiss watches in the United States did indeed drop considerably from 1929 through 1930.[39]

The legislative debates had been followed abroad with great interest, and countries lodged a formal protest against the act. Some countries retaliated immediately. In Italy, a government-controlled press led campaigns against purchasers of American automobiles, and Mussolini announced that "Italy will defend herself in her own way." He used state trading organizations to direct oil and timber imports from America toward Russian suppliers.[40] In Canada the U.S. tariff helped the Conservative party under Richard Bennett win an election victory on a "Canada First" tariff platform. After the July election the new government immediately put up rates on textiles, agricultural implements, electrical apparatus, and meats, as well as a substantial range of other American products.

Switzerland, whose watch trade encountered rates of 194 to 266 percent, also launched boycott campaigns. Sales of American typewriters and automobiles dropped in 1930, and sales of German typewriters increased at the expense of the U.S. product. In addition, the Swiss federation introduced higher duties. But the American share of the Swiss automobile market still stayed at over half in 1931, and the dramatic break of Switzerland with the MFN system in September 1931 was justified not as a reaction to anything American, but rather to the German government's use of a passport tax to stop German tourism in Switzerland.[41]

The most international response to American developments was the French foreign minister Aristide Briand's pan-Europe plan. It began in 1929, when twenty-seven European countries voted at Geneva to consider a federal link that would provide in economics an equivalent to the work of the League in politics. Briand thought the union would "secure not only political but also economic peace among nations," and the resolution developed the theme of an economic underpinning of political peace. "No one today doubts that the lack of cohesion in the grouping of material and moral forces in Europe constitutes politically the most serious obstacle to a development and to the efficiency of all political and judicial institutions on which the first attempts at a universal organization of peace are founded."[42] The possible tasks of the new federation involved the control of cartels and international organizations, the coordination of public works, and the development of backward regions.

The project had an unmistakably anti-American accent, even before the terms of the Hawley-Smoot tariff had been finalized. American exports had surged into Europe, and Briand feared the emergence of a perpetual dollar gap because of the different rates of productivity growth in Europe and North America. Currency depreciation as a means of responding to differential productivity had been discredited by the history of the early 1920s; and thus trade policy needed to make the adjustment.

Such a course involved going outside the MFN framework in order to create separate European rates and preferences. The French liberal newspaper *L'Ere nouvelle* explained the thinking behind Briand's scheme by depicting Europe as ground to pieces by the MFN principle: "prevented by the MFN clause either from organizing itself vis-à-vis the United States, or from proceeding with regional agreements, lost in a labyrinth of individual treaties, condemned to die between the too-rich America and the Russian commercial monopoly, whose dumping measures are merely, in sum, the exaggeration of warring methods universally honored."[43] The paradoxical conclusion was that only by abandoning MFN, the great principle of the nineteenth-century liberal trading environment, could world tariff levels be cut. This principle remained after 1930 as an essential ingredient of French trade philosophy, and it reemerged in 1931 and 1932 in the form of schemes for regional preferences and federations, most importantly in 1932 in the Tardieu scheme for southeastern European preference.

In late 1930 a series of regional conferences discussed the agricultural situation of eastern Europe. More successfully, the Scandinavian countries and Belgium, Luxembourg, and the Netherlands signed in 1930 the Oslo Convention, agreeing not to increase tariffs or to introduce new ones without notifying the other signatories. In the most effective regional agreement, the Ouchy Convention (June 1932), Belgium, the Netherlands, and Luxembourg agreed to impose no new tariffs and to reduce existing levels by 10 percent each year.

The broad outlines of Briand's vision, however, ran into a dead end: because of British opposition, and the Labour government's commitment to dealing with the United States; and through the opposition of mostly British officials at the League who saw the general and international principles of Geneva threatened in economics as well as in politics by particular and narrow alliances.[44] Even the very modest legacy of Briand's scheme, a European plan for agricultural credit support, failed, and the British and German governments delayed their ratification.[45]

The trade dilemma and its political ramifications had thus become acute before the events of 1931: the German-Austrian plan for their own regionalism in the shape of the customs union, the following central European banking crisis, and the British abandonment of the gold standard and move to tariff protection.

The bank and currency crises of mid-1931 precipitated a new round of responses on commercial policy. After July 1931 most European and many non-European countries revised or reconstituted their tariff systems.

The most spectacular turnaround occurred in the United Kingdom, which had for a century and a half been the leading international proponent of laissez-faire principles in commerce. The question of a tariff had already been widely discussed before the 1931 crisis; advocacy of a tariff policy was, for instance, one reason why Maynard Keynes was less sympathetic to devaluation. Tariffs might be a more efficient way of coping with international price differentials. Although Ramsay MacDonald remained prime minister, the National Government formed after the October 1931 elections was dominated by protectionists, and in particular by Philip Snowden's successor at the Exchequer, Neville Chamberlain.

In November and December 1931 three temporary orders imposed higher duties on a number of manufactured goods. In February 1932 imports of nonessential agricultural products were reduced, and in March 1932 these ad hoc barriers were replaced by a 10 percent ad valorem duty, with additional tariffs following this general imposition. The British pressure groups reacted enthusiastically. The Federation of British Industries passed a resolution commending the change in commercial policy, "realisation of which will go far to restore British industrial activity and to promote mutually advantageous trading relations primarily with the rest of the Empire, and secondly, with such foreign countries as are willing to negotiate commercial agreements upon an equitable reciprocal basis."[46]

After 1932 the British tariff system was as far as possible depoliticized, not so much in order to prevent the political logrolling that had led to Hawley-Smoot, but rather to limit the infliction of political wounds. The National Government contained passionate free-traders (Home Secretary Sir Herbert Samuel and Lord Privy Seal Philip Snowden, now known as Lord Passfield), compromising free-traders (MacDonald himself, President of the Board of Trade Sir Walter Runciman; and Foreign Secretary Sir John Simon), as well as committed protectionists (Chamberlain and Major Walter Elliot, the minister of agriculture). Their disputes, which crossed traditional party divisions, in the winter of 1931–32 came close to tearing the government apart, and a solution to the tariff question became essential for the political survival of the National Coalition.

The scope for pressure increased as the divisions became more apparent. The steel industry, having suffered from chronic problems of overcapacity throughout the previous decade, presented an important memorandum to the cabinet urging the case for protection.[47] In 1932 the steel men fought to extend protection of steel to supplies for the shipbuilding industry, thus raising costs there. Then in turn those hurt by protection responded: the shipbuilders, and furnituremakers whose imported raw materials had become suddenly more expensive and who at the same time faced protection in foreign markets. Setting tariff rates raised many thousands of questions of this kind, relating to the balance between trade and the industrial "mix." "Unless," one member of Parliament wrote to the chancellor of the Exchequer, "the Tariff Commissioners are really going to be supermen and give decisions at the rate of hundreds a day, I am afraid some of the manufacturers are going to have a difficult time."[48]

But as pressure politics became a commonplace, politicians tried to insulate themselves from a direct impact. A new agency, the Import Duties Advisory Committee (IDAC), composed of nonpolitical experts, heard evidence and set rates. On the whole, this attempt to prevent the operation of business pressure succeeded: there is actually an inverse correlation between the degree of concentration of an industry and its ability in the 1930s to secure effective protection.[49] The IDAC involved itself in formulating a business strategy: it used its ability to give tariff protection to the highly fragmented iron and steel industry in order to force through amalgamations and rationalizations. In 1935 it also used the threat of a rise in the tariff in order to give British steel producers a bargaining weapon in their dealings with the International Steel Cartel. Finally, it followed a regional policy: rates of effective protection are highly correlated with industrial representation in depressed areas.

The general political aim behind British protectionism lay less in a general recovery strategy than as a response to the highly regional growth of unemployment in the British Isles. Secondly, the government wished to change the direction of trade and to increase the links with the empire. In Neville Chamberlain's world view, inherited from his Tariff Reform father, tariff meant empire: "There is no article of your food, there is no raw material in your trade, there is no necessity of your lives, no luxury of your existence which cannot be produced somewhere or other in the British Empire."[50] The framework for the expansion of trade within the empire was created at the Imperial Conference in Ottawa (July 1932). Here again, pressure group politics operated. The Candian Manufactures Association sent a group to check any concession by the Bennett government. The London *Times* commented on the "tremendous and varied pressure employed by industrial interests convinced that a diminution of their tariff preserves means, if not ruin, grave embarrassment."[51]

In practice, largely because of Canadian insistence, British policy involved higher tariffs against nonimperial goods: the 10 percent duties previously charged on fruits, dairy products, vegetable oils, and rice were replaced by specific duties of between 33.3 and 100 percent.[52] In order to facilitate the development of the imperial link, Britain's foreign tariffs were consolidated and fixed for a five-year period. The high levels set gave a bargaining weapon, used quite effectively in British dealings with some non-empire raw material and food exporters. Runciman presented tariff policy to the British cabinet as just a "pillar round which negotiations were to be opened up."[53] It was a British response to the French attempts at securing European preference areas. Ottawa made final Britain's conversion to protection, and made nearly impossible her position at the approaching World Economic and Financial Conference. The outcome led to the resignation of Samuel and Snowden from the cabinet, on the grounds that the National Government had had no mandate from the electorate for anything but an emergency tariff.[54] In explaining the threat to the London conference, Chamberlain could only fall back on the device of blaming the Americans: "Some members of the Canadian Government, however, living under the shadow of a powerful neighbour given to sudden and ruthless imposition of trade barriers, had evinced a strong opposition to any such general policy [of lowering tariffs] and could not bear the thought of lowering their tariff barriers against the United States."[55]

Other countries followed the same course and tried to use tariff policy to stop the international transmission of deflation (price collapse). In December 1931 Greece imposed a new additional tariff, at ten times the previous level, on imports from countries with which no commercial treaty existed. In February 1932, after acrimonious political debates about the extent of agricultural protection, the German tariff was raised yet again. France turned to trade with the empire in an even more dramatic way than did the United Kingdom. Whereas in 1925 10.5 percent of French imports came from French overseas territories, in 1936 that proportion was 28.6 percent. In the mid-1920s, 14.6 percent of French exports had gone to the overseas possessions; in 1936 33.4 percent did.[56]

Most important, however, there was a move away from tariffs as the easiest way of regulating external commerce. Quota systems offered an easier answer in that the immediate cost to the consumer looked much less, and the political benefits might be commensurately greater. In this, France led the way. From mid-1931 to July 1932, the French parliament extended quotas over 1,100 items in the tariff code. But similar measures were implemented in Turkey, Austria, Sweden, Estonia, Greece, Poland, Switzerland, Czechoslovakia, and to a more limited extent also in Britain, Belgium, Germany, Norway, Denmark, Rumania, and Italy. Australia, Brazil, and Japan also introduced quota systems.

Another way to control trade in the depression was the creation of import monopolies of the type already pioneered by the USSR. Persia took over entirely the Soviet system, but Uruguay, Estonia, Latvia, Switzerland, Czechoslovakia, Belgium, and Turkey also created some monopolies, and in Sweden the wheat trade was regulated in this way.

Finally the capital flight and currency runs of 1931 meant a necessity of imposing exchange control. In almost every case, the countries introducing the new measures explained that they were intended to curb speculation and not to interfere with legitimate commerce. In practice, however, in the first place, it was hard to tell the two apart, in that legitimate importers often accelerated their imports in the hope of making exchange profits. Secondly, the possibility of regulating trade in this way, semisecretly and without such a great likelihood of retaliation, proved very tempting. The German system of exchange control was one of the most complete, and at the beginning there was a distinction in allocating exchange for imported goods between products that were essential, necessary "up to a certain extent," and unnecessary. The central bank, without ever revealing the lists on which it based its decisions, allocated some exchange to would-be importers of the second category, and refused exchange to the third group.

The result of the move away from tariffs and to quotas, and the increased use of exchange control as a weapon of trade policy, was a bilateralization of trading relationships, and also, as bilateral exchanges became crucial in negotiations, a linking of trade and debt issues.

Creditor countries tried to recover their debts through commercial agreements. The first of these arrangements was the Swiss-Hungarian clearing agreement of December 1931. As long as Hungarian receipts in Swiss francs did not reach the amount of payments due for purchases of Swiss goods, one-third of the sums received would be allocated for the payment of commercial debts. In 1932 Germany negotiated similar clearings with Bulgaria, Estonia, Greece, Rumania, and Yugoslavia, allowing preferential tariffs for fixed quantities of imported wheat in order to allow surpluses for debt repayments.

The involvement of political issues—the questions of war debts and reparations—further complicated the discussion of commercial issues. As a League report piously put it: "Cruel is the conflict between human intentions guided by the spirit of Geneva and the brutal force of realities."[57] Politics, British prime minister MacDonald believed, drove nations apart; but common action in the face of the world depression for the sake of promoting recovery might restore harmony. "Economics and trade," he noted in his diary, "are the deepest rock foundations of politics."[58] He set out to apply this doctrine at the conference over which he presided in the summer of 1932.

At the Lausanne reparations conference in 1932, the question of inter-Allied war debts was deferred, principally because the United States would not reach an agreement before the presidential elections in November. One of the ways of masking the reason for the deferral also offered a possibility of tackling the trade issue in its broad context; these were to be the themes of a world economic conference held in 1933.

Such a conference had been suggested from time to time by American diplomats as a way of bringing the European continent to its senses, as well as achieving the more specific goal of defusing objections and avoiding retaliations in response to the Hawley-Smoot tariff. In October 1930 Undersecretary William Castle had urged an economic conference to provide "tangible political and economic satisfaction of American interests." The British took this up enthusiastically and passed it on to Germany as a way of defeating the European integration side of the Briand plan; and the Germans thought it might open a way to make the United States interested in the financial side of economic questions, and in particular the end of reparations. The German foreign minister then urged his ambassadors to sell the plan as a strong platform for Hoover's campaign for reelection as president.[59] Later, in December 1931, Ambassador Frederick Sackett made a more concrete proposal of this kind to German Chancellor Heinrich Brüning.[60]

By 1933 the realities had changed substantially. Hoover had been defeated, and the Germans had already achieved their aim of ending reparations at Lausanne. As the date for the London World Economic Conference approached, the prospective participants realized that a large meeting could not be expected to produce any significant result unless a substantial basis had been laid by preliminary commissions and committees presenting draft contracts and agreements.

These began in late 1932 in Geneva under the auspices of the League of Nations; they represented the last major attempt to deal with the international policy questions of the depression in an international framework. Separate financial (that is, monetary) and economic (that is, trade) subcommittees met to work out the respective agendas.

The problem was that each saw the other's field as crucial. All the speakers at the Financial Subcommittee agreed that "freer trade was a prerequisite of a return to normal economic conditions and of a return to the gold standard."[61] At the Economic Subcommittee, the British government's chief economic adviser, Sir Frederick Leith-Ross, took the opportunity to present the view "that the financial breakdown was the occasion rather than the cause of the present crisis. For ten years the world has been attempting to adjust the balance of payments by lending and borrowing instead of buying and selling."[62]

Trade issues immediately affected the political obligations of governments of the participating states, and thus the experts felt uncomfortable about making firm commitments. The U.S. ambassador to the Geneva Disarmament Conference, Norman Davis, who also represented the United States at the economic talks in Geneva, informed the Geneva Organizing Committee that he "had got the impression from conversations with the experts that it was difficult to agree on an agenda because of embarrassing political questions which were involved. He thought the policies of Governments were partly responsible for the present trouble, and these questions would have to be faced."[63] But every government looked at different targets. For the British, the obstacles to agreement lay in the U.S. tariff and in the extent of German, French, and Italian agricultural protection, since this stimulated agricultural overproduction and reduced the ability of the Danubian states to sell. Thus the debt crisis stemmed from agricultural protection. This British strategy of addressing trade issues rather than monetary ones arose out of the view that there should be no stabilization of sterling.

On the other hand, in the view of Ottawa and the system of imperial preferences, it was a rather weak bargaining position, and easily criticized by other states who saw Ottawa and the sterling devaluation as causes of the depression. Britain had only half completed the tariff system announced at Ottawa, and did not want any interruption of the process. Ottawa's chief British architect, Neville Chamberlain, in consequence referred to the world economic meeting as "this miserable conference." Although MacDonald never wanted to acknowledge the fact, the consequence fatally handicapped British preparations for the London conference. Britain would not compromise the turn to empire. As a result, British preparations suffered a decisive blow when Sir Walter Layton, the editor of *The Economist*, resigned from the Geneva Preparatory Committee before the meetings even began and published the text of his letter to the prime minister: "In the absence of a radical change in the world's commercial policy—in which this country's attitude could be an almost decisive factor—I do see the possibility of a really satisfactory outcome of the conference on the monetary side."[64]

For the other powers, the decisions taken in Ottawa meant that negotiations with Britain stood little chance of success. The German Foreign Ministry trade expert, Hans Posse, wrote that "it has not yet become clear to the English how they have damaged us in good measure by the direct and indirect contents of the Ottawa agreements."[65]

The trade discussions at Geneva certainly produced some proposals. The chief of the League's Financial Section, Pietro Stoppani, produced a well-worked-out scheme for allowing greater quantities of grain to be exported by the Danubian states—Rumania, Yugoslavia, Hungary, and Bulgaria—to industrialized Europe (Germany, France, Italy, Austria, Switzerland, and Czechoslovakia) by allowing a partial circumvention of MFN clauses. In addition, it provided for conventions of European scrap-iron and coal producers.[66] But the trade side looked again and again to the monetary experts to provide schemes for debt relief and currency stabilization. In this way, a stalemate set in.

Leith-Ross made the point very clearly:

> The Financial Sub-Committee thought action in the monetary sphere was dependent on greater freedom in the movement of goods, while the Economic Sub-Committee considered that no progress could be made in economic matters until financial and monetary questions were settled. The President had said that work in the two spheres should proceed on parallel lines. It was a quality of parallel lines that they never met. It might be more correct to say that a vicious circle had been created and the question was how to break that circle.[67]

The result was that the preparatory work in Geneva achieved very little. In practice, the financial side of the conference came to overshadow trade: both currency questions and war debts proved immensely divisive. The French default on war-debt repayments in December 1932 increased the tension between the United States and continental Europe. Secretary of State Henry Stimson passed on the following message to MacDonald from President Hoover: "Tell MacDonald that I believe that the civilization which he speaks of can only be saved by the cooperation of Anglo-Saxons, we cannot count on other races."[68]

The second attempt at preparation took place among politicians rather than "experts" in Washington in April and May 1933. The key to Roosevelt's approach was a tariff truce to last for the duration of the conference: a proposal that Whitehall interpreted as an underhand way of wrecking the Ottawa agreement. The debt issue was widened in Washington by the German central bank president's attempt to win consent for a German moratorium on the servicing of long-term private foreign debt. And the monetary issue was raised in an acute form by the announcement of the U.S. gold embargo while MacDonald and Leith-Ross were still at sea.

By the time the conference actually met, on 12 June 1933, in the London Geological Museum, there were too many parties interested in killing it off for the negotiations to stand much of a chance of success (though on the whole they also wanted to make sure that the blame fell on someone else). The conference resembled nothing so much as an Agatha Christie novel in which there are too many suspects in a murder—all with highly plausible motives and unconvincing alibis.[69]

Even the smaller powers joined in the disruption. Austria saw the conference as an ideal stage for (a quite legitimate) warning against the dangers of a new German expansionism. Chancellor Engelbert Dollfuss ended his major speech with a moving but provocative citation from Schiller's *Wilhelm Tell:* "Es kann der Frömmste nicht in Frieden bleiben / Wenn es dem bösen Nachbarn nicht gefällt" (Even the most pious cannot rest / When his evil neighbor is a pest). Irish minister of land and fisheries Joseph Conolly likewise addressed British iniquities in Ireland.

But the most mischief came from the major powers. The British insistence on war-debt reduction, which they believed to be the original raison d'être of the conference, around which the sumptuous icing of debate about trade and currency had been built, meant that they did not want the debate to widen. Chancellor of the Exchequer Neville Chamberlain stressed that the conference would not be considered successful if it did not satisfactorily resolve the war-debt issue.[70] But the president's instructions to the U.S. delegation quite explicitly excluded either formal or informal discussion of war debts as well as disarmament.[71]

Germany saw the most important issue as the international regulation of short-term debt through conversion to longer maturities and interest-rate reduction. Reichsbank president Hjalmar Schacht believed that in Washington he had come close to convincing President Roosevelt of the merit of the German demand, but that he had been frustrated by the intervention of the State Department. The Germans were heavily committed to massive agricultural protection, and in consequence doubted whether the agricultural tariffs could be lowered.[72] The mission to the conference included Schacht, who after Washington no longer took the discussions very seriously, and Food and Economics Minister Alfred Hugenberg, who did not believe in international trade. The latter's inclusion occurred despite warnings from the professionals in the German Foreign Office—Foreign Minister Konstantin von Neurath and State Secretary Bernhard von Bülow—that it would lead to disaster.[73]

Hugenberg did not fail to produce public explosions in London: rabid denunciations of the Soviet Union, and also most spectacularly a memorandum on 16 June calling for the restoration of German colonies and also for German land for settlement in the East, at the expense of Russia. The goal was to "open up to the *Volk ohne Raum* areas in which it could provide space for the settlement of its vigorous race and construct great works of peace." There was no point in world cooperation. "The world economy is a simultaneous co-existence of independent national economies . . . whoever is of the opinion that the individual economies can only be cured from the world economy is putting things on their head."[74] Tariff reductions were irrelevant to the task of economic recovery, which would take place only on the basis of national economic planning.

On the fringes of the conference, German representatives used the opportunity to negotiate bilateral trade treaties with anyone who cared to listen—for instance Turkey.[75] At the same time, Britain went over to a form of bilateralism because of concern about debt issues. Just before the conference, it had negotiated a "payment" agreement with Argentina in which a proportion of foreign exchange received from exports to Britain would be reserved for debt payments. Later Britain made similar agreements with Uruguay, Brazil, Hungary, Rumania, and Germany.

Secretary of State Cordell Hull's main interest in London, as elsewhere, concerned the reduction of tariff barriers. He wanted the conference to enact the idea he had already raised during the 1932 presidential campaign: a worldwide 10 percent tariff cut and a tariff truce. He hoped to come to London with a draft of reciprocal trade agreements legislation authorizing the administration to negotiate reductions on an MFN basis. At the beginning of April, Roosevelt had declared that he would ask Congress for the authority to conclude reciprocal trade agreements.[76] But in the end he refused Hull's demand, because it might endanger congressional support and erode the rest of the New Deal program. In addition, there were conflicts between the domestic program and international policy. Provisions in the Agricultural Adjustment Act, for instance, violated the proposed tariff truce (producers of seven basic commodities were given federal subsidies financed through a tax on processors: for the sake of equity, this was accompanied by a parallel tax on imports of foreign products processed from the commodities).[77]

By the time the conference was in its fifth week, the participants realized that the position was hopeless, and that further negotiations meant nothing more than a means of drawing out disagreements.[78] On 27 July the conference went into recess, and Hull made a rather resigned final speech: "A reasonable combination of the practicable phases of both economic nationalism and economic internationalism—avoiding the extremes of each—should be our objective." In practice, the participants ignored the tariff truce: Britain raised schedules on fifty items, claiming that it had made applications for these before the truce came into effect on 12 May. In September the Netherlands and Sweden, and then in November Britain withdrew from the truce. This was the end of the last major attempt at international cooperation on trade issues.

There were two alternative strategies to cooperation. The first was the course adopted in the United States, and associated with Hull, which used tough bilateral negotiations as a way of opening closed economies. The second was Schachtianism, and took its name from the central banker of Weimar Germany whom Hitler appointed as minister of economics. Schachtianism, too, rested on a bilateral approach to international relations, but treated this primarily as a way of exercising power politics.

Hullianism and Reciprocal Trade Agreements

The author of the House Ways and Means Committee minority view on the Hawley-Smoot trade bill in 1929, Cordell Hull, included in his report the statement that "American foreign policy can no longer ignore the fact that since 1914 we have changed from a debtor and small surplus Nation to the greatest creditor and actual or potential surplus-producing Nation in the world."[79] Eight million "idle American wage-earners" had been the victims, the "effects of the long years of virtual airtight tariff or similar protection."[80]

As Roosevelt's secretary of state he embarked on the task of tariff reduction with a notorious single-mindedness. In the 1930s, many observers concluded that the constant humiliations inflicted on Hull indicated that he was an irrelevancy in the Roosevelt administration, a "futile idealist who is allowed to make speeches which don't represent the Government's position."[81] Most historians have accepted this verdict, but it is an unfair one.

Hull's approach recognized the responsibility of the United States for economic and political developments in Europe. It was a position formulated even more dramatically by his friend Ambassador William E. Dodd, who wrote to the secretary of state: "The tariff policy 1923–1930, the dangerous loans of 1923–1928, and the refusal of the Senate, 1921, to live up to the expectations of the election of 1920 are, therefore, the basic causes of Mussolini and Hitler, of British and French economic autarchies."[82] From the beginning of the administration, Hull believed that the tariff held the key to foreign policy. One of his first proposals was to alter the composition of the Tariff Commission in order to isolate it from special (that is, protectionist) interests by adding a Consumer Counsel who might object to proposed duties and conduct additional and supplementary investigations into the effects of a particular tariff.[83]

The scheme for a reciprocal trade bill to coincide with the London conference failed, but later in the year Roosevelt asked Hull to draft legislation on tariff reduction. The main point of the new bill was to transfer the initiative on tariff reduction from Congress to the executive, and it was defended on the grounds that this made negotiations with other powers much simpler. Congress had "thoroughly demonstrated by the Smoot-Hawley [sic] Act that there are enough commitments from members from the local standpoint relative to the rate situation to preclude and prevent the carrying out of any definite and certain emergency reciprocity policy."[84] A new policy would be in the national interest, for tariff reductions, as well as tariff increases, could be part of a sustained effort of economic nationalism: a bargaining for easier access to foreign markets by American goods. There was thus a substantial industrial lobby, concerned with exporting, prepared to support the new legislation. Some commentators have seen the first New Deal as the result of a historic compromise in which internationally minded and capital-intensive export business, led by figures such as John D. Rockefeller, Walter Teagle of Standard Oil, and Gerard Swope of General Electric, accepted the Wagner National Labor Relations Act, the Social Security Act, and free trade.[85] But on the whole business groups played a secondary role in the debate about the Reciprocal

Trade Agreements Act (RTAA). Some groups were in favor: the National Automobile Chamber of Commerce and the American Manufacturers Export Association; others were opposed: the National Association of Manufacturers, the American Mining Congress, and the National Wool Growers. Larger firms were in general more sympathetic to the RTAA principles and less demanding of protection.[86]

Like the British IDAC, the institutions created by the act aimed at a depoliticization of the tariff-setting and bargaining process. The interests were not to be allowed the degree of influence wielded in the debates over Hawley-Smoot. A new Executive Committee on Commercial Policy determined the broad line of commercial strategy and applied it in the case of the bilateral negotiations. According to the chairman of the Tariff Commission, R. L. O'Brien, the new system tried to "substitute the national welfare for special favors. It offers fair hearing to every interest but permits no single one to be guiding. It provides, in an atmosphere removed from the inescapable turmoil of the political arena, for a study by commodity experts and economists, of every tariff rate in whose preservation or change there is a promise of general gain."[87]

After a formal announcement of the intention to negotiate a commercial treaty, the State Department issued a detailed survey of trade relations, including lists of the individual commodities affected. There followed a six-week period for the submission of written statements, and after eight weeks the Committee for Reciprocity heard evidence. Each set of negotiations was supervised by a separate committee, armed with studies by the Department of Commerce on the concessions that could be agreed and by the Tariff Commission on concessions that might be offered.

The RTAA mechanism incurred considerable political disapproval. The greatest protests came not from the interests but from the politicians who had made a living representing them. Arthur Vandenberg protested that the bill would allow "Washington bureaucrats" to "identify so-called 'inefficient industries' and put them out of business by their fiat." The RTAA proceedings were dubbed "Star Chamber." In the 1936 campaign Senator William Borah argued that farmers were the victims of the new tariff policy. In 1937 Republicans in the House of Representatives claimed that Hull was acting like Mussolini or Hitler in pretending that the "whole performance of constitutional government, particularly in the legislative end, is venal and unworthy"; or again that the RTAA "permits the lowering of our tariffs without reference to domestic production costs, and thereby jeopardizes all American agriculture, labor and industry; undermines the American wage level, which is by far the highest in the world; and threatens our American standard of living."[88]

Hull did in fact successfully mobilize professional economic advice against the interest groups. The cotton textile industry, for instance, remained in a state of acute crisis throughout the 1930s—the result of over-expansion, the shift of industries from the North to a lower-wage South, competition from new factories, vulnerability to changes in fashion, and a hopelessly fragmented industrial structure that frustrated attempts to rationalize. Industrial representatives responded with insistent demands for protection, especially against low-cost Japanese imports; they pointed out that Japanese imports had risen from 1.16 million square yards in 1930 to 7.29 million in 1934. But Herbert Feis's Office of the Economic Adviser in the State Department worked out that protection could at the most lead to an increase of 5 to 6 percent in the production of cotton goods by American mills.[89]

This is not to say that the administration was insensitive to the political side of tariff reductions. Especially before elections, the issues proved highly sensitive. One response was the use of opinion polls to gauge responses to the reciprocal agreements. The Gallup polls in the Midwest corn and dairy states showed only between 9 and 17 percent of farmers favorable; but Hull's answer was that there needed to be more agreements with industrial states—such as Britain—in order to reduce prices of imported goods and make farmers see the potential gains from liberalizing commerce.[90] In November 1938 this treaty was indeed concluded with a Britain by now eager for political support in the face of the growing European crisis. From a purely economic viewpoint, the United Kingdom had little to gain from American trade concessions, but weighed an economic price against a political gain.[91]

Between 1934 and 1940 the State Department negotiated in all twenty-two reciprocal trade agreements, which shifted trade in the direction of the new accords; thus in 1935, the first year in which the results became apparent, U.S. exports increased by 7 percent, but exports to those countries with which agreements had been concluded rose much more sharply: exports to Cuba went up by 33 percent, and to Belgium and Sweden each by 16 percent. In 1938, for sixteen countries with trade agreements, imports from the United States had grown by 39.8 percent since 1934–35; while imports from Germany (which had no trade agreement but rather a conscious policy of reorienting trade) had risen by only 1.8 percent.

An inseparable part of the movement of liberalization and trade expansion was an avoidance of any link between trade and debt issues. The debt pileup and the subsequent rash of defaults, in the administration's view, had been the result of private action—chiefly by East Coast bankers—and the federal government had no responsibility to mount any rescue. In 1933 a Committee of Foreign Bondholders was established as an equivalent to the British Council of Foreign Bondholders to protect the interests of creditors. But the insignificance of the U.S. institution was widely recognized. "The fact that among the rather undistinguished group of gentlemen invited to discuss the creation of the new organization, no persons seem to have been included with any outstanding knowledge either of foreign finance in general or of the defaulted loans in particular, is no doubt due to Governmental animus against Wall Street."[92]

The new State Department did indeed try to make a clear break with the past. A characteristic view was offered by the U.S. ambassador to Mexico, Josephus Daniels, who consistently argued that involvement in debt collecting would be highly damaging. "Why should our Government undertake this work and press collections due to those who pressed loans upon South American governments and got big rake-offs? We have not taken the laboring oar to secure other creditors. Why jeopardize larger trade in these countries by helping to collect money due to private parties?"[93]

The outcome of the U.S. experience of the 1930s was a shift in perceptions about what government should and should not do. It *should not* protect the private interests of financiers and creditors, and should not make itself vulnerable to private pressures from special producing interests in Congress. It *should* act to guarantee overall fiscal and monetary stability, and it should set general conditions in which an expansion of U.S. trade might be facilitated. Both of the latter processes proved to be a crucial part of the establishment of a secure framework for the world economy after 1945. The U.S. path was quite distinct from the approach of other major countries.

Schachtianism and Bilateral Economics

Germany also moved away from reliance on interest groups in the making of foreign economic policy, with the centralization of the Nazi state, the ideological purging of industrial pressure groups, and their reconstitution as part of an "organic state." Some historians have emphasized the bureaucratic confusion of policymaking in 1930s Germany—the proliferation of institutions without clearly defined, or with overlapping, definitions of competence. But this problem had existed already during the Republic, and in trade policy had been solved through the creation (in 1925) of a Trade Political Committee (Handelspolitischer Ausschuss), which the Foreign Office chaired and in which the Ministries of Finance, Economics, and Agriculture were represented. To these traditional governmental sources of bureaucratic friction were added others specific to National Socialism. The Four-Year Plan under Hermann Göring, the Army leadership, and the Foreign Political Organization of the Nazi party all intervened.

The most severe disagreements arose over the extent of export orientation. Economics Minister Schacht isolated himself more and more by arguing against excessive autarky, and pointed out the high costs incurred in building up domestic substitute industries. In 1936–37 he engaged in, and lost, a bitter conflict with Göring over the use of low-grade German domestic iron ores in steelmaking.[94]

But there was a general German consensus on the desirability of diversifying trade away from northwestern Europe and North America. In part this was a consequence of the debt issue, since large surpluses in bilateral transactions were applied, as under the 1934 British-German Agreement, to debt servicing. Germany stood to gain by running down these surpluses, particularly as the pace of export growth slackened in consequence of the strength of domestic recovery.

A reorientation toward South America and southeastern Europe had already been demanded by industrial and banking pressure groups, notably the Central European Economic Association, or Mitteleuropäischer Wirtschaftstag, since the depression.[95] These demands played at least some role in the calculations of the Trade Political Committee. In the 1930s, in the conditions of exchange control that had been imposed since the financial crisis of 1931, prices could be manipulated in a system of multiple exchange rates to direct trade to particular partners, according to an overall political strategy.

Italy and Japan also introduced centralized administrative systems for administering with quotas and quantitative restrictions. Japanese trade, like that of Germany, changed direction. There had been a positive balance of trade with the United States in 1929 of 260 million yen; in 1932 there was a negative balance here of 65 million yen and in 1934 of 371 million. Instead Japan exported more to colonial areas in Asia and Africa, and also to South America.[96] On the other hand, Japan, more or less uniquely, avoided bilateralization.

The economic interests that had been squeezed out of trade negotiations sometimes came back through international production and cartel arrangements. Discussions on wheat continued in London in 1933 even after the collapse of the World Conference. The United States, originally fiercely opposed to the idea of export quotas on wheat, made two significant concessions:[97] it accepted the idea of internationally negotiated crop reductions and also agreed to preferences for Danubian producers. But throughout the negotiations, the major exporters realized that any agreement they might reach would be useless without the cooperation of European importers,[98] and the scheme broke down when the major importing countries had harvested unusually abundant crops. Other agreements also came into difficulty. Sugar was regulated in 1931 by the Chadbourne Agreement, but this expired in 1935 and was not renewed. The participating countries— Cuba, Java, Czechoslovakia, Poland, Hungary, Bulgaria, Peru, and Germany—reduced their production of sugar by half from 1930 to 1935, but the nonparticipating countries, in particular the United States, responded merely by increasing domestic output.

Seventy-five percent of the world's copper production (again with the exception of U.S. output) was regulated and restricted by a convention of 1935. The United States limited itself to a pledge not to increase exports, and the world's total output in the event remained unchanged—although prices recovered somewhat as a result of the rearming boom.

Tea regulation (by the International Tea Committee of 1935), by allowing exports as a share of a standard figure, fared rather better, although again—as in the case of wheat and sugar—there was substantial tea-growing in areas that were not covered by agreement (Japan, China, the USSR, and French Indo-China).

Tin (under the International Tin Agreement of 1931) and rubber (May 1934) were regulated by allowing variable export quotas that increased over the course of world recovery. The schemes had a much greater flexibility than had the earlier rubber scheme (the Stevenson Plan). Prices rose steadily, provoking U.S. protests at unfair management of the market.

Such international agreements involved a mix of private and state interests. They were usually worked out at a governmental level, but individual producers and associations played a prominent part in setting the strategy. Even in private cartels—such as the International Steel Cartel—governments used other policies in order to achieve advantages for their industries. Thus in 1935 British steel producers reached a relatively favorable agreement with the ISC because their government had proposed introducing a penal high tariff on foreign steel products.

This was the un-American way of going about business, and Hull saw the proliferation of planned trade support plans involving the acceptance of preferences and quotas as both a threat to the overall chances of liberalization and an attack on the interests of the United States as a major consumer of raw materials. Those schemes that worked most successfully infuriated U.S. policymakers; those that failed did so because of U.S. action.

The tendency to move trade policy out of the reach of democratic politics and pressure groups and into executive control occasionally occurred for laudable reasons—one being that 1920s logrolling protectionism had resulted from an excess of democracy; but always in the background lay the power political calculations that increasingly determined trade policy. Nowhere was this clearer than in the history of the trading relations of southeastern Europe and South America with the great powers. Germany's relation with southeast Europe and the Balkans and with South America accounted for around a third of the total number of instances in which trade-balancing provisions were included in trade treaties.[99]

The tendency toward a bilateralization of trade in the 1930s was by no means a German peculiarity. Indeed the best available index of bilateralism indicates that British trade shifted more in this direction than did that of Germany.[100] But bilaterism was quickly demonized, and it looked politically convenient for democracies to attack it. At the 1933 World Economic Conference, the chief economic adviser to the British cabinet, Sir Frederick Leith-Ross, tried to argue that the bilateral approach was only a negotiating strategy. But after 1933, Britain rapidly extended bilateralism. The British argument remained that this had been forced on the country by the rest of the world: in particular, the measure was presented as a reaction to the German suspension in 1934 of service on the Dawes and Young Loans. Britain indeed initially refused to provide the League of Nations inquiry on bilateralism with statistical material on the grounds that this was not a British policy and that Britain had not entered into any clearing agreements.[101] But in practice there was a major expansion of British trade in the 1930s to the weaker Scandinavian countries (Denmark and Finland) and to the Baltic states, and these countries experienced a dependence on trade similar to that established by Germany in the case of southeastern Europe.[102]

Germany had developed exchange control as a temporary response to the emergency of 1931. The first clearing agreements, which established a model for subsequent developments, had been concluded between Switzerland and Austria and between Switzerland and Hungary. The theory of clearing agreements had been expounded most elaborately in 1931, at a central bankers' meeting in Prague, by the governor of the Austrian Nationalbank. These precedents provided the basis for German clearing agreements of 1932. The temporary response developed into a permanent system in 1933, after the Nazi seizure of power. In June 1933 Germany imposed a moratorium on all foreign debt repayments (except the interest and amortization on the 1924 Dawes Loan and interest payments on the 1930 Young Loan).

The low point of the German depression as measured by an index of industrial production occurred in the summer of 1932. As the domestic recovery became more vigorous, the trade problem that had plagued the German economy in the 1920s reemerged. Despite the attempts to control imports by allowing quotas of foreign exchange based on 1931 figures, imports mounted without any corresponding rise in exports. In the spring of 1934, imports of some raw materials were rationed. The central bank's reserves continued to disappear, and in September 1934 Hjalmar Schacht, now installed by Hitler as acting economics minister as well as Reichsbank president, introduced a "New Plan," requiring importers to obtain Devisen certificates issued by control boards under the supervision of the Reichsbank. The New Plan provided a much more suitable instrument for the management of trade than the impromptu mechanisms devised in 1931 as part of the apparatus of exchange control. Since this time, systems of managed trade have been dubbed "Schachtianism."

Schacht publicly defended his approach as a necessary response to the peculiar interconnectedness of the global economy, which had discredited all the older theories of economic management, and in particular laissez-faire. He presented a fascinating reversal of the argument that free trade and a common monetary standard should be the accompaniments of an integrated world. Quite the contrary, he argued: "the world has become too small, people and goods are crowding in on each other so much, that a self-steering economy in the sense of the automatism of the gold standard or the theory of free trade is no longer possible."[103]

The clearings under the Schachtian system of managed trade did not mean that trade necessarily balanced bilaterally. In fact Germany built up considerable debts in bilateral trade balances as its export performance still lagged behind the growth of imports. The relationship with Germany's clearing partners depended to a great extent on the measure to which they were prepared to tolerate these balances, and in this way in practice to finance German recovery.

Working out who derived which benefits from these transactions has been a theoretically difficult task, because the transactions between economies under exchange control did not occur at world market prices. In, for instance, the German-Hungarian relation, Howard Ellis has shown that both import and export prices were considerably above world levels. Thus in 1936 Hungary exported butter to England at an average price of 114 pengö/quintal, but to Germany at 204. Hungarian imports of raw coffee from England cost 78.10 pengö/quintal, but from Germany 106.50. Individual comparisons of this kind indicate that the premium paid by Germans exceeded that paid by the Hungarians.[104]

In addition, there were at least several hundred different Mark rates. Under the New Plan, trade was financed through Aski Marks—the word is an acronym for Foreigners' Special Account for Domestic Goods. They were available on different terms for German exports to different countries.

The overall result of the management was a diversion of trade away from countries still practicing a liberal or modified liberal economy (trade subject only to tariff or quota restraints) and toward other clearing countries. The depression altered the pattern of trade from international to greater reliance on domestic sources, and also toward the formation of an economy of blocs. Both moves are associated with welfare losses, since the substitutions are more costly than the preferred options expressed in the free system.

By the spring of 1938 Germany had concluded bilateral trade treaties with twenty-five countries. In general, Germany turned away from trading with industrialized countries, and both exported and imported more with poorer and less developed producers of raw materials and commodities. The share of European industrialized countries in German trade, which after the Second World War proved to be the chief source of German trade expansion, fell sharply. Instead, Germany developed trading relations with what has been called a "Reichsmark bloc": Bulgaria, Greece, Hungary, Rumania, Turkey, and Yugoslavia. It appeared to some German policymakers as a functional equivalent of the sterling bloc of countries that had followed the British floating in September 1931. (The equivalent is not an exact one, since there was no tie of the southeastern European countries to

Germany through an exchange-rate regime, but rather through finance and clearing agreements.) The share of German imports of this bloc rose from 5.6 percent in 1933 to 18.5 percent in 1939, and the share in exports rose over the same period from 3.8 percent to 18.3 percent.[105] With some partners the rise was much more dramatic, and in these cases the increased trade with Germany constituted a major political factor. Thus Yugoslavia in 1932 had taken 18 percent of its imports from Germany, and 11 percent of its exports went to Germany. The equivalent figures for 1937 are 32 percent and 22 percent. In Hungary the extent of the dependence was even greater: 22 percent of imports in 1932 came from Germany, but 55 percent in 1937. Of Hungarian exports, 15 percent went to Germany in the first year, and 43 percent in 1937. Bulgaria had an even greater dependence on German trade.

Such figures inevitably raise the question of dependence. But who was dependent on whom? Many commentators in the 1930s assumed that Germany could exploit a position as a monopsonist, since Britain and France had closed their markets off and adopted imperial protection. The Royal Institute of International Affairs concluded that the German system "amounts to the exploitation of the bargaining-power of the stronger partner in a trading system which has been reduced to bilateral barter."[106] The agricultural producers of southeast Europe thus had no other large markets open, and were forced into a dependence on Germany. Rumania, with a more diversified export structure, in which strategically significant petroleum figured prominently, had greater bargaining power and was less heavily bilateralized in trade with Germany.[107] Such conclusions are undermined by an analysis of the terms of trade, which developed unfavorably for Germany. (The dependency theory would require Germany to extract a terms-of-trade advantage.) Some countries, notably Hungary, ran export surpluses with Germany and then used the acquired Reichsmark reserves as a base to finance a monetary expansion. Germany offered goods to some of its trade partners on what even critics of German power called "incredibly generous terms with almost negligible downpayments."[108] This picture has led the historian Alan Milward to comment on "the successful exploitation of Germany's economic weaknesses before 1939 by the small economies of central and south-eastern Europe."[109]

If this analysis is right, it still raises the question of why a powerful state such as Germany allowed itself to be exploited (or, less emotionally, why it paid prices higher than those prevailing on world markets). Trade decisions relating to the European area had a strong foreign policy component. The political dimension is clearest in the case of the two countries that would be the primary victims of Nazi aggression, Czechoslovakia and Poland. The Czech economy was much less complementary to that of Germany than those of its less industrialized neighbors. In 1933 the German Economics Ministry explicitly excluded Czechoslovakia from the German trade offensive in southeast Europe. The clearing agreements concluded with Germany in the early 1930s restricted trade, rather than allowing it to expand.[110] When Czech industrial production began to appear crucial to building an effective basis for a German war economy, Hitler simply dismembered the country and stripped industrial assets into German-controlled corporations. There was no prior attempt to bind Czechoslovakia into a German economic bloc, or *Grosswirtschaftsraum*, and no wish to make any foreign policy concessions. By contrast, in the early years of the German dictatorship, when Hitler's strategy depended on a foreign policy rapprochement with Poland, Germany paid higher than world market prices too for Polish products that were not really required by German consumers.[111] Favorable trading relations, large German purchasers, generous supplies of exports—these were weapons in a struggle to bind countries politically to Germany. In other words, Germany was paying an economic price in order to establish political dependence, not the other way round.

In large part, the motives for the diversion of trade stemmed from power politics. The economist Albert Hirschman has demonstrated how establishing dependence in trade relations becomes easier when a number of conditions are met: if the trading partner is a small country; if trade is directed toward poorer countries; if the exports supplied are manufactured goods with a high degree of product differentiation, so that the supply cannot easily be switched; and if the export prices of the trading partner are driven up above world levels by the promotion of high-cost production and through exchange-rate clearing.[112] All these conditions describe aspects of 1930s trading practice. Most dramatically, Germany changed the direction of trade and also encouraged the development of new high-cost products such as cotton in Egypt and Brazil. Hirschman showed that the German trade pattern in the 1930s was unique in the extent of the transformation, and that the states of Balkan and southeastern Europe displayed a higher degree of concentration of trade that made them vulnerable to "peaceful conquest." Germany paid—through import prices well over world market levels—in order to secure economic influence; it was for Germany an exchange of money for power.

To what extent was this trade-off a result of "plans for economic conquest actually laid down in advance"? Hirschman's answer in 1945 was that "it seems probable that the amazing coherence of German policies was due only in part to detailed planning stemming from economic analysis and that an important role was left to experimentation of actual policies."[113] The move to southern and eastern Europe followed not just from a power calculation, but also from a trade vacuum in the area, which the British, French, and Italians were unwilling to fill. In fact the increased regional concentration of German trade was already evident in 1928, before the depression. In the 1930s a previous tendency simply became much more pronounced.[114] Moreover, the increased links with Latin America reflect the logic of a world of clearing agreements, which brought debtor countries to trade more with each other.

In the long run, there was no consistent German strategy, since military expansion and occupation eventually destroyed the entire logic of the previous German approach. Henry Kissinger concluded that "Versailles and Locarno had smoothed Germany's road into Eastern Europe, where a patient German leadership would in time have achieved a preponderant position by peaceful means, or perhaps even have had it handed to it by the West. But Hitler's reckless megalomania turned what could have been a peaceful evolution into a world war."[115]

Unlike in the case of southeastern Europe, the major industrial countries were in competition with each other in their dealings with the much larger and more significant South American economies. The closer ties of Latin America with Germany followed from three considerations.

In the first place came supply considerations. The export economies of the continent were seriously threatened by the collapse of primary prices at the beginning of the decade. Particular groups associated with exporting interests played a prominent part in political life, and tried to negotiate settlements that allowed guaranteed markets for their products. These agreements involved accepting trade diversion in order to gain security for export markets.

After 1932 primary product prices recovered slowly; but an index showing the ratio of agricultural to nonagricultural prices (1929 = 100) remained for Argentina at 60 until the middle of 1935. Only the United States, Chile, and Canada reached their 1929 ratios again over the course of the 1930s.[116] Thus with the exception of Chile, all Latin American countries continued to suffer from the movement of terms of trade throughout the 1930s, and could reckon that they would continue to do so in the foreseeable future. But they could find particular advantages from the sales of some strategic goods. Animal fat from Argentina—or in the eastern European case Rumanian oil—became highly desirable goods, and the strength of the market could be used to bargain for advantages for other sales.

Second, the pattern of demand shifted. The imperial powers directed trade away from South America as a consequence of imperial preferences and domestic protection. The share of the British Commonwealth, colonies, and protectorates in British imports rose from 30.2 percent in 1929 to 39.0 percent by 1935, and for British exports from 44.4 percent to 47.6 percent. France's diversion of trade to empire was much more dramatic.[117] Though the share of South America in British imports held up relatively well, it dropped in the French case. And both countries imported substantially less from southeast Europe.

Finally, it was political calculation that determined the extent of the movement into the bloc economy. Most Latin American countries had built up considerable debts during the 1920s, which became much heavier in real terms because of the extent of price deflation. Erika Jorgensen and Jeffrey Sachs speak of the "rising mountain of sovereign debt claims" in the 1920s.[118] In view of the combination of price collapse and consequent difficulty in debt servicing on the one hand, and the almost complete failure of world capital markets on the other, default became a highly attractive option. The first came in Bolivia in January 1931, followed by Peru in April and Chile in August. By 1934 only Argentina, Haiti, and the Dominican Republic kept up debt service.

The economy of debt played a major part in the trade switch. The contrast between the experience of the two largest South American trading economies, Argentina and Brazil, is remarkable. Argentina largely kept up debt service and attracted refunding loans from Britain. In return the Argentine government concluded a trading agreement with Britain that offered the British access on very favorable terms. Brazil on the other hand defaulted on debt and changed the direction of trade dramatically, from a historical connection to the United States to an increased engagement with Nazi Germany.

Argentina was affected by the decline in prices of agricultural goods but left the gold standard quite early, in December 1929, so that the internal price structure could be decoupled from the international order. There were as a result no significant financial disturbances in the course of the depression: though a few banks were threatened, notably the Banco Español del Rio de la Plata, they survived with the help of the government's banker, the Banco de la Nación. And the trade effects of devaluation were also on the whole beneficial: by mid-1931 there had been a clear improvement in exports and a fall in imports. The Finance Ministry issued an optimistic report, concluding that "the economic readjustment necessitated by the world business depression is taking a very satisfactory course in Argentina. The country certainly knows how to face bad times and does so with an unwavering confidence in the following future."[119]

The sterling devaluation, the British emergency tariff, and the Ottawa Conference gave a shock to this process of adjustment. In October 1931 Argentina responded to the end of gold in Britain with the imposition of exchange control on a German model. In this system, all exporters were obliged to sell their exchange to the control office, the Comisión de Control de Cambios, at a fixed rate; and importers needed a prior permit from the Control in order to buy at the fixed rate. On the other hand, they were still free to bid on an open market for exchange, and the open-market price could in effect be set by the number of permits that the Control might be prepared to issue. The office also allocated exchange in 1932 in line with the practice of the Central European controlled-exchange countries, reserving only a certain proportion to debt repayments. For the first ten months, 15 percent of receipts were allocated to the service of the foreign public debt, and 12 percent for the service of privately contracted debts.[120] The result of exchange control as applied in 1932 was that unpaid commercial debts to German and particularly British creditors accumulated.

At the beginning of 1933, Argentina appeared to the British financial community as the biggest of the Latin American debt crises. The blocked accounts owed to British creditors in the whole of the continent amounted to £15.3 million, and of this £8.6 million was owed by Argentina.[121] On the other side, Argentine exporters suffered from the tariff increases: a third of British imports were now subject to duties, whereas none had been in 1930, and before Ottawa 83 percent had still been free. The quantitative restrictions imposed by Britain required a drop of 35 percent in frozen meat shipments and a "temporary" reduction of 10 percent for chilled beef.[122]

Two parallel teams worked to find a solution to this problem in traditionally warm British-Argentine relations. The first was a British mission theoretically to advise Argentina on the setting up of a new central bank, but in practice to give general economic advice. This was led by a Bank of England official, Sir Otto Niemeyer.[123] At the same time an Argentine group in London led by Julio Roca negotiated with the president of the Board of Trade, Walter Runciman.

Niemeyer's solution to the Argentine problem was temptingly obvious. The service of short-term, mostly commercial and mostly British, debt should continue, while long-term debts should be renegotiated or even written off. Niemeyer's right-hand man on the Argentine mission, Henry Clay, expressed himself very freely:

> The proper solution of their difficulties is for them to default on their dollar loans. People who lend money to South American republics to save them from the necessity of covering their current expenditures by taxation deserve to lose their money: and the saving on foreign exchange would just about put their balance of payments right. Unfortunately we can't persuade them of this course. International bankers are great humbugs. They are always preaching to debtor countries the absolute necessity of balancing their budgets, and when the debtor countries don't balance their budgets, but run up a big floating debt, they issue a loan for them to fund the floating debt.[124]

Niemeyer was just as honest, he thought, about the holders of Argentine railway debt in Britain. He constantly wrote back urging the British creditors not to press their case too hard. "I think Whitehall and railways overstate strength of their bargaining position," he cabled. "Railways may easily be left with their pesos if they do not face realities."[125] His answer was to set up a central banking structure that would prevent Argentina from relaunching on the 1920s cycle of overborrowing and threatened default. "I believe it to be of supreme importance that the Argentine should get a better system under way now, *before* the tide turns and she is once more inundated with American financial carpet baggers: also before the present Government, which is mainly sound money and in favour of independent banking, gives way to people with more extensive and political ideas."[126]

The Argentine government, and particularly Finance Minister Alberto Hueyo, distrusted and disliked Roca and told Niemeyer that his mission was not really professional: "mainly ceremonial and doubt if equipped for serious technical discussion."[127] When the Roca mission started offering startling concessions to the British on trade, Niemeyer was surprised and incredulous: "I doubt if authorities will confirm or could implement what Mission is said to acquiesce in, at any rate unless there are some substantial reciprocal trade concessions not so far indicated."[128]

In fact the Roca mission was prepared to use the British trade figures as the basis of negotiations, and proposed a funding of the frozen remittances and an allocation of exchange for debt settlement. By 20 March, in spite of Hueyo's threat to resign, Roca was willing to reach an agreement with Britain.[129] Concluded in April 1933, it provided for £12 million sterling bonds to unfreeze the British assets. Argentina would revert to the 1930 levels of tariff in all goods in which Britain was interested, and maintain free access for British coal. Of 388 items submitted by Britain in the negotiations, Argentina reduced the rate in 347 cases.[130] The British concessions looked much more modest: there would be no restrictions on the import of chilled beef for quantities below the level of 1931–32; and no new tariffs on meat, bacon, maize, linseed, and quebracho (a tree bark with medicinal uses).

It is not surprising that these negotiations and their outcome were bitterly criticized in Argentina, or that Roca and his economic adviser, Raúl Prebisch, were held responsible for the sacrifice of Argentine interests simply in order to keep the meat trade open. Niemeyer believed that the arrangement had done great harm in Argentina: "I have never," he wrote, "seen any set of negotiations conducted so badly by both sides, and it is a thousand pities that the Board of Trade, who obviously knows nothing whatever about the Argentine, did not take any advice from local people . . . I suppose the truth is that Runcy, being as usual too indolent to master the real position, has got into a position in the Cabinet from which he cannot retreat without loss of face." Runciman in fact argued mostly about the benefits of the agreement to the City and financial interests, and faced a substantial opposition from the minister of agriculture (supported by the home secretary and the secretary of state for Scotland), who claimed that "the agricultural industry was being sacrificed by rentiers."[131]

In the event the Roca treaty did not dramatically increase British exports to Argentina over the three years in which it operated (see Table 3.1).

The treaty has widely been interpreted as a victory of Argentine meat interests, whose economic significance was rather less than their colossal political power (even in the late 1920s, meat accounted for only just over a tenth of Argentine exports). But the Ottawa reductions in British frozen meat imports remained, and even went up when in 1935 the Roca treaty

Table 3.1 British-Argentine trade, 1933–1935 (millions of £)

	1933	1934	1935
British imports	41.7	47.0	44.0
British exports	13.3	14.9	15.6
Balance	−28.4	−32.1	−28.4

Source: Memorandum, "The Roca Agreement," 7 May 1936, Bank of England OV 102/6.

was renegotiated. The Argentine proportion of frozen and chilled beef imported into the United Kingdom fell: in 1929 it had been 77.4 percent of British purchases abroad, in 1933 it was 74.4 percent, and in 1935 64.2 percent. By 1937 it fell further, to 61.5 percent, while Britain's empire trade increased correspondingly.[132]

Hueyo resigned because of the way his revenue from customs duties had been reduced by the treaty commitments, and the British increased the sense of Argentine humiliation by issuing a postage stamp commemorating the hundredth anniversary of the occupation of the Falkland Islands. But the purpose of the agreement was not to expand trade. Prebisch, whose work it had been, explained the thought behind the policy in these terms: "Argentina had resolved to pay its external debt and come out of exchange regulation, and the radical means applied were the best way of doing this. At the same time, there is a policy of keeping up Argentine exports and the preservation of the best clients, and here he announced that he was opposed to the newly developing powerful tendencies towards industrialization and autarky."[133]

In fact in the 1930s industrial production grew at a dramatic rate (6.5 percent annually from 1933 through 1938). Import substitution produced quite visible results. Of all Argentine consumption of manufactured goods, 41.3 percent had been imported in 1913, and 40.5 percent in 1929; but the ratio fell to 25.3 percent in 1937. As a specific example, in 1930 there were 60,000 cotton spindles, and by 1936 300,000.[134]

The U.S. share of Argentine imports fell abruptly, but American goods (in particular machine tools and engineering equipment, but also arms) were replaced by German products. Weapons and machine tools are an ideal export in terms of committing the importer to a trade dependence, since they constitute a system of specifications, which cannot easily or costlessly be exchanged for products using different specifications, for another country.

In addition, German firms regarded Argentina as a lucrative export market. They were eager to present Germany as offering an alternative to British or American economic imperialism. A representative of the large chemical company, IG Farben, wrote optimistically about the possibilities in South America, and especially in Argentina: "The general situation in South America, which is characterized by an increased national consciousness and the effort to establish independence from foreign influence, allows Germany to present herself as an exemplar."[135] At the beginning of 1934 Germany had felt left out of the Argentine market. The exchange office gave favorable treatment in the allocation of exchange to importers of British as well as French and Czech goods, but discriminated against the products of Germany and the United States.

In July 1934 a German-Argentine treaty followed the model of the 1933 British treaty. Argentine exports would be increased, and trade would be diverted to Germany: for instance, Argentina now took German rather than Canadian paper imports. In the exchange-control framework, a special account was created (Account "M") for orders that would not otherwise go to Germany: machinery, locomotives and locomotive parts, and even the notorious mouth organs (in July 1937 the German embassy reported that of the 11.4 million RM trade under Account M, 57,000 RM worth of mouth organs had been shipped).[136]

Germany desperately needed food imports—particularly wheat and fats—but the exchange allocation represented a great difficulty. In 1936 the issue of fat imports underlay the major conflict between Economics Minister Schacht and the Nazi party: in particular Robert Ley, the leader of the German Labor Front, and Hermann Göring, minister-president of Prussia and the creator of the 1936 economic Four-Year Plan. Schacht had been opposed to the allocation of scarce foreign exchange for food imports and believed that the only way of securing additional imports was to launch an export offensive.

This was the task of a special mission led by a private German businessman, J. A. Kulenkampff, who in November 1936 left his firm to work for three years as "Adviser to the Reich Government and to German Missions in order to promote German exports to South America." Already in the summer Kulenkampff had negotiated with Prebisch (now director of the new Argentine central bank) about doubling trade with Germany by using Sondermark and ASKI Mark accounts at a discount. The mission initially produced a considerable friction between the new adviser and German firms in the hemisphere (since Kulenkampff tried to avoid unproductive competition between German enterprises) and also with regular diplomats.[137]

The experience of the 1936–37 trade offensive was less than satisfactory in Argentina. There were great delays in shipping German goods, and frequent Argentine complaints about irregular payment. In late 1936 trade suffered because of fears that there would soon be an outbreak of major European war.[138] The steadiest part of German supply to Argentina turned out to be weaponry, and shipments continued even after September 1939 until the Atlantic blockade made this trade impracticable.[139]

Argentina had the most modern army of any South American state and presented a great potential threat to her northern neighbors, including Brazil. The threat increased after the Chaco war, in which Argentina supplied Paraguay in the conflict with Bolivia. Brazilians felt nervous. The possibility of obtaining German arms—and the support for this trade from the politically significant military leadership in Brazil—is one explanation for the much greater success of the German export offensive there.

Brazil's exports were much less diversified than Argentina's. In the 1920s, one crop, coffee, accounted for two-thirds of exports; and coffee suffered especially severely in the world depression. Sales in 1930 were worth 30 percent less than in 1929. The initial reaction was to allow the currency (milrei) to depreciate against gold, from July 1930, in order to separate domestic and external price levels; and to suspend foreign debt payments.

On 1 September 1931 Brazil halted sinking-fund payments on all levels of government bonds (federal, state, and municipal) held abroad. In March 1932, after a lengthy series of discussions with Sir Otto Niemeyer, whose advice was similar to that given in Buenos Aires, the federal government alone funded its debt—a solution that was disadvantageous to the United States, since the bulk of U.S. investments were in state and municipal issues. Unlike Argentina, the Brazilian government took Niemeyer's advice very seriously. Through 1933 the Roosevelt administration actively tried to reach a more comprehensive settlement, but again Niemeyer urged against a settlement and ran down the Americans as "bad bankers."[140] He succeeded in limiting the Brazilians to a £10 million refunding operation to unblock short-term commercial credits.

The Aranha Plan of 1934 regulated the bond position and reduced payments severely. Soon even this, however, appeared too generous: the Brazilian financial structure was still very shaky, and in 1935 rumors circulated that the plan would be suspended. After President Vargas' November 1937 coup and the introduction of an authoritarian state, he suspended debt service once again and allowed payments to resume only in July 1939. Brazil could do this without fear of great American retaliation because of the apparent reluctance of 1930s governments to link trade and debt issues.

Brazil's debt difficulties did not reflect a depressed economy, but rather one that grew so quickly that it found it hard to produce export surpluses. The major motor of growth lay in domestic demand.

Much more explicitly than Argentina, the 1930s Brazilian governments under the presidency of Getúlio Vargas (first military, then democratic after 1934, and finally from 1937 authoritarian) followed a strategy of industrialization. Vargas himself was particularly interested in the development of steel production, but also in textiles and cement. The tariff structure was calculated to facilitate this development: import tariffs on cement equipment, for instance, were eliminated in 1932 so as to allow the development of a domestic industry; while a highly protective general tariff limited imports. During the 1930s the Brazilian economy grew at a spectacular rate.

Germany attracted Brazil most immediately and directly as a major purchaser and consumer of coffee. German chemical companies (IG Farben, Böhringer, Hansamühle Hamburg) experimented in addition with the extraction of proteins and fats from coffee beans scheduled for destruction under market regulation schemes.

But German trade also offered Brazil an apparently convenient and attractive way out of dependence on export monoculture. The rapid development of cotton growing in the northern provinces after 1933 could not have taken place without a German market, and without the reorientation of German trade away from previous dependence on North American cotton. In 1929 Brazil had exported 49,000 tons of cotton, and in 1932 less than 1,000 tons; but by 1936 there were 200,000 tons while Egyptian exports held constant and U.S. exports fell (in 1937 they were still 22 percent below the 1929 level).[141]

Germany's alternative to a U.S. supply—the expansion of imports from Brazil and Egypt—was less satisfactory, and involved substantial costs. Egyptian cotton was of high quality, but very expensive; and low-quality Brazilian short-staple cotton required expensive alterations to German spinning equipment in order to produce a yarn that might be acceptable.

Faced with a shortage of currency, Brazil found imports needed as part of the industrialization drive difficult to obtain; and negotiations over blocked accounts offered a way of obtaining difficult materials (in addition the director of exchanges was an "integralist" with strong sympathies for the form of social organization being evolved in Nazi Germany). In November 1934 Germany used the threat of buying less cotton in order to win longer-term contracts for the supply of German goods. This agreement, never published in order not to offend Washington, led to a rapid growth of German imports and to the accumulation of a substantial Reichsmark balance to Brazil's credit.

Finally, there was the Brazilian response to the Chaco war. The Brazilian army was poorly equipped compared to that of Argentina, and Brazilian generals tried to buy weapons in the 1930s in order to modernize. Destroyers came from England, submarines from Italy, and airplanes and artillery from Britain, Italy, and the United States. German equipment—heavy artillery, aircraft, and lighting equipment—offered a valuable complement. There was often a barter element to German supplies: thus in 1936, the military manufacturer Krupp won a big order in which 500,000 sacks of coffee were exchanged for arms.[142]

In June 1936 a Brazilian-German trade treaty included cotton exports and expanded German purchase of coffee to 1.6 million sacks annually. In order to accommodate this amount of coffee, Germany agreed to reexport to southeast Europe. At the heart of the trade under the 1936 agreement lay a massive subsidization through the use of multiple exchange rates. Calculating machines were thus 30–35 percent cheaper than those supplied by the American International Hollerith Company, air compressors 25–35 percent cheaper, printing machinery up to 50 percent cheaper, and rails 20 percent cheaper.

The result was a dramatic expansion of German exports. In 1929, 17.8 percent of Brazil's imports of finished products came from Germany, in 1934 26.1 percent, and in 1936 36.9 percent. The share for iron and steel goods was 68.6 percent, of coal 22.5 percent, and of cement 44.0 percent. As German exports went up, they squeezed out British and American products (see Table 3.2).

The expansion of German trade rested also on a substantial amount of corruption. Two-fifths of the 1936 treaty coffee was exported from Brazil by the Sociedade Internacional de Commercio Limitada (SOINC), run by Olavo Egydio de Souza Aranha, who had played a prominent part in the negotiation of the treaty. Souza Aranha had contacts with Vargas, and also

Table 3.2 Share of Brazil's total imports, 1913–1937 (%)

Year	Germany	Britain	United States
1913	17.41	24.40	15.77
1924	12.25	23.87	24.16
1925	13.28	22.27	24.64
1926	12.64	19.02	29.16
1927	10.68	21.23	28.64
1928	12.46	21.50	26.57
1929	12.69	19.15	32.10
1930	11.31	19.41	34.16
1931	10.45	17.45	25.01
1932	9.01	19.20	30.20
1933	11.25	19.44	21.18
1934	14.02	17.14	23.67
1935	20.44	12.41	23.36
1936	23.50	11.26	22.12
1937	23.90	12.10	23.00

Sources: League of Nations, *International Trade Statistics, 1937* (Geneva, 1938), and previous issues.

with the military: the foreign minister, José Carlos de Macedo Soares, believed that he had been personally responsible for winning the order for Krupp rather than Bofors, the Swedish firm that had taken orders for Krupp until 1935 because of the Versailles Treaty limits on Krupp's range of production. Souza Aranha also extended his influence in the cotton business, and secured the intervention of the key German ministries—the Economics Ministry and the Auswärtiges Amt—to eliminate a rival Hamburg importing firm.[143] In 1937, despite this substantial range of privileges for SOINC, Souza Aranha demanded more, and started reminding the Germans that Japan was offering better cotton prices, and that the United States still had a powerful position in Brazilian trade. Germany responded by allowing yet more privileges to SOINC: the company now began to act for German firms in repurchasing German bonds domiciled abroad.

Not surprisingly in the light of this mixture of political influence and private advantage-seeking, German and SOINC trade had powerful enemies: notably Vargas's confidant Oswaldo Aranha, first finance minister, then ambassador to Washington, and finally foreign minister. Confronted with the SOINC arrangement, he asked President Vargas, "Don't you think there is something fishy about this?"[144] He remained a constant advocate of the trading link with the United States, and in Washington in 1937 negotiated a new program for debt relief, and U.S. funds for the establishment of a central bank, in return for trade concessions. Vargas announced the formation of a "Good Neighbor" committee in order to further Brazilian-American trade and "to give special attention to examination of the German-Brazilian agreement to determine in what respects it is injurious to Brazilian-American relations."[145] After Foreign Minister Souza Costa visited Washington for the conclusion of the agreement, a final joint communiqué with Cordell Hull read: "a number of minor complementary measures are advisable in order to safeguard its principles and benefits in view of the form of trading pursued by some other countries. Accordingly they undertake to protect these principles and benefits against outside competition that is directly subsidized by governments." The United States sold up to $60 million in gold in exchange for Brazilian dollar balances, the milrei was stabilized against the dollar, and further stabilization loans were held out.[146] In fact this agreement, claimed to be "a forerunner of postwar foreign aid,"[147] did not break the German trade relationship with Brazil.

It did, however, complicate the politics of trade. In November 1937 an attempted coup led to the creation of a more authoritarian state, dubbed the *estado novo*. Vargas suspected involvement in the coup by Germans who wanted to expand their share of military procurement. In addition, the personality of the new German ambassador to Brazil, Karl Ritter, caused great difficulties. His mission initially was a sign of the importance Germany placed on the development of the Brazilian link. He was Germany's most experienced trade negotiator, but he lacked any more general diplomatic skills or any inclination to camouflage his belligerent nationalism. His relations with the Vargas government suffered because of his extensive contacts with the German settlers' Nazi party. A new revolt in May 1938 against Vargas by the Integralists (Brazilian fascists) had some contacts among the German settlers, and in the aftermath of the uprising seven directors of the Deutsche Süd-Amerikanische Bank were arrested. Brazil then demanded the expulsion of Ritter.

This clash also had repercussions in trade. In July 1938 Brazil abruptly put an end to the barter arrangements with Germany, although the business began anew in November. Oswaldo Aranha was now foreign minister, and American diplomats and businessmen looked forward to better relations with Brazil. A confidential report by a U.S. bank stated: "Much is expected of him and he has already given evidence of being pro–United States, if not anti-German, which may be very helpful to the American exporting community in its struggle with Germany over the Brazilian market."[148] In the summer of 1938, American firms for the first time bought large amounts of Brazilian cotton.[149] In February and March 1939, Aranha visited Washington once more to negotiate further U.S. credits: $19.2 million to unfreeze the trade balance, $50 million to finance new Brazilian purchases from American suppliers, and additional investments for rubber and quinine plantations in Brazil. The Hull strategy of turning a blind eye to debt problems in the hope of reaping gains in commerce and politics at last yielded results, rather belatedly.

The political influence of Germany all over the continent became even more suspect than that of the United States. At a meeting of German diplomats concerned with South America, each described the fear that Germany was following "power political purposes" in her trading policy. The German ambassador to Chile noted that the "xenophobic attitude previously directed against the United States is now turned against Germany."[150]

The political resentment against the dramatic German expansion of commerce in Latin America and southeastern Europe probably set an upper limit for the dependence: any expansion in southeast Europe beyond that required military force rather than economic pressure. Trade hegemony on its own could not work forever as an instrument of power politics.

But in the meantime bilateralism in trade developed as the major obstacle to the restoration of a world economy trading on liberal principles in the 1930s. The world was divided into several blocs: the imperial systems of Britain and France, the free-trading environment of idealistic Hullian principle, and the clearing and barter world of German trading practice.

By the mid-1930s this was widely recognized as the major problem of the international order. Clearing agreements depressed prices outside the clearing, and their opponents, such as Niemeyer, argued that their tendency was "to prevent the internal adjustments which would necessarily have to be made one day." Another way of making the same point was to argue that it was the monetary problem of artificial exchange rates that created the trade-political problem. In 1935 the League Secretariat concluded: "In fact, devaluation of over-valued currencies has ceased to be hush-hush. When I say over-valued currencies, I do not, of course, mean the Swiss or French francs or the Guilder [the remaining gold currencies], which may or may not be over-valued. I am thinking of those whose value can only be maintained by means of artificial control."[151]

The Soviet Trade Monopoly

The Soviet experience presented a complete contrast with that of the rest of the world economy. It was easily the most dramatic case of "artificial control," and apparently the most successful. Escaping from capitalist crisis had been one of the rationales of Joseph Stalin's adoption in the 1920s of the strategy of "socialism in one country," in place of the alternative vision expounded by Leon Trotsky that looked for an international spread of revolution. And what a powerful rationale it appeared to be as the rest of the world slid into apparently ever deeper depression!

Even before the choice for socialism in one country, already in the early days of the revolution in April 1918, the Soviet system had established a foreign trade monopoly. Such a monopoly was demanded by Lenin in a memorandum of 10 December 1917, as the third of nine points about fundamental economic policy.[152] In Soviet practice, the trade monopoly was run through the creation of a series of state-owned companies created after 1925 and specialized in trade with a particular range of products: Exportkhleb for the export of grain and seeds, Exportles for forest products, or Stankoimport for the import of machine tools.

Stalin made the trade monopoly that he inherited from Lenin a central part of his own economic vision. Especially in 1927, just before the turn to rapid industrialization by means of the Five-Year Plan, it formed a central element in his turning away from prices and the market. This was a time of great vulnerability, for while the rest of the world was booming, Soviet growth was faltering. The British government raided and closed down the Soviet trade delegation in London as a center of espionage. Stalin now argued that the trade monopoly served several purposes: it aimed at preventing economic and political blackmail, protecting new socialist industries, and stopping the subjection of the Soviet economy to a dependence on the rich industrial countries. Stalin explained in 1927:

> for the workers, the abolition of the monopoly of foreign trade would
> mean a refusal to industrialize the country, to build new factories and
> plants and to enlarge the old ones. That would mean an inundation of
> the USSR with goods from capitalist countries, a decrease in industry be-

cause of its relative weakness, an increase of unemployment, a decline in the standard of living of the masses, a weakening of the economic and political positions. For peasants this would mean the transformation of our country from an independent one into a semi-colonial one with an impoverished peasantry.[153]

At the Fifteenth Congress of the Communist Party in the same year, A. I. Mikoyan stated that the trade monopoly was the "impregnable condition of the building of socialism in a capitalist environment."[154]

These arguments used a theory of the "development of underdevelopment," in other words of the tendency of rich countries to use trade as a weapon to lock poorer peoples out of the charmed circle of industrialization and prosperity. Such a theory subsequently became the intellectual underpinning of import substitution strategies throughout the developing world.

The practical consequence of Stalin's policy was a move toward semi-autarky. Already in the 1920s, the share of Russia in world trade fell in comparison with the prewar era, and the size of trade relative to the Russian economy also decreased. In 1914 Russia had accounted for 3.7 percent of world trade, but in 1926 that ratio was 1.2 percent. Whereas before the war, trade had been 13.2 percent of Russian production, the equivalent ratios in the mid-1920s were less than 5 percent.[155] The composition of trade also shifted. The Soviet Union became a major importer of machinery required by the industrialization strategy. Before the war, imports of industrial equipment and raw materials for the textile industry had been 27.4 percent of the total, while by 1931 these two categories accounted for 74.6 percent of Soviet imports. Such imports were paid through the export of primary commodities, especially grain and wood and wood products; but industrial products also began to play a greater role in Russian exports.[156]

During the depression, at just the time when prices were locked in a seemingly endless cycle of decline, Soviet grain exports surged. During the mid-1920s Soviet grain exports had fallen off. The brutal terror with which grain was extracted from the countryside in the period of collectivization, even at the price of widespread famine, was justified by the Soviet leadership as the only means of financing the machinery imports necessary for industrialization, since foreign credit was so difficult to obtain. Official figures showed an almost tenfold increase in the value of grain exports from 1930 to 1931.[157] The brutal policy of surplus extraction for export, cynically described as "primitive socialist accumulation," was the Soviet answer to the miseries of the capitalist world depression.

The effect of the new trade strategy was to separate Russia altogether from the world price structure. The chervonets was convertible for only a brief period in the 1920s, from the spring of 1924 to the spring of 1925. After that, the exchange was controlled.

The separation of world and domestic prices set in motion a process in which prices lost any relevance for economic decision-making. The Soviet economy turned into a mixture of command and terror on the one hand, and transactions based on barter on the other. The elimination of foreign prices made planning simpler, and some analysts have even argued that it was a prerequisite for Soviet planning. Jacob Viner wrote at the beginning of the 1950s: "The less the degree of dependence of a national economy in its ordinary operations on trade with other countries, the less, *ceteris paribus*, will be the difficulties of setting up and operating a comprehensive national economic plan. There is planning logic, therefore, in the marked association in recent years between the movement toward comprehensive economic planning and the movement toward autarky, most conspicuous in Soviet Russia but by no means confined to it."[158] Some theorists later argued that a socialist economy would actually benefit from competitive advantage in the same way as did a market order;[159] but in practice in the post-1945 era socialist trade within Comecon was increasingly subject to political and other irrational dictates. External trade control was not the reason for Stalin's decision to impose collectivization of agriculture and rapid industrialization, but it provided the only basis on which such a choice would not have produced immediate disaster.

The isolation of a nonprice economy was intended to protect the economy from the unplanned shocks of an unstable capitalist order. The decision to make the external trade control the "shield and the joy of our young socialist country" was followed almost immediately by the great Western economic collapse.[160] This was the moment of the greatest contrast between the Soviet course of rapid industrial expansion, in the first Five-Year Plan (1928–1932), and crisis and depression elsewhere. Inevitably this contrast formed a major theme of Soviet propaganda, and a major attraction of the Soviet model. Stalin and his economists, in particular Eugen Varga, eagerly identified the Western misery as the predicted general crisis of capitalism. Varga developed a law to show that the previous solution to capitalist crises, the discovery of new markets, had reached a natural limit. Since there were no virgin territories, a chronic depression would follow. This theme was taken up in Stalin's triumphalist report in June 1930 to the Sixteenth Congress of the Communist Party:

> Recall the state of affairs in the capitalist countries two and a half years ago. Growth of industrial production and trade in nearly all the capitalist countries. Growth of production of raw materials and food in nearly all the agrarian countries. A halo around the United States as the land of the most full-blooded capitalism. Triumphant hymns of "prosperity." Groveling to the dollar. Panegyrics in honor of the new technology, in honor of capitalist rationalization . . . And what is the picture today? Today there is an economic crisis in nearly all the industrial countries of capitalism.[161]

Soviet economic growth was indeed impressive in the period 1928–1940: it amounted to an annual rate of between 5 and 11 percent (depending on the choice of price level adopted); although a price of the chaos that accompanied the rapidity may have been the subsequent distortions and stagnation of the post-Stalin era.[162] During this era, the Soviet experience had a substantial impact on the world, both in terms of the specific trade impact, and through a general idea about the character of the national economy.

During the depression, the Soviet market played a quite important role for some engineering and machinery producers. Even before the world depression, the USSR had become the world's second-largest importer of machinery (after the United Kingdom).[163] The peak year of Soviet imports was 1931 ($569 million); after that imports fell away dramatically as the goal of socialist autarky was more nearly attained. Imports in 1936 were less than a quarter of those in 1931.[164] In 1931 27.5 percent of U.S exports of industrial equipment (and for particular products the ratio was much higher: 73.8 percent for foundry equipment and 97.4 percent for turbines) went to the Soviet Union. Four-fifths of Germany's engineering exports at the end of 1930 were to Russia. The Soviet press pointed out that "while bourgeois economists seek a way out of the economic crisis without result, the Soviet Union will conclude agreements with Germany that create jobs for many thousands of German workers."[165]

An obvious concern for the USSR's trade partners was the security of Russian credit. As the Five-Year Plan and collectivization began in political chaos, some observers predicted an imminent Soviet collapse. German banks, which had in the mid-1920s organized syndicated credits for German-Soviet trade, sounded warnings in 1929. At the beginning of 1931, New York bankers told the U.S. State Department that "the Russian credit system will crash immediately."[166] In consequence, security in credit relations could be achieved only by state-to-state treaties. During the depression the German government concluded two state-guaranteed trade credit agreements with the USSR (the so-called Pyatakov agreements). There was a strongly political element to the German government's calculations, in addition to the hope that the Soviet deal might create some desperately needed employment. The labor minister argued that "for reasons of general policy, it appears correct to stake more on the Russian card than previously"; while the president of the central bank thought that a foreign policy consideration should prevail. "Other countries must be shown that in order to pay reparations Germany must make this type of deal."[167] In this sense, Soviet trade marked for Germany too the beginning of a movement away from trade as a result of contracts between private-sector agents and toward trade as a measure of government planning in the service of overall macroeconomic purposes.

The most important legacy of the dramatic industrial triumph of the Five-Year Plan was a mindset about economic development that subsequently became a generalized blueprint for Soviet-style development. International entanglements such as trade or finance were held to be economically but also politically damaging. By the middle of the 1930s, as the USSR was well on the path to armed autarky, the previous internationalism became the subject of Stalin's nationalist suspicion. In the early 1920s Lenin had seen foreign firms and investors as an essential help in the economic development of Soviet Russia. By the time of the Five-Year Plan, "bourgeois experts" had become the subject of suspicion and political attack. Many of the officials from the trade administration of the 1920s and of the First Five-Year Plan were victims of the terror of the late 1930s. Grigori Pyatakov, accused of espionage for the Germans as well as sabotage, was the central figure in the most prominent show trial of 1937.[168]

In the end, national power objectives rather than rational economics remained the most powerful vindication for Stalin's experiment. This was the basis for the strategy's international appeal too. Stalin's leading Western biographer wrote that by the end of the 1930s, "Russia's industrial power was catching up with Germany's . . . To the world it was important as the first truly gigantic experiment in planned economy, the first instance in which a government undertook to plan and regulate the whole economic life of its country and to direct its nationalized industrial resources towards a uniquely rapid multiplication of the nation's wealth."[169]

To some critics, in and outside Russia, a miracle based on the propagandistical manipulation of plan targets ("hortatory planning") and artificial money seemed more like a cheap conjuring trick. Mikhail Bulgakov's great satirical novel of the late 1930s, *The Master and Margarita*, contains scenes in which Satan visiting Moscow in the guise of a magician changes worthless paper into rubles, and rubles into foreign exchange. The victims experience horrible nightmares in which inquisitors demand the surrender of foreign exchange.

The philosophy underlying this magic remained the Soviet guide to the economics of the postwar world. The international economy, as it currently existed, could only be regarded as an obstacle to socially just development. Such an interpretation actually provided the basis for the Soviet rationale for the perpetual opposition of socialist and capitalist blocs, in other words for the Cold War. In the great speech of 9 February 1946, in which Stalin moved decisively to confrontation with the West, he stated: "It might be possible to avoid military catastrophes, if there were a way of periodically reapportioning raw materials and markets among the countries according to their economic weight—taking concerted and peaceful decisions. But this is impossible to fulfill in contemporary capitalist conditions of world economic development."[170]

The Legacy of 1930s Trade Practices

Although at the end of the 1930s it was still just possible to speak of a "world market," the enclaves within this world system operating under special rules increased. The Soviet approach looked ever more attractive. Not just German trading policy, or the British regime of trade preferences, but the whole world economy was moving toward Schachtianism. Tariffs in the 1920s had reduced the rate of growth of international trade, but the availability of capital flows to finance major trade imbalances removed some of the most acute constraints on development. These restraints became immediately apparent once capital flows were reduced, and the push to protection gathered momentum because the unavailability of new capital made the costs of protection for the national economy very much less damaging.

Thus there existed an initial link between debt crisis and exchange control. After the debt crisis of 1931 in South America and Europe, the abnormal behavior of trade in the 1930s was less the result of the spread of tariffs than of the extension of bilateral and barter trading practice. There was also a connection between the spread of exchange control and the imposition of authoritarian rule. The influence of the RTAA at the time in stemming this development was slight. Germany and its trading partners developed a relationship that redirected trade and reduced the global total. In the light of the weakness of the MFN system with unconditional clauses, and its tendency to produce tariff increases as a result of the combination of bargaining processes and desires to raise levels of domestic industrial output, reciprocal bilateral negotiations offered the only way out of the trade impasse. In this way, they offered the only hope of also restoring better financial relations.

Some indication of the redirection of trade as a result of the formation of economic blocs emerges from a calculation of the share of U.S. trade with Germany and Britain (both of which formed their own blocs) as a proportion of total world exports. For the pre-crisis period, 1926–1930, this had been 5.7 percent. It fell during the depression, to 4.4 percent in 1932, and continued to fall to 3.5 percent in 1934, with only a small recovery by 1937 (3.7 percent), and then another setback with the recession of 1938.[171]

Another indication is provided by the data on bilateralism in world trading calculated by the League of Nations for the early 1930s. Bilateral trading practices were promoted by the increase of quotas and clearing agreements, both of which often explicitly aimed at securing bilateral balances in trade (rather than triangular or more complicated relationships), as well as by MFN agreements giving concessions limited to narrow ranges of goods that in practice were the subject of bilateral trade between the partners in the agreement. For twenty-two countries, accounting for approximately 70 percent of world trade, commerce was divided in the way summarized in Table 3.3.

The increase of bilateralism after 1931 is certainly apparent. But the most striking single feature of the calculation is the reduction from 1931 of the line "balance of merchandise trade" (the sum of the twenty-two countries' trade deficits or surpluses: the extent to which their trade was not balanced either bilaterally or multilaterally). The total fell in the first place because of the collapse of the world payments system, and the con-

Table 3.3 The bilateralization of trade, 1929–1935 (%)

	1929	1931	1932	1933	1934	1935
Bilateral merchandise trade	71.7	68.1	69.4	71.3	71.9	74.2
Balances of total merchandise trade	9.9	16.4	15.6	14.4	13.0	12.0
Triangular merchandise trade	18.4	15.5	15.0	14.3	15.1	13.8

Source: League of Nations, *Review of World Trade, 1935* (Geneva, 1936), p. 65.

sequent impossibility of financing large imbalances (outside specifically agreed clearing arrangements of the kind Germany negotiated with southern and eastern Europe). As it became impossible to sustain unbalanced trade any longer, countries tried to achieve a balance, which could be achieved only through reduction of the overall level.[172] The League table demonstrates the limits placed on trade by the breakdown of the world's capital markets.

The need to balance external accounts brought governments directly into the regulation of trade relations. Trade policy in the 1930s became much more tightly controlled by governments, and much less vulnerable to the leverage of pressure and interest groups, which had taken so prominent a role in the 1920s. The political economy of tariffs in the interwar years thus moved in a different direction from that taken by monetary policy.[173] There the results of depression were the discrediting of central banks, the diminution of their power, and a greater responsibility of governments and a greater policy flexibility after abandoning the gold-standard regime. Monetary policy is less susceptible to interest pressures, to "small-group action," but it may allow the development of structures of interest representation. The new monetary policy made possible new social pacts—from the Matignon pact and the New Deal at the democratic end of the political spectrum to the reordering of German social life under National Socialist totalitarianism.

The flexibility that monetary reform gave allowed the interest groups to change their attention to macroevents—and in particular to abandon the minutiae of tariff negotiations. The focus on large-scale policy, however, required exceptionally broad and wide alliances, and not the specific haggling that characterized the formation of tariff legislation. Thus the prominence of the money issue actually helped to diminish the importance of private group pressures that had played such a prominent role in launching the world on the protectionist path in the 1930s. Instead it held out the prospect of large-scale corporatism within a framework made possible and stable by monetary stability or mild monetary expansion. One of the most important elements in the move, finalized only after 1945, to a cooperative rather than a conflictual pattern of political and social relations was the combination of macro-thinking prompted by monetary changes, and the discrediting of micro-thinking associated with the disastrous trade history of the 1920s and 1930s.

The military outcome of the Second World War meant that the Hullian rather than the Schachtian vision shaped the postwar world. Article VIII of the IMF's Articles of Agreement required a transition to convertibility in the current account, making impossible the use of exchange control as a means of trade direction. It was, however, far from being a complete triumph. Schachtianism continued to be widely practiced. Countries had multiple exchange rates. Europe did not remove restrictions on the current account until 1958. Many parts of the Hullian vision were stillborn. The projected International Trade Organization never materialized in the immedaite postwar era (the World Trade Organization of 1996 was a very distant descendant). Until the Kennedy Round of the 1960s, the GATT did little to reduce tariff protection.

Regional trade agreements had an exemption from the GATT, and in the late 1950s Europe started to move toward a formation of regional blocs, with the European Economic Community and European Free Trade Area. The competence of the GATT was progressively restricted. Two of the most contentious trade areas, textiles and agriculture, where industrialized countries faced the greatest potential competition from the developing world, were by the 1960s effectively removed from the GATT.

The breakdown of the par value (or Bretton Woods system) in the early 1970s threatened new trade disorders, as countries feared that competitive devaluation—the characteristic ill of the 1930s that Bretton Woods was supposed to remedy—would bring unfair competition. Major exchange-rate misalignments, such as the massive dollar appreciation of the mid-1980s, indeed triggered new efforts at protection. Nontariff barriers proliferated. The major industrial countries, the United States and the countries of the European Community, forced their trade partners to reduce exports through so-called voluntary export restraints.

The push to trade liberalization of the 1980s and 1990s came not so much through interests, but through an intellectual conversion analogous to the triumphal journey of nineteenth-century Manchesterism. A case for freer trade was made with most intellectual force first in the case of the developing economies.

At the same time as trade liberalization advanced, the movement to regionalism gained a new vigor. Some of its advocates saw regional integration as the best way of advancing a global agenda.

The competition between regional and global visions thus continued in the postwar world. By the late 1990s, regionalism looked increasingly frayed. The Asian economic crisis after 1997 increased the incentives for rapid opening. In Europe, the slower growth of the European Union in comparison with the United States made the protected aspects of Europeanism seem less attractive. But there is also a countermovement. In the nineteenth century arguments about free trade emphasized peace as much as concrete economic benefits. Peace appeared too as the major argument in the second half of the twentieth century for regional integration; the most stunning success in this regard was the conversion of the Franco-German antagonism that had produced three destructive wars into economic and increasingly political cooperation. The globally integrated economy went with a different vision of peace, that of the *pax americana*. The greatest challenge to that vision comes not from any sort of economic argumentation, but from discontent: in the center, the United States, at the notion that foreigners have achieved unfair advantages from the American security umbrella, and have not "properly" opened up. That feeling is most pronounced in regard to Asia, and especially to Japan. Outside the United States, the discontent arises from the belief that America interprets its mission arbitrarily and finds rule-based and consensual approaches to problemsolving deeply unappealing. Such arguments provide the underpinning for advocates of new regional solutions that inevitably carry overtones of characteristically 1930s trade arrangements.

4

◆

The Reaction against
International Migration

A backlash against international migration was already well under way at the beginning of the twentieth century. It was in part a product of increased democratization, and the associated emergence of a new radical populism. Objectors to global integration argued, to some extent correctly, that living standards and labor incomes were being eroded by continuing immigration. After the First World War, however, the discussion became much more intense, and labor standards constituted a central part of analysis of relative economic performance. Currency fluctuations helped to focus attention on international differences in labor costs.

Unemployment and Depression

The main way in which the depression is still remembered, at least in industrial countries, is through the demoralizing experience of mass unemployment, with its concomitants of soup kitchens, dole lines, "buddy can you spare a dime?," hunger marches, and broken families. This experience made unemployment and its avoidance the central political issue of a generation, and led to a call for the protection of national labor. In the United States, industrial unemployment averaged 37.6 percent in 1933. In Germany and the United Kingdom, the peak had been reached a year earlier, with an average of 43.8 percent and 22.1 percent respectively.[1] The British prime minister, the Labour politician Ramsay MacDonald, noted at Christmas 1929, at the beginning of the slump: "Unemployment is baffling us. The simple fact is that our population is too great for our trade . . . I sit in my room in Downing Street alone and in silence. The cup has been put to my lips—& it is empty." A few months later, in his country residence, he felt no more sanguine. "Is the sun of my country sinking? . . . We have to adjust ourselves & meanwhile the flood of unemployment flows & rises & baffles everybody. At Chequers one can almost see it & hear its swish in the figures I have been studying."[2]

Explaining why an economic shock like the depression and the financial panics of the era produced so much unemployment requires an examination of the dynamics of the labor markets. An important reason why gold-standard monetary shocks had such a profound effect on real output and employment rests on the observation that nominal wages were "sticky" and thus that the monetary contraction led to rises in real wages. If the economic structure had been more flexible, and money wages had fallen in line with prices, there would have been a much smaller impact on output.

Explaining this phenomenon requires a cross-national comparison. The clearest and easiest result from econometric testing is that gold-standard countries were more exposed to the rise in real wages, while devaluation eventually offered a way out of the trap of wage costs. This is part of the argument presented with different tests by Barry Eichengreen and Jeffrey Sachs, by Ben Bernanke and Harold James, and by Bernanke and Kevin Carey.[3]

But within the national responses there are some differences. One explanation for such variations looks at institutional arrangements. An objection to letting money wages fall along with prices is that there were many prices that were fixed for long periods—especially rents and mortgage payments—and thus a wage cut would impose a sacrifice on workers unless it were accompanied by a general reduction in costs.[4] Such a general round of reductions, however, could be accomplished only by massive government interventions in price-setting, and very few countries were prepared to go that far. (An exception is Germany, where the Emergency Decree of 8 December 1931 reduced wages along with interest rates and mortgage payments. It was not a popular measure, and provoked massive protests.)

What are the institutional explanations for different labor market responses? One obvious candidate is the power of organized labor. But some highly unionized countries displayed quite substantial flexibility in wage issues (especially if the gold-standard constraint was lifted). Australia was the most highly unionized country in the world, as measured by the share of workers in unions (45.7 percent in 1929, compared with 33.9 percent in Germany and 33.8 percent in Sweden, and with 9.3 percent in the United States).[5] But from 1929 to 1932 the nominal wage fell by 20 percent, and changes in production and unemployment were correspondingly mild: a 9 percent fall in real GDP and a 9 percent rise in unemployment).[6] The Australian machinery for centralized wage determination, in which wages were set in response to previous price changes, proved an effective and politically uncontroversial mechanism for reducing wages (although of course real wages remained more or less constant on the basis of such a formula).[7] On the other hand, the United States, with a very low rate of unionization, had a very dramatic rise in unemployment. It is clear that union presence or power on its own is a poor explanation of depression-era unemployment.

A second institutional factor is the way in which lessons of previous economic events had been received. In the United States, wages responded much less quickly to demand shocks in 1929–1933 than they had in the short but very severe postwar depression of 1920–21. The widely learned lesson of the early 1920s was that wages had fallen too rapidly, and had thereby intensified the depression. President Hoover in the Great Depression tried to persuade companies not to cut wages in response to falling demand, since he believed it was above all necessary to maintain consumer purchasing power. At least some large employers (General Motors and International Harvester) appear to have followed his advice.[8]

A third answer might lie in institutional arrangements that strengthened or hardened the position of labor negotiators. In both the British and German case, fiercely fought historiographical debates have focused on this issue. In Britain, an argument was made during the depression era that the high level of unemployment benefits (the "dole") and the availability of benefits to the short-term unemployed increased the long-term rate of unemployment. At its lowest in the interwar period, unemployment was as high as in any year before the First World War. In his contemporary book on the depression, Lionel Robbins claimed: "The cartelisation of industry, the growth of the strength of trade unions, the multiplication of State controls, have created an economic structure which, whatever its ethical or aesthetic superiority, is certainly much less capable of rapid adaptation to change than was the older more competitive system. This puts it very mildly . . . The post-war rigidity of wages is a by-product of Unemployment Insurance."[9] This view was set out more systematically at that time by Edwin Cannan and by Jacques Rueff.[10] At the end of the 1970s it was revived—to great controversy—by David Benjamin and Levis A. Kochin, who focused their account of the impact of the insurance acts of 1911 and

1920 on the search process: the existence of benefits allowed workers to continue searching for better-paid jobs for a longer time, and thus drove up the general wage level. They tried to demonstrate how inflexible the British economy had become, so that in the depression era nominal wages fell by only 3 percent and unemployment increased by 22 percent (a quite dramatic contrast with the Australian experience).[11] The subsequent debate substantially modified the initial argument, which had been insufficiently attentive to the microeconomics of the labor market. Heads of household suffering unemployment were less likely to be satisfied by benefits (which were substantially lower than their previous wages), but the search argument applies better for dependent family members.[12] An explanation for the strikingly lower rates of youth unemployment in interwar Britain may also depend on wage structures, which paid much lower rates to workers under eighteen and twenty-one, so that many young people were laid off when they reached an adult age.[13]

For the German case also, an argument that had been frequent in the interwar period was revived in the late 1970s, by Knut Borchardt. Wage increases, which were not matched by comparable productivity gains, turned Weimar into a "sick economy." Nominal hourly wages, as set by wage agreements, were 33 percent higher in 1929 than they had been in 1925, and actual earnings were 37 percent higher. These were equivalent to real increases of 22 and 26 percent respectively.[14]

The major cause of the German wage push was a combination of trade-union power with a state arbitration system, in which binding settlements could be imposed on the participants in a labor dispute. Since a tendency in such arbitration is to split differences, workers could generally reckon with increases. Some contemporaries insisted on the ability of the political process to influence wage negotiations. In particular, the socialist politician and economist Rudolf Hilferding coined the idea of a "political wage." In the historiographical controversy that followed Borchardt's article, Theo Balderston and Johannes Bähr tried to show that the arbitration system merely reproduced the logic of the labor market (which might be read out of the actually paid wages, as compared with those fixed in agreements).[15] Since the supply of labor was fixed, Balderston argues, the rise in wages reflected the strength of demand, especially for German exports, in the boom years of the late 1920s.

This argument—and indeed the similar debate in Britain—of course depends on the assumption that the labor market is of a fixed size. It is striking that in none of the literature critical of the Borchardt thesis is there any reference to the restriction of the labor market by migration controls. Yet this was a major feature, one that distinguished the interwar economy from that of the more fully globalized prewar period. This in short was yet another policy area where a major and destructive reaction against globalization set in and distorted the economic structure.

Immigration Law

During and after the First World War, immigration was generally much more restricted; the model for such restriction was provided by the United States. In 1917 the Immigration Act excluded a wide class of aliens as undesirable: idiots, the feeble-minded, epileptics, those of "constitutional psychopathic inferiority," drunkards, paupers, beggars, sufferers from tuberculosis or other "loathsome diseases," polygamists, anarchists, prostitutes, laborers under contract or those whose passage had been paid for, and Asians (with a geographic definition of origin). Those excluded by earlier acts (Chinese and Japanese) were again excluded. A parallel Act, the Burnett Act, also imposed a literacy test.

The American discussion of the 1920s drew on the resentments that had already been expressed before the First World War, and directed against the so-called "New Immigrants," who were—the stereotype went—economically motivated (rather than politically or ideologically, as the older immigrants had—largely erroneously—labeled themselves). The two Restriction Acts of 1921 and 1924 aimed at altering the ethnic and national mix of immigrants and at greatly restricting the overall flow. The 1921 act reduced the annual number of immigrants from over a million to a maximum of 357,803 and stipulated that the maximum number of immigrants of any nationality should be 3 percent of the foreign born of that nationality resident in the United States in 1910. But the 1921 act did not restrict land immigration, via Canada and Mexico; this loophole was remedied by the 1924 act. That act took the crucial base year back to 1890, in other words before the large Mediterranean and Russian and east European emigration of the 1890s and 1900s. The quota was now set at 2 percent of the foreign-born individuals of that nationality in the continental United States as measured in the census of 1890.

Obviously this legislation was not completely and immediately effective. Smuggled immigrants amounted to an annual 50,000–100,000. There were some striking instances of large-scale avoidance. In 1924, for instance, the French colonial authorities in Tunis expelled some 10,000 Italians as part of a clampdown on criminality, and the U.S. secretary for labor reported that they were "welcomed with open arms by the United States."[16]

What economic effects followed from the new policies of restriction? In the nineteenth century, construction activity had been linked to waves of immigration. For the 1920s, on the other hand, construction was the weakest point in an otherwise booming economy. From 1926 through 1929, at the height of 1920s prosperity, spending on construction fell by $2 billion, and the sector remained very weak during the depression and the recovery of the 1930s. Another measurement of the feeble character of building is given by the lumber industry: by 1929 output was only 91 percent of the 1925 peak level.[17] Nevertheless, despite the obvious precedent of the nineteenth-century experience, traditionally historians have been unwilling to see reduced construction in the 1920s as an outcome of immigration policies. One calculation, for instance, suggests that a laxer immigration regime would have raised housing investment by less than one percent.[18] This is too restrictive an estimate. But such estimates should not lead us to minimize the extent of the impact of immigration on economic growth, for they systematically exclude any consideration of the effect of immigration on labor market behavior.

The primary motive for the change in the U.S. stance reflected the impact on the labor market of large numbers of poor and unskilled immigrants. The first congressional votes on a literacy test, which was approved by both the House of Representatives and the Senate but was vetoed by President Grover Cleveland, came in 1897. In 1915 both House and Senate again voted for such a measure, by larger margins, and Woodrow Wilson vetoed the bill. In 1917 anti-immigration votes were sufficiently numerous to override the presidential veto. The pressure to stop immigration had little to do with the war. It was a result of the surge of immigration in 1900–1910, which had a discernible impact on the wages of less skilled workers. Economic circumstances and voting patterns in Congress were linked. Whereas in the large East Coast cities, with large immigrant communities, there were pro-immigration majorities, elsewhere workers moved to an anti-immigrant position. They directed their hostility precisely against the less qualified immigrants, who posed the greatest competitive threat, those from eastern and southern Europe.[19] As a consequence, it is possible to see the development of anti-immigration sentiment as motivated solely by a quite rational perception of the dynamics of the labor market, without any additional racist argumentation.

But there was also a distinctly "racial" cast of argument. At the 1927 Geneva world population conference, an American, C. B. Davenport, explained the U.S. goal of "the preservation of a reasonable degree of homogeneity in the population of the United States. Possibly," he continued, "the lesson learnt in the great war in Europe, of the strong differences in feeling between different nationalities in Europe, led us to dread lest there should come about that which seemed imminent, namely, that we should have represented in the United States groups which should make it a little Europe, with warring nationalities included."[20]

The other classic countries of immigration soon adopted similar discriminatory measures. Canada listed "preferred" countries (Belgium, Denmark, France, Germany, Netherlands, Norway, Sweden, and Switzerland) whose citizens were admitted on the same terms as those of Britain; and then "non-preferred" European countries, whose peoples could come only as agricultural laborers or domestic servants.[21] South Africa after 1930 virtually halted immigration from "non-preferred" countries altogether. Australia, at the instigation of its powerful labor unions, negotiated limits on the passports issued to immigrants from east European countries and Italy.

An International Solution

Migration was clearly an international issue, and restrictions reduced potential living standards in the countries of emigration. But attempts to deal with the regulatory issues on an international level largely failed.

The discussion of international measures to deal with fears and accusations of unfair competition and wage pressure exerted across national frontiers began in the nineteenth century. Sometimes the memorandum presented by the enlightened New Lanark factory owner Robert Owen to the international Congress of the Concert of Europe at Aachen (Aix-la-Chapelle) is considered to be the beginning of international labor legislation. Owen wanted the principles of enlightened industrialism to be extended from Britain throughout the world. Instead of competing with other countries, Britain should "extend the knowledge which she has acquired of creating wealth or new productive power, to the rest of Europe, to Asia, Africa and America."[22] Owen invited the congress statesmen to see the progressivism of New Lanark as a model for widespread international emulation. The proposition is an obvious one: good reforms by one state could be undermined by unenlightened policy in other countries. Low-cost competition would make the improvement of living conditions impossibly expensive and bankrupt enterprises that wished to be humane. During a discussion of child labor legislation in France in 1838–39, the economist Jérome Blanqui suggested an international treaty "adopted simultaneously by all industrial countries which compete in the foreign market."[23] Louis René Villermé, a surgeon employed as an inspector of textile factories, suggested a "holy alliance" of manufacturers, "not only in his vicinity, but in all countries where his goods are sold . . . to bring to an end the evil with which we are afflicted instead of exploiting it to their profit."[24]

The first really systematic move occurred in 1889, when the Swiss government issued invitations to a preparatory conference on international labor legislation. As a federal country with intensive cantonal legislation, Switzerland was a natural laboratory for such initiatives: one canton would not be well advised to pass a particular piece of labor legislation unless the same agreement was reached in the others. At the initiative of the new German emperor, Wilhelm II, the conference was eventually held in Berlin, not Switzerland, and in the event produced no concrete outcome. The next Swiss initiative was much more successful: in 1905 and 1906 conferences in Bern produced an agreement for the prohibition of night labor by women, as well as a ban on the use of white phosphorus in matches. At the time of the meetings, Austria, France, Germany, Great Britain, Italy, the Netherlands, and Switzerland already had a ban on night working. The major aim of the discussions was to bring "backward" states, notably Japan, into an international system, and thus prevent cheap and exploitative labor practices posing an unfair economic threat.

The next development was a response to a dramatic failure of international working-class solidarity. Many socialist and labor leaders had seen in concerted action, across national boundaries, a chance of improving labor standards, but also of preventing war. In August 1914, however, there was little protest, and most of the European working class seemed to be swept up in the fervor of war enthusiasm. As the war went on, however, every belligerent country bought labor peace and increased munitions output by a promise of a better postwar world. The German economic planner Walther Rathenau explained that "the trenches cannot be paid for with a deterioration of the standard of living."[25] This sentiment was generally shared. Very soon after the outbreak of the European war, the American

Federation of Labor passed a resolution calling for a meeting of labor representatives as part of a future peace conference, "to the end that suggestions may be made and such action taken as shall be helpful in restoring fraternal relations, protecting the interests of the toilers and thereby assisting in laying the foundations for a more lasting peace."[26]

The second plenary session of the Paris peace conference on 25 January 1919 passed a resolution appointing a commission "to inquire into the conditions of employment from the international aspect, and to consider the international means necessary to secure common action on a permanent agency to continue such inquiry in cooperation with and under the direction of the League of Nations." The major drafting initiatives came from the British, but this was also one area of the conference's activities that attracted some German support. After the military breakdown, and in the context of a rapid democratization and an extension of rights to labor representatives, the German Labor Office saw in international labor action one of the most attractive aspects of the whole peace process. In February 1919 the German government submitted a draft program for labor provisions in the peace treaty, which included an expression of the right of every worker to work and reside where he could find employment, and called for a ban on prohibitions of emigration and immigration. Immigrant workers should have the same conditions and wages as local workers.[27] The French proposals also made a great deal of the freedom of migration.

Labor issues were placed in Part XIII of the Versailles Treaty, which established an International Labour Organization (ILO), with a permanent International Labour Office. Its Governing Body of twenty-four would have twelve representatives of governments, six of employers, and six of workers (in 1922 it was enlarged to thirty-two, after a struggle about the representation of non-European states). The ILO had a sanctions mechanism for enforcing conventions, analogous to the general practice of the League. A member could submit a complaint that another member was not in effective observance of a convention. The Governing Body had the power to appoint a commission of inquiry, whose report would be published by the League; within a month of the report, the parties to a dispute were obliged to accept the report or to refer the matter to the Permanent Court of International Justice, which could impose economic sanctions on "defaulting governments."

Trying to provide international guidelines for working conditions offered one path to a solution of labor problems in the context of a global economy. Another approach—a more ambitious project even than attempting to coordinate labor legislation—lay in the control of population movements. In Paris, some delegates—in particular from countries of emigration such as France, Italy, Japan, and Poland—wanted to bring the ILO into controlling and regulating migration. But such proposals raised objections from the countries of immigration, in particular the United States, which thought that immigration should be subject to a consideration of national interest. Subsequently Italian delegates at the annual conferences frequently raised the issue of a world redistribution of the factors of production, in which countries with surplus agricultural land should accept the workers of countries with no unoccupied land.[28] In 1921 the League of Nations and the ILO held an international congress on migration in Geneva, but its deliberations were crippled by the refusal of Australia and Argentina (large recipients of immigration) to send delegations. The Brazilian delegation announced that control measures were urgently needed to "discipline migration in the higher interests of mankind."[29]

With such failure, the ILO inevitably restricted itself to the field of labor conditions. The first international labor conference, in Washington in 1919, discussed the extension of the 1906 Bern Conventions, the protection of female labor, and the application of the eight-hour day or forty-eight-hour week. There was a substantial Asian presence at the conference, with delegations from China, India, Japan, Persia, and Siam. In 1919 in Paris, the Japanese delegate had explained

> that the Government and people in Japan were much concerned with labour questions, but their conditions were very different from those of Western Nations, and therefore there might be certain measures of reform embodied in proposed conventions which were necessary for a large number of other countries, but which, if adopted immediately and unconditionally, would be contrary not only to the interests of industry, but also to those of the workers themselves in Japan. Consequently, in accepting and carrying out such proposed reforms . . . Japan should have the opportunity of subjecting their execution to a period of delay or of introducing some exceptions or modifications.[30]

In the 1920s the Japanese textile industry raised the issue of inequality of labor conditions as a factor in competition. But increasingly the Labour Office recognized that if it were to take the competition issue as a basis for its activity and the enactment of new conventions, it would be doomed to failure. In 1927 the director's report argued that "Possibly, in the last resort, the whole system of international conventions which sprang from the traditions and precedents of the pre-war period correspond to conditions of international competition which no longer exist today in precisely the same form."[31]

By the beginning of the 1930s the Hours of Work convention had been ratified by 18 countries, the Unemployment Convention (on reciprocity in unemployment insurance) by 24, the Convention on the Employment of Women before and after Childbirth by 13, the Women's Night Work Convention by 27, the Minimum Age (Industry) Convention by 23, and the Night Work (Young Persons) Convention by 27 countries. From 1919 to 1934, 44 conventions and 44 recommendations were adopted; but most were adopted at the first three conferences, and the ILO principles proved increasingly difficult to translate into practice. General conventions, say on hours of work, which were always treated with caution and skepticism, and required repeated reaffirmation at the international institutional level (in 1930, a new convention on the eight-hour day and forty-eight-hour week was instituted), were generally less significant than rather concrete measures, with regard to issues such as industrial hygiene.

In the course of the world depression, as unemployment mounted, the issue of hours of work became increasingly controversial. At the beginning of 1932 the Governing Body of the ILO urged the extension of the Washington Hours of Work Convention. The eight-hour day could be a foundation for the abolition of overtime and the reduction of working hours before workers would be dismissed in response to bad business conditions.

In 1932 the report of the ILO director urged the redistribution of work and the increasing use of short time, as well as the maintenance of wages and the regulation of migration through international agreements. Such initiatives had an increasingly unreal air. While some governments, notably the Hoover administration in the United States, tried to keep wages up, in order not to reduce purchasing power further, in most countries the pressure went the other way. In the light of a diagnosis of the crisis that emphasized the difficulties posed by falling investment levels, the Genevan cures involving wage maintenance did not look attractive.

Professor Alfred O'Rahilly of the Irish Free state provided a neat epitaph on the initial work of the ILO in 1932:

Now the factors governing the world today are entirely beyond the control or competence of this Organization. The fact is deplorable, but undeniable. This Organization was designed for a world which has practically ceased to exist; a world of comparatively stable prices and profits, of industrial expansion and colonial exploitation; a world of big powers and submerged nationalities. Today we are living in a world of fluctuating prices and collapsing profits, an era of industrial contraction and resurgent nationalism, when production has outrun consumption and the machine is ousting man, and usury—miscalled finance—has whole nations in its grip. And in spite of the creation of these two great international organizations, the League and ourselves, the world today has economically disintegrated, ever since the war, into fragments and powder—men, money, goods, petrified as if by the trick of a cinema photographer.[32]

Continental Problems

As transoceanic migration became harder because of increased restrictions, initially intracontinental migration surged. In the 1920s many Italians who might otherwise have gone across the Atlantic went to work in northern and western Europe. Both oceanic and continental migration was shorter term now, in that there was more return migration. Forty-one percent of Italian emigration was "continental" in 1920; by 1938 the share was 80 percent. But even such migration fell off abruptly in the depression, when the new (continental) countries of immigration launched their own restrictions. In 1932, at the height of the world depression, 16,000 people were turned back at the Swiss frontier on the grounds that they had insufficient funds to support themselves.[33]

The European country with the highest levels of immigration was France, where the movement was more politically acceptable than elsewhere. It could provide a remedy to the French demographic weakness, which had put the country at a disadvantage in its historic rivalry with Germany. In addition, immigration compensated in some manner for the great losses of the war. In 1911 aliens had constituted 2.86 percent of the population; by 1921 the share had risen to 3.78 percent. With more reconstruction it went higher, to 6.15 percent in 1926, and to 6.91 percent in 1931. Unlike other countries, France made immigration easier. Already in 1889, there had been automatic naturalization for children born in France to alien parents who had also been born in France, and optional naturalization for other children born in France. In 1927 naturalization was made possible for aliens who had been in France for at least three years.

The largest single national share of the immigrants to France was Italian (in 1926 Italians constituted 31.7 percent of aliens; 15.7 percent came from Russia and Poland, and 13.5 percent from Spain). National groups were recruited for particular activities. The Mine Owners Committee sent recruiting missions to Poland, and in 1919 a Franco-Polish emigration treaty regulated the process of migration. By 1923, for coal mining in the department of Pas de Calais, 39 percent of all underground workers and 53 percent of hewers were Polish. While Poles tended to work in mining, Italians worked in construction and agriculture. With such high proportions of foreign workers, foreign countries—rather than French workers—began to complain about unfair competition. One British survey of population developments at this time, for instance, referred to the "complaint heard in foreign countries that France was building up a new form of slave state."[34]

Germany followed much more restrictive policies in the 1920s, both in comparison with prewar practices and in comparison with those of its western neighbor. In the first decade of the twentieth century almost 600,000 Italians came to Germany.[35] Almost all were repatriated quickly after the outbreak of war in 1914. There were Poles, especially in eastern agricultural work and in the coal mines of the Ruhr valley. Before the war, some attempt had been made to restrict movement and to provide for central registration. The employers' associations took on this task in 1907. The postwar Weimar Republic moved quickly to the establishment of a major series of welfare reforms, and trade unions were powerfully represented in government and decisionmaking. It was much more of a workers' state. Correspondingly, inward movement, which might have upset the precarious political equilibrium, was discouraged. The Employment Exchange Act of 22 July 1922, which set out to guarantee the rights of German workers to welfare benefits, regulated foreign recruiting. Foreign labor was to be employed only if there was an actual shortage of German labor. A treaty between Poland and Germany in 1927 restricted migration to agricultural workers and permitted only temporary and seasonal movements. Each worker needed a contract with a specified employer before he was permitted to set out. In return, limited rights to sickness and accident insurance were provided.

Did the different migration experiences of France and Germany change the dynamics of the labor market? Most analyses of the problems of the Weimar economy, while emphasizing the problems caused by high wage settlements in the later 1920s, in the circumstances of a stable, gold-ex-

Table 4.1 Nominal wages of skilled male workers in 1929 as a share of 1926
wages, various countries (%)

Country	Weekly	Daily	Hourly
France	119	—	119
Germany	117	—	118
Japan	—	96	—
Poland	—	138	—
Switzerland	—	99	—
United Kingdom	100	—	100
United States	103	—	103

Source: Calculated from *International Labour Review* 26 (1932): 248–254.

change standard currency, have not attributed a great role to the absence of
substantial inflows of foreign workers.

Table 4.1 shows that the behavior of French and German wages showed
little difference, but that the major distinctions lay between countries with
and without inflationary experiences in the first part of the decade. Japan,
Switzerland, the United Kingdom, and the United States all had more or
less stable wages, while the continental European countries, where inflationary expectations had been built into wage bargaining, continued to experience quite substantial wage increases during the stabilization period.[36]
The political drama of a return to the gold standard apparently did nothing to change the actual behavior of unions and industrial bargainers.

When the labor market turned more difficult, many of the foreign workers in the host countries left by themselves. In 1927 and 1931, departures
from France exceeded arrivals.

Particularly populist politicians of the right—but also labor organizations and the parties close to them—saw immigration as a threat to living
standards and welfare rights. The French socialist statesman and director
of the International Labour Office, Albert Thomas, told the 1927 World
Population Conference, held in Geneva, that a "rational migration" policy
was needed to deal with the demographic problem, since "of all demographic phenomena, migration is the most susceptible to direct intervention and control." Thomas compared the policies of the United States
and France to protection by customs tariffs. In his peroration, in which
he raised the possibility of an international supreme migration tribune,
Thomas said: "An attempt should be made to tackle the migration prob-

lem, and this attempt should be made internationally. The question is one of peace or war. If no action is taken, fresh wars, perhaps even more terrible than those which the world has recently experienced, will break out at no distant date."[37]

Countries that had previously sent large numbers of emigrants now found that aggressive imperialism might be an alternative. Both Italy and Japan had experienced high rates of emigration. Both now tried first to organize their emigrant groups. In 1927 Foreign Minister Dino Grandi started an official campaign against emigration. Italian subjects were allowed to leave with the intention of settling abroad only if they were moving to be with a near relative or had a contract of employment (which immigration restrictions in host countries made it increasingly difficult to obtain). The restrictions were briefly relaxed in 1930 as the depression affected Italian labor markets and outward migration shot up (88,054 in 1929, but 220,985 in 1930 and 125,079 in 1931). At the same time as obstacles were placed on outward migration, Mussolini announced a new campaign to increase natality (which was unsuccessful: the number of births per 1,000, which had fallen from around 30 in the early 1920s to 27.5 in 1927, continued a remorseless decline, to 25.6 in 1929 and to 23.4 by 1934).[38]

Russia, which adopted radical policies in every other regard, also tried almost completely to prevent emigration. This stance was defended in terms of ideology. "The socialist state," its representatives announced, "considers people as its most valuable asset."[39]

There was a corollary to the increasingly popular principle that movements across national frontiers should be prevented. If there were intolerable pressures within the national frontiers—which had previously been dealt with by the export of goods or of people—they could be answered in the new environment in which goods and people could not move only by shifting the frontiers themselves. Is it a coincidence that the countries that turned dramatically and destructively to military expansion in the 1930s were countries that had previously been large suppliers of emigrants?

Japan rationalized the push into Manchuria after 1931 in terms of the need to find room for settlement in a world in which Japanese export industries could no longer find markets. It would be a "lifeline" for the supply of raw materials, the extension of a new market for Japanese goods, and a means of relieving Japan's rural overpopulation. Japanese business described the schemes for the state-led economic development of

Manchukuo, the Japanese puppet state, as a "solution to the current dead-lock," and an "escape from depression." The development occurred along Soviet central planning lines, with mostly public-sector investment—but the large industrial trusts, the *zaibatsu*, bought the bonds floated by the state of Manchukuo.[40]

Mussolini justified the invasion of Abyssinia, which meant the definitive break of Italy with the League of Nations system, as a recreation of the Roman empire, but also as a search for an outlet in Africa for the surplus Italians. Previously they had moved across the Atlantic and weakened the fabric of Italy. Now Italians would build the new empire around the Mediterranean ("our sea"). In 1932 the Italian foreign minister, Dino Grandi, had explained to the Senate that a nation of 42 million could not be "confined and held captive within a closed sea." Libya would be the initial destination. The colonial undersecretary explained state-led colonization as a necessary reaction to the depression, with decisive methods needed to "speed the completion of the truly grandiose undertaking that is purposed." Africa would be the new destination for Italian emigration and national self-assertion. "Africa, with its huge territories, its unexplored mineral and agricultural wealth, its possibilities—in vast zones—for European colonization, its growing capacity as a market, truly constitutes a necessary complement, the supreme resource of our old continent, which is demographically too dense and economically too exploited."[41]

In Germany the nationalist literature opposed to the Versailles settlement had complained in the 1920s that the German people were cramped by the country's territorial losses. One of the most influential novels of the 1920s was Hans Grimm's *Volk ohne Raum* (People without Space), published in 1926, of which almost 600,000 copies were printed by 1939. The title made the point clearly: Germany no longer had sufficient space. But the author believed that "the German needed room and sun and inner freedom in order to become good and beautiful."[42]

Hitler took up the popular theme of the need for an outlet for population. In his programmatic account of his political beliefs, *Mein Kampf,* he explained that "The right to possess soil can become a duty if without extension of its soil a great nation seems doomed to destruction."[43] He contrasted the German experience with that of the United States, with a boundless frontier, or of the west European colonial countries, Belgium, Britain, France, the Netherlands. In his unpublished foreign policy statement, subsequently known as *Hitler's Secret Book,* he maintained: "Regardless of how Italy, or let's say Germany, carry out the internal colonization of their soil, regardless of how they increase the productivity of their soil further through scientific and methodical activity, there always remains the disproportion of their population to the soil as measured against the relation of the population of the American union to the soil of the Union."[44] The United States had been so productive, not just because of its natural riches and the vast extent of its territory, but because it attracted the most valuable immigrants from Europe. Emigration had correspondingly deprived Germany of the most courageous and resistant Germans.

Immediately after his appointment in January 1933 as chancellor of Germany, Hitler explained the basis of his future policy to a private meeting of army leaders. There were in his view two alternative solutions to the German problem. A first option was that Germany could develop industrial potential by reviving the export economy after the ravages of the depression. But at the beginning of the speech, he had emphasized the limited capacity of the world market to absorb exports. So the second alternative was "perhaps—and probably better—conquest of new living space in the east and its ruthless Germanicization."[45]

The theory of *Lebensraum* depended on what appeared to be a rational economic analysis—rational, that is, in the context of the depression and depression economics. In the past, countries had expanded their population on the basis of an inadequate agricultural production by selling industrial manufactures in exchange for food imports. As every country adopted its own industrialization strategy, and as world trade in manufactured goods diminished, it would become ever harder to sustain imports on this basis. Germany's economic difficulties would thus grow from year to year. Consequently, the deduction went, it was necessary to increase agricultural production by any means, including the conquest of new territory.[46]

At the secret conference in which he laid down the schedule for a future war, on 5 November 1937, Hitler explained that the destruction of Czechoslovakia and Austria would be only a first step in a strategy of creating *Lebensraum* in the East. But the initial conquests would be purged: there would be "forcible emigration" of one million people from Austria, and two million from Czechoslovakia.[47]

The quest for expansion as a substitute for emigration is most striking in smaller countries such as Poland, given the complete absence of political realism associated with the endeavor. As the map of Europe began to be open to challenge in the 1930s, Poles formulated demands for increased territory as a means to settlement. After the Munich agreement of September 1938, which awarded the Teschen area to Poland in the context of a much more dramatic cession of Czech territories to Germany, the semiofficial Polish newspaper *Gazeta Polska* spoke about the need to go further and establish a "common Polish-Hungarian frontier." The Party of National Unity distributed leaflets in Warsaw demanding "the immediate attachment to Poland of all the areas under the Czech yoke," and the deputy minister for aviation took up the claims for a common frontier with Hungary.[48]

National frontiers—defended and extended vigorously—would produce genuine communities in a world otherwise threatened by international forces. In this sense, the nation was a defense mechanism against the evils and sins of a global world. A nation could build an improved sense of justice.

A new world of passports and visas was the most obvious manifestation of the generally changing attitudes to migration. The new realities were especially shocking in central and eastern Europe, where large multinational dynastic empires (the Romanov, Ottoman, Habsburg—and also the German Hohenzollern empire) were broken up. In Joseph Roth's great novel *Die Kapuzinergruft* (The Vault of the Capuchins) (the burial place of the Habsburg dynasty, perhaps the longest-lasting secular survival of the concept of supranationalism), a seller of horse chestnuts says: "Now we need a visa for each country." A Polish count then comments: "He is only a chestnut roaster, but he is quite symbolic. Symbolic for the old monarchy. This gentleman once sold his chestnuts everywhere, through half of Europe one might say. And everywhere, where his roasted chestnuts were eaten, was Austria, and the Emperor Francis Joseph reigned. Now there is no chestnut without a visa."[49]

The result of the new policies and legislation was a dramatic decline in emigration from those areas with high population increases, and which had figured prominently in the prewar emigration statistics. Large parts of eastern, southeastern, and Mediterranean Europe, where birth rates and the growth of the labor force were very high, now sought alternative strategies for the employment of "surplus population." The development of industry and a search for export markets was one such approach, but it required an openness of export markets (which was increasingly threatened) and also open capital markets. For Poland, for instance, the growth of the labor force was such that a more than threefold growth in industrial employment (at an annual rate of at least 6.6 percent) would have been needed to absorb it. Given productivity increases, industrial output would have had to rise even faster. But these are difficult targets at the best of times—and in the interwar climate impossible, because of the instability of the export markets and of capital markets.

In the peripheral or industrializing countries with rapidly expanding populations, restrictions on immigration to richer territories depressed wages and prices and made the financial structure more vulnerable to debt deflation. In the industrial countries, the link of demographic developments and depression is not as clear. But they constituted one factor in the demand for the protection and control of labor markets, and in the demand for "national labor." Restrictive labor practices in turn contributed to the lessened flexibility of labor markets, and hence to a general vulnerability to monetary contraction.

5

♦

The Age of Nationalism versus the Age of Capital

It is easy to sum up the conventional wisdom that quickly emerged in response to the problems of the global economy. Everything that was moving across national boundaries—whether capital, goods, or people—really had no business to be doing that and should be stopped. If it could not be stopped, it should be controlled, in accordance with a definition of national interest. At every population conference, delegates accepted that sovereignty involved the choice of who might be admitted to a particular country, in accordance with the national interest. Trade was to be regulated so as to maximize domestic employment. Central banks began to redefine their job of monetary management in accordance with national priorities.

The central bankers, and others, interpreted the large sums that flowed as a response to the signals they sent as "capital flight," a term with moral overtones, implying desertion and national betrayal. Estimates of capital flight for Germany in 1930 amounted to a sum equivalent to an eighth of national income, in France for 1938 of a quarter. These short-term capital movements were so substantial that they endangered regulators' ability to control the national economies. Such flows created the basis for a myth that "mobile international capital" was undermining the national economies.

In the 1920s and early 1930s the nature of the discussion became even more radical. Adolf Hitler excoriated attempts by Weimar politicians to explain away the German depression as an outcome of international factors. In the election campaign of July 1932 he stated: "They can't say that the crisis is a result of international economic factors. Now the international is supposed to be dangerous. But they always had such good international relations, why don't they use them for Germany? There's so much international, so much world conscience, so many international contracts; there's the League of Nations, the Disarmament Conference, Moscow, the Second International, the Third International—and what did all that produce for Germany?"[1]

Why was internationalism so dangerous? Because governments and central banks attached so much prestige to the reestablishment of the fixed parities of the gold standard, they opened a window for the speculators who did not believe that their policies might be successful. In the nineteenth century there had been few cases of abandonment of the gold standard: once the system had already collapsed in 1914, once governments faced the intractable budgetary difficulties of the postwar era, short-term movements began to follow a quick-entry, quick-exit strategy.

The logic of the attachment of prestige to a difficult economic objective was that the speculator became a state and national enemy. Sometimes the attacks were linked with class conflict: the left in France attacked the "deux cent familles" who frustrated the reforms of the center-left coalition (cartel des gauches). The British Labour party believed that it had been undermined by a "Bankers' Ramp." The national resentments of the wartime era were frequently transferred to discussion of peacetime social relations. In wartime Russia, speculators were thought of as Germans. At the beginning of his 1922 novel To Let, John Galsworthy describes his "man of property," Soames Forsyte: "the habit of condemning the impudence of the Germans had led naturally to condemning that of Labor, if not openly at least in the sanctuary of his soul."[2]

Sometimes the objections to speculation were racially based: speculators were identified as cosmopolitan, Jewish, or alien. Such racial identifying of the sins of speculation intensified with a geographic progression eastward across the European continent. Since the middle of the nineteenth century, with the evolution of a new, dynamic, and unstable sort of market economy, Jews had been identified with finance capitalism. At the beginning, the critique often came from the political left. In France the left-wing revolutionary Alphonse Toussenel in 1845 wrote Les Juifs, rois de l'époque: Histoire de la féodalité financière. In Germany the Saxon revolutionary Richard Wagner wrote in "Jewry in Music" (1850): "In the present state of affairs, the Jew is already more than emancipated. He rules, and will continue to rule, as long as money remains the power before which all our actions lose their force."[3]

With the First World War, price controls, inflation, and the evolution of a black market, large numbers of people were obliged to take up speculative, illegal, or semilegal activities simply in order to survive. Such actions conflicted with traditional ideas of what business conduct was legitimate. One powerful argument on why anti-Semitism flared up so poisonously during and after the First World War is that Germans widely took up activities that had previously been defined as Jewish, that they hated themselves for the breach of traditional values, and that they responded by transferring their hatred to the members of the ethnic group associated with the stereotype of bad behavior.[4] The new anti-Semitism then sought an external target with ever-increasing aggression. One example of such a transition, in someone who played a crucial role in the development of the Nazi state's anti-Semitic policy, is Joseph Goebbels, who seems to have learned Jew-hating as a clerk with the Dresdner Bank during the great inflation of the early 1920s.

The stereotypes and the behavior of the vulnerable minorities reinforced one another. Faced by mounting anti-Semitism, Jews tried to move their capital out of many central European countries; and as they fell foul of new legislation to control speculation, they reinforced the stereotype of the "Jewish" speculator. (For instance, in Hungary, in the year *before* the introduction of anti-Semitic legislation in 1938, 112 of the 187 currency offenses prosecuted were committed by Jews.)[5]

After the outbreak of the major financial crises of 1931, central banks transformed themselves once more: no longer apostles of internationalism, they secured a happy bureaucratic raison d'être as the implementers and invigilators of increasingly complicated schemes for exchange control. This role was facilitated by a turnaround in economic thinking, not just in Nazi Germany—where autarky became a guideline for policy—but in almost every country.

The Mentality of Exchange Control: A Case Study

One detailed case should suffice to show how worry about capital mobility interacted with security concerns to produce a doctrine of economic control, as well as a deeply divided political culture. Nowhere was the debate about capital flight and its link to national strategic weakness conducted more intensely, even paranoiacally, than in France. France after 1931 was hit by successive waves of capital inflow (as central European capital looked for a secure haven) and outflow (as investors became nervous about France's political, social, economic, and military stability). A secure military defense was needed in an increasingly insecure world. However, through its effect on the budget and thus on financial confidence, rearmament rocked the already unsteady French boat yet further. By early 1936 it had become very difficult to sell French government bonds to the public.[6] Policymakers had to weigh the relative merits of military preparation and financial stability: excessive military spending might actually make France more vulnerable because of a financial threat to influence politics.

This was not new in 1935 or 1936. Germany had already used economic diplomacy in 1932 as a way of maneuvering France into accepting the Lausanne reparations settlement. German efforts to use finance to influence French policy became more intensive after Hitler's seizure of power. Already in December 1933, during one of the early runs on the franc, the French domestic intelligence agency, the Sûreté Générale, presented evidence that Germany was launching a speculative attack. It reported that

> Dr. Schacht and the Berlin bankers Fritz Mannheimer and Arnold formed a syndicate for a bear speculation using two brothers in France, Zélik and Grégori Josefowitz (alias Zebovik), who "had received a mission from the Führer to especially work the Paris market." French banks in their turn joined in the attack with the motive of overthrowing the ministry. They sent treasury bonds and commercial paper to the Banque de France for discount and used the proceeds to buy gold.[7]

In March 1936 a new speculative attack on the franc followed the remilitarization of the Rhineland and accompanied the Popular Front elections (the first round was held on 26 April, the second on 3 May). The army general staff anxiously surveyed a large range of German newspapers to try to establish how German propaganda was working against the French position; the German press, the French soldiers discovered, was proud to announce that the Banque de France discount-rate increase of 28 March showed that "the confidence of French capital has been shattered."[8] As in previous speculative attacks in central Europe, rate rises were read by the market as a sign of weakness, not of strength.

The military and security aspects made it much more urgent for France to attempt to obtain a currency stabilization. In 1935 and 1936 the Banque held frequent talks with the Bank of England about ways of preventing currency speculation.[9] In March and April 1936 the panic was so great that the Banque de France lost control of the money market altogether.

In 1936 a new center-left government, the Popular Front, under Prime Minister Léon Blum, took power after the April elections. But its financial policy dilemma had already existed for over a year before the elections that put it in power, and had been exacerbated by German action in March. To make their problems worse, the Popular Front leaders, in the course of the political campaign before the elections, had made promises that tied their hands on the issue of devaluation. The Communists campaigned against devaluation, claiming it meant an expropriation of wage earners for the benefit of capitalists. There was, they said, a conspiracy between French capital and foreign interests. One of the most emotive headlines of the party newspaper *Humanité* read: "The Fascists Organize the Hemorrhage of Gold." The Communist leader, Jacques Duclos, wrote: "The evildoing potentates of the Bourse and the Banque, having robbed the country through deflation, now wish to rob her through devaluation." Devaluation meant a way of avoiding a property tax on the rich.[10] But the (non-Socialist) Radicals took a similar line. Edouard Herriot, scarred by his memories of the financial crises of 1924 and 1932, announced in an election speech in Lyons: "Devaluation, that would be I know not what dangerous road toward zero."[11] The Socialist leader, Léon Blum, accommodated the beliefs of his allies by keeping to a slogan, "Neither Devaluation nor Deflation," which seemed to give no room for policy maneuver. In public Blum had always opposed the idea of devaluation. Instinctively he preferred capital controls: in late 1934 he had told the Chamber of Deputies in response to a pro-devaluationist speech by Paul Reynaud that devaluation could be prevented by putting an end to "the worst of the scandal," foreign-exchange speculation.[12]

In private, however, he and other Socialists had contemplated devaluation, but only in an internationalist setting that would not leave France humiliated or on its own.

After April 1936 the financial panic demanded some kind of action, and it became apparent that the choice lay between franc devaluation and exchange control. Both possible choices had unpleasant aspects: devaluation was humiliating, but exchange control distorting. There were also non-economic, security, aspects. This debate formed the core of a famous and influential conversation between Blum and Emmanuel Mönick, the French financial attaché in London. Mönick argued powerfully that exchange control presented a "German path" that would bring France close to the German war economy, whereas an agreement with the United States and Britain would prepare a path for a parallel political collaboration of democracies against dictatorship. "If we follow the German path, we are beaten from the start, because our country does not possess the same resources in manpower and raw material that our neighbor across the Rhine enjoys."[13]

For a considerable time there existed uncertainty between these two courses. In the early summer, devaluation seemed certain. In late June, Mönick went to Washington to negotiate a new parity,[14] and in July Blum visited London to agree the basis for a devaluation and a tripartite currency pact.

In fact nothing happened until a new franc crisis in September. Many policy measures implied a preference for exchange control rather than devaluation. The position of the Banque de France in particular was highly ambiguous. One of the most important steps taken by the Popular Front was the reform of the Banque de France, which effectively ended its autonomy. The governor (whose appointment had already been highly political) was replaced. A new statute ended the role of the regents of the Banque, who had represented the old financial and banking oligarchy, which had been vigorously attacked by the Popular Front. As the regents departed, the new governor, Ernest Labeyrie, gave them a lecture on how it was the duty of the Banque to obey the elected government of the Republic. Labeyrie also believed that money markets and speculation should be controlled; by the summer of 1937 he was being described as a "victim to his anti-speculation mania."[15]

Labeyrie adopted a corporative approach to the issue of capital flight, obliging Roger Lehideux, the representative of the French banking association, to send out a circular instructing French banks not to give credits for speculative purposes. The Banque de France also began extensive investigations into the mechanisms of capital flight, seeking an answer to the question that obsessed central bankers in the 1930s: who did it?

The Banque now kept a day-to-day account of the gold transactions on the Paris market. A surprisingly large amount came from just one bank, Lazard Frères, which accounted for 16 percent of the movement to London, 9.5 percent to New York, and 13 percent to Brussels in the second half of May 1936.[16] At the same time, we know from other sources that Lazards already began in 1935 to exercise some pressure on the government to devalue the franc;[17] in other words, the bank was moving its money in a bet against the French franc. The Banque's inquiry of 1936 went much deeper: it looked at regional variations in capital flight. The police started to attack the speculators. One inspector examined activity in the Lille-Tourcoing-Roubaix area (on the frontier with Belgium). He found plenty of small-scale activity, thousand-franc notes being taken across the Belgian frontier, but also much more systematic movements. Most of the textile businesses ran down their current accounts during the franc crisis; and at the same time the leading banks (Banque Nationale pour le Commerce et l'Industrie, Crédit Commerciel, Banque Joire, Lloyds Bank) gave large credits to the textile owners, which allowed purchases of raw material in foreign exchange.[18]

Such police operations were intended to prepare the way for an exchange control, which could be implemented only on the basis of a great deal of local and particular knowledge. In June 1936 Vincent Auriol, the new Popular Front finance minister, issued a decree imposing penalties for the nondeclaration of capital held abroad, and authorizing the government to take action against those who attacked the state's credit (that is, those who organized the flight of capital). In an address to the Chamber on 20 June he ruled out the possibility of devaluation. On 11 June the French financial attaché in Berlin had sent in a memorandum drawing on Germany's experience with exchange control since 1931, and explaining in detail how it could be applied.[19]

Then came more dramatic foreign political events: the eruption of the Spanish civil war, German lengthening of military service, and a need to prepare a new French armaments program.[20] The result was devaluation after a new franc crisis. Auriol now defended devaluation as a better alternative than exchange control.[21]

But the devaluation did not guarantee stability or make the franc immune to further attacks. The recognition that the best way to restore stability lay in *permitting* capital flows (because illegal exchange operations would continue anyway) required a change in the leadership of the Banque de France, and indeed in the whole direction of French economic policy (a reversal of policy that would not really be achieved until the late 1950s). Pierre Fournier, the deputy governor of the Banque, replaced Labeyrie, and represented a much more traditional style of management. He had argued that a large proportion of French capital was now abroad in the aftermath of the franc panics, about a third being in the United States and half in

Britain.[22] The only way of getting it back would be a liberalization and a revocation of the Lehideux circulars.

The fundamental cause of French instability, the massive public deficits, partly the result of armaments spending, remained, and consequently there was little chance of a long-lasting stabilization; 13.8 billion francs in treasury bonds were written off, but there was still a new legal ceiling on government spending, and the military budget went on rising. When new budget deficits were predicted for 1937, the outflow of capital began once more. On 13 February the government was forced into retreat.

A £40 million British loan provided temporary relief, while Blum declared a "pause" in the radical social and economic program of the Popular Front. Traditional liberals such as Jacques Rueff (who had become general director of the debt administration in November 1936) took the lead in directing the policy not just of the Finance Ministry, but also of the nationalized Banque.

No policy measure brought respite for France: not the devaluation of the franc to a new parity (the "franc Auriol"); not the Tripartite Pact with Britain and the United States that accompanied it, which promised coordination of monetary policies; and not the liberalization of capital movements and the encouragement of flight capital to return through tax incentives and the issue of reserved government paper on favorable terms.[23] The monetary crises continued, and as a result France suffered from financial instability, continued worries about the instability of the franc, and restrictions on military spending imposed by the need to keep the franc stable and respect the sentiments of small investors as well as foreigners.

The U.S. government left no doubt that it considered that French arms spending lay at the bottom of French troubles. U.S. Treasury secretary Henry Morgenthau told Roosevelt: "The world is just drifting rapidly towards war. We patch up the French situation every so often but with the constant increased percentage of their budget going for war purposes we really cannot help them. The European countries are gradually going bankrupt through preparing for war." At the same time Morgenthau asked the British chancellor of the Exchequer for "suggestions whereby he and I might make some start to stop the arming that is going on all over the world."[24]

The franc continued to jitter. In March 1937, after the Blum pause, the Germans attempted once more to destabilize the franc by massive sales on the Amsterdam market.[25] The instability of the government increased international anxiety about France.[26] In June, new drains brought down the Blum government, and a new administration under Georges Bonnet carried out a further devaluation and a floating of the franc. It also cut defense spending, and the new air force program was severely pruned.[27]

By 1938 the United States estimated French capital flight at $2.5 billion, $1 billion of which had gone across the Atlantic. Morgenthau now proposed to help France by locating where exactly this money had gone, since the movements "may gradually undermine the basis of the Tripartite Pact [while increasing] the danger of a movement toward autarky and political dictatorship." He thought that France should simply "make it a jail offense not to take your money back."[28]

Blum came back in March 1938 with a government formed just before Hitler's *Anschluss* of Austria. He intended to use rearmament as an economic stimulus, and the result was a new franc panic. Within a month, Edouard Daladier succeeded him with an administration still committed to arms, but also now to the removal of the limitations on production imposed by the forty-hour week (the most spectacular social achievement of the Blum government).

In July 1938 a memorandum from the office of the prime minister explained the grounds for the new attack on the franc. The immediate cause was an article written by Charles Rist and published in London that presented a grimly realistic account of the state of French government finance: the reaction was such that "the capitalists once more doubt the stability of our money." But once again the Italian and German radio and press devoted their attention to the embarrassment of the franc.[29] The author recommended a drastic budget reform involving an end to the amortization of the national debt and an increase in the efficiency of tax collection through the strengthening of the Finance Inspectorate and the publication of tax returns.

The rather more conservative reign of Georges Bonnet and later Pierre Marchandeau in the Finance Ministry, the presence of Fournier in the Banque de France, and the new strength of the Banque's position made for greater calm. The Banque now worked no longer through direct pressure on the government but through a new and intimate relation with the leading firms in the Paris market. A large part of the influence operated through personal connections with the leading Paris banks. By mid-1937, of the great banks only the Société Générale had no former governor or deputy governor in a prominent management position. Whereas at the time of the German *Anschluss* in March 1938, and during the May war scare over Czechoslovakia, there had been financial panics in France, the markets remained rather steady during the Sudeten crisis in September 1938 and before and after the Munich Agreement. By early 1939 a large part (around 30 billion francs) of the flight capital had returned.[30] The returning capital was mobilized for defense purposes through a new institution set up in 1938 by Marchandeau, the Caisse Autonome des Investissements de la Défense Nationale.[31]

It was only after the two devaluations and the removal of the Popular Front's major social legacy that greater sums could be devoted to armaments without causing an immediate panic. But this was in 1939, and it was then rather late. The price of maintaining gold too long through the 1930s involved the security, and eventually indeed the existence, of the French Republic. The lesson learned from the experience was that controls were needed to defend France's national interest against the security dangers posed by hot money flows. The experience of the 1930s convinced many observers, not just in France, that speculative money was immoral and dangerous. By the late 1930s, and especially in the war years, a consensus emerged that the instability of the 1920s international economy, and thus also the way in which the financial sector served as a transmitter of depression, was a consequence of unstable capital flows. This is not a particularly popular view today, when the orthodoxy among economic historians (expressed most powerfully by Barry Eichengreen in *Golden Fetters*) now holds that the fixed exchange-rate regime (rather than the mobility of capital) provided the chief systemic vulnerability.

In the 1930s, both the positions on the causes of the financial sector vulnerability and the depression were argued in serious and highly intelligent and persuasive books. The best interpretations on both sides were published by the League of Nations. The modern argument was presented very skillfully by Gottfried Haberler in *Prosperity and Depression*. The best exposition of the view that capital flows were destabilizing comes later—in Ragnar Nurkse's *Interwar Currency Experience*—and this view also decisively shaped the deliberations about the postwar monetary order in Bretton Woods.[32]

Why did Nurkse's interpretation win the debate (for the moment), when really, at least judged from the modern perspective, it should not have? The answer is not to be found simply in economic debate, but in the way in

which political and security concerns became mixed in with the economic analysis.

National Economics

In the world of the 1930s, everything was to be national—labor and goods, but also capital. John Maynard Keynes brilliantly described this development in his 1933 essay "National Self-Sufficiency," which was quickly translated into German: "I sympathise, therefore, with those who would minimise, rather than with those who would maximise, economic entanglement between nations. Ideas, knowledge, art, hospitality, travel—these are the things which should of their nature be international. But let goods be homespun whenever it is reasonably and conveniently possible; and, above all, let finance be primarily national."[33]

The collapse of the economy now brought a turning away from the market. Even moderate and pragmatic analysts, such as the director of the League of Nations' Economic and Financial Section, Sir Arthur Salter, believed that the future lay in regulation and control.[34] With the encyclical *Quadragesimo Anno* in the crisis year 1931, the Catholic church looked for a "third way" between capitalism and socialism.

Increasing regulation and planning encouraged those who saw the function of the state as being to externalize the costs of economic adjustment: to impose those costs on those outside the national community. The state's duty lay in protecting its citizens and in ensuring that the inhabitants of other national communities suffered as much as possible. This was of course quite the opposite of the traditions of classical economic liberalism, in which there is a mutuality of gains.

The path away from the market and toward control was frequently also a path to political dictatorship. The most obvious examples were in Russia and Germany. But the sentiment that democracy had failed in fulfilling a basic social need was widely shared by many democrats. In his diary in February 1940, for instance, André Gide noted: "One must expect that after the war, and even though victors, we shall plunge into such a mess that nothing but a determined dictatorship will be able to get us out of it."[35]

Military spending appeared to be the most effective way of breaking out of the vicious circle of depression economics. This was the basis of recovery policy in both Germany and Japan, although in each case the rearmament was complemented by civilian-oriented programs: the expansion of motorization in the German case, and a strikingly successful export offensive, aided by the sharply devalued yen, in the Japanese case.

One of the most obvious lessons of the depression seemed to be that the state should sponsor an industrial drive in the strictly planned setting of a national economy. The hyperindustrialization of Stalin's Russia was only the most extreme example. This lesson appealed especially to economists who experienced personally and directly the mixture of power and pressure in 1930s trade relations: so that Raúl Prebisch, who had helped negotiate the Anglo-Argentine agreements, or Thomas Balogh, who thought about the consequences of German-Hungarian trade, learned then taught that trade was manipulative. The healthiest development required import substitution, and Prebisch and Balogh were eager to sell this message in quite inappropriate contexts in the postwar world. Prebisch became the chief proponent of import-substitution industrialization as a way of dealing with terms of trade that would otherwise be hopelessly set against the developing world.

Balogh serves as a prime (if somewhat extreme) illustration of how the economic lessons of the Great Depression were mislearned, with often disastrously inappropriate conclusions. In the late 1930s he studied the German economy and realized that it had not become as autarkic as its propagandists would have liked. He therefore concluded that its economy could not stand the strain of major conflict, and would collapse quickly in the event of a war. In 1947 he predicted a permanent dollar shortage which the Europeans would not be able to overcome and which would stymie any chances of a European recovery. When Germany in 1950 adopted a stabilization program that laid the basis for the trade-sustained *Wirtschaftswunder* of the 1950s, he foresaw that it would bring the quick collapse of the West German economy. In the 1970s and 1980s he predicted a new great depression of the 1930s type.[36] All these prognoses appear in retrospect quite risible. All followed from the same logic.

At this time the nation-state with its control mechanisms was supposed to provide guarantees against threats from the world economy. But was not the protection more dangerous and destructive than the threat?

In the nineteenth century there had been a rapid process of globalization, which met almost immediate resistance. The interventionist state derived a great deal of its legitimation from the process of globalization, and became increasingly an impediment to integration. It was in the Great Depression that those who opposed the freedom of migration, and of goods and capital transactions, saw the opportunity to move the pendulum back. The strong nation-state and the free flow of capital now stood as polar opposites.

Three underlying economic propositions justified the new policy stance:

- That international trade was in a process of secular decline. This proposition had been formulated by Werner Sombart in 1903. It became commonplace in the 1930s.
- That international financial flows were destabilizing.
- That economic development required social change and mobilization, which could best be achieved through the intensification of solidarity based on awareness of common ethnic features. In practice, a sort of racism underlay much of the doctrine of development elaborated at this time, for which the term "national socialism" (understood more widely than in respect to the specifically German phenomenon of "National Socialism") seems appropriate.

6

◆

Conclusion: Can It Happen Again?

There is a paradox about the rapid shift of the last ten years toward market economies. The integrated world economy is shaken by crises—stock exchange upsets, debt crises, Mexico's "tequila effect," the "Asian flu," contagion in Russia and South America. The dramas lead to more and more unease about "globalization"—or alternately, as its critics call the process, "neoliberalism," "turbocapitalism," "casino capitalism," "disordered capitalism," "capitalism pure," "Anglo-Saxon economics." With every crisis, an initial reaction claims that the new events spell the end of a particular model of liberal economics, the so-called Washington consensus. But despite the shocks and the shrieks, there is no interruption. On the contrary, the drive to the market becomes faster; and its former critics are converted into proselytes. Experiments in heterodoxy are ever shorter-lived. While the Mitterrand government experimented for two whole years from 1981 to 1983 with a French alternative to Reaganomics and Thatcherism, a similar experiment in a new ideology of demand management lasted only five months in Germany in 1998–99 with the brief tenure of Oskar Lafontaine as finance minister.

Each major recent crisis has produced arguments that a new Great Depression, and with it a collapse of globalization, is possible or perhaps even likely. As yet, it has not happened. The risks, as spelled out in the previous pages, emanate immediately from the financial system, and from the possibility of contagious financial collapse in a well-integrated world. What made the Great Depression "Great" was a series of contagious financial crises in the summer of 1931 and the subsequent trade response. But the policies that were followed built on a backlash against globalization that had been developing progressively since the last third of the nineteenth century. That backlash identified globalism with change and sin, and held that moral regeneration required national cultures.

Some of these associations have been broken apart in the course of the twentieth century. Thomas Friedman's recent book sensibly treats the veiled Islamic woman who also uses the Internet as an icon of modern globality.[1]

This phenomenon of the strength of internationalism at the end of the millennium is so perplexing because it seems almost natural that there should be, perhaps not immediately but certainly in the foreseeable future, some backlash against global capitalism. It is tempting to see the world economy as moving over long historical stretches like a giant pendulum, in phases of liberalization followed by a rejection and the reimposition of controls. And many people ask: why don't we attempt to control the economic process more?

New Conflicts

We are now in the middle of a second Industrial Revolution, which has produced in the eyes of some analysts a new economic paradigm, of continued crisis-free growth. The combination of very rapid technical progress with global competition limits the possibility for inflationary crises, which plagued the world during much of the twentieth century (after the collapse of the international gold standard). Some commentators conclude that there has been a "death of inflation."[2]

The technology revolution will transform society as much as did the first Industrial Revolution, which beginning in the late eighteenth century drove workers out of the fields and into the factories. It was that first revolution which shaped the push and pull of expectations about government that swung the intellectual pendulum. But that world is changing.

It is always easiest to see the transformation around us and in our own lives. These changes make us aware of the extent to which our own activities are caught up with the destiny of billions throughout the world. The drama of the economic transformation requires an institutional reordering—not an abandonment, but a complete rethinking of many aspects of traditional politics as developed over the past century.

At home, the new industrial order is emptying factories—and people are in increasing numbers working out of their homes again. Anxiety about the extent and the conditions of part-time employment fueled massive public support in the United States for the summer 1997 strike at the delivery firm United Parcel Service. Europe currently has one and a quarter million "teleworkers," connected electronically to the outside world; and nearly half of these are in the United Kingdom. The large corporation of the midcentury is now squeezed by a much more competitive world, and it passes the squeeze on to its employees. Companies such as General Motors or IBM no longer offer the guarantee of jobs for life. The big companies themselves are unstable. Of the Fortune 500 companies in 1980, one-third no longer had an independent existence in 1990. Then the pace of extinction became even quicker, so that of the companies in 1990, two-fifths had disappeared by 1995.[3] As a result, fewer and fewer people expect the security—or perhaps the drudgery—of lifetime work with one employer.

The result of such changes is a fundamental alteration of many social and also political certainties. It is easiest to see the consequences in the politics of our own society. Shifts in employment patterns have undermined the basis for class identifications and for the fundamental political dynamic of the past century and a half. In the politics that followed the Industrial Revolution, owners voted for the parties of the right, which wanted to preserve and strengthen notions of property; and workers supported parties of the left, which tried to redistribute property. The great success of the ballot box over the last century and a half is that it replaced the barricade and the street as a way of fighting the war about property. The new Technology Revolution has made that war irrelevant and replaced it with a battle over ideas and ethics and the control of technologies. Many old-style parties struggle to maintain their legitimacy. The result is a different sort of politics.

Does this mean a new set of enemies? Certainly Patrick Buchanan, or Ross Perot, or Jean-Marie Le Pen, or Jörg Haider, or Vladimir Zhirinovsky, or Mahathir Mohamad thinks so. Mr. Mahathir has perhaps been the most emphatic recently. Speaking about foreign speculators, whom he blames for Malaysia's financial collapse, he stated: "I say openly, these people are racists. They are not happy to see us prosper. They say we grow too fast, they plan to make us poor. We are not making enemies with other people, but others are making enemies with us."[4] In fact he has his own kind of racism, which views the activities of Chinese businesses in Malaysia with suspicion, as part of a movement for the creation of an economic "greater China."

Even some of the most powerful makers of the new international society, such as George Soros, are terrified of the implications of the new enemy culture. The repercussions in the international arena were felt even before the fall of Communism. Conventional military conflicts between industrial countries became unthinkable while substitute "trade wars" increased. By the late 1980s, surveys regularly showed that far more American citizens were afraid of Japan than of the Soviet Union. It is striking that this was exactly the kind of thinking that underlay the new approach to economics of the 1920s and 1930s.

New Fears

As in the interwar period, many people see in internationalism (rather than in the new technology that which links countries but also has far-ranging other effects) the source of a major challenge. Globalization has become a favorite target of people who call for more economic activism in promoting some particular vision of a social order, shaped in accordance with local conceptions and prejudices.

The new world has produced some powerful and persistent myths. The most widespread of these is that all dramatic economic changes, whether desirable or undesirable, are the product of "globalization." It is easy to demonstrate the false assumptions behind much of the alarmism, at least as regards the present:

1. That unskilled jobs are disappearing solely because of competition from foreign low-income producers. Most unskilled jobs are in the service sector, where international competition for obvious reasons is not easy.
2. That wages for unskilled workers are falling as a consequence. Most recent studies in fact argue that the effect of international competition is relatively limited: for the United States at most one-fifth of the reduction in unskilled earnings can be accounted for in this way. But such analysis does correctly identify the way in which globalization may eventually make for a greater equalization across national boundaries of returns to labor as well as returns to capital.[5]
3. That trade is dominated by cheap imports from low-income countries. In fact most trade is between industrial countries.
4. That there is a limit to the amount of goods that the world can ab-

sorb, and that we face a glut in consequence. In fact there is no evidence that consumption rates are falling in most countries—indeed, the contrary is the case. In the United States, personal savings rates, which are correlated inversely with consumption, have fallen by half since the 1960s.

The fundamental economic story is much simpler than these myths. Maybe it is even more comforting. We have just become more efficient at producing. It is because of this improvement that over the past fifty years something of the old integrated world economy that reigned before the First World War has been restored. In fact the direction of causation runs in the opposite direction to the one usually supposed, in which international opening leads to a spread of technology. It was in fact technical changes and efficiencies of scale that have made purely national markets relatively inefficient, and created pressures on business to rationalize by spreading across borders. Much of the shift to "globalization" has thus been a consequence of corporate strategies and the dramatic expansion of the scope of multinational corporations. Even in a world deeply suspicious of economic internationalism, firms began to produce and distribute across national frontiers, in order to realize the gains offered by new techniques.

The move to globalism surprised many commentators, who in general assumed that it was either undesirable (that business is best "homespun," to use Keynes's famous term) or impossible because of the dynamics of protectionist pressure groups. At regular intervals since the publication of David Ricardo's *Principles of Political Economy* in 1817, analysts have predicted the imminent death of free trade. Such observers have been confronted with a constant series of astonishing and incomprehensible events. It is worth taking a moment to think of the startling turns in modern economic history.

The first surprise concerns the opening of trade. It can be read as a suspense drama, with a new twist to the narrative on almost every page. The GATT was a compromise. It achieved its greatest successes in the 1960s, largely at the cost of reducing its extent so as to exclude some of the most contentious trade items—textiles and agricultural products. By the 1970s, after the collapse of the Bretton Woods par value system, most writers agreed that the GATT was moribund. The Tokyo Round was protracted and spotty. In the mid-1980s the leading experts concluded that the GATT was "in a state of breakdown." The ministerial meeting of 1982 had failed. The Uruguay Round looked doomed to failure as the United States and the European Community became locked in a politically complex struggle over agricultural pricing and subsidies. Even in 1993, on the eve of the final agreement of this round, a major text produced by a GATT official had as its theme "the weakening of a multilateral approach to trade relations," "the creeping demise of GATT," and the fact that "the GATT's decline results from the accumulated actions of governments."[6] But then came the astonishing extension of multilateral principles to intellectual property, trade-related investment, the creation of a more complete conflict-resolution procedure, and the institutionalization of multilateralism in the World Trade Organization. At that time the commentators were skeptically insisting that the United States would ignore the new institution, and instead continue a unilateral exercise of power through the application of Super 301 (the 1989 extension of the president's power, under Section 301 of the 1974 Trade Act, to take retaliatory action against trading practices deemed "unfair"). But when the first ruling came against the United States, the United States accepted it. In 1998 everyone gave reasons why the financial services agreement could not be realized. Then, apparently unpredictably, at the last moment it came about.

The second startling development, which accompanied the trade revolution, is the liberalization of capital movements. At the time of the 1944 Bretton Woods Conference almost every economist believed that volatile capital markets—hot money—had been the contagion mechanism by which the Great Depression spread internationally. It was highly unlikely that international capital flows would resume quickly. The bankers had seen their credits frozen and their reputations attacked; the badly burnt fingers of the bondholders were still clutching the defaulted and worthless paper issued by governments all over the world. But even if capital movements did by some unlikely chance resume, there should be international and national policy instruments available to control them. There was no equivalent to the requirement of the 1944 Bretton Woods agreements to liberalize current-account transactions. In fact, however, it was really quite hard to put such limitations on capital; the offshore markets developed and eventually brought down the Bretton Woods regime. However, many capital controls remained in force and impeded capital flows. It is only recently that the consensus that embraces trade liberalization has been extended to the capital account.

Capital flows remain very volatile; and indeed each crisis brings fresh calls—even ingenious schemes—to reintroduce some measure of control or to discriminate between useful and speculative, destructive movements. After the great European Monetary System crises of 1992–93, there were demands for some variety of sand in the wheels. The Mexican peso crisis of 1994–95 produced in the view of otherwise quite sane commentators the verdict that this was a consequence not of human error, but of "the collapse of an economic model." Malaysian prime minister Mahathir Mohamad in 1997 blamed international speculators and the hedge funds. He was not alone.

Labor flows remain the most controlled part of the international economy. In the classical Industrial Revolution, before 1914, these had been relatively free, although starting in the 1880s the United States attempted to control Asian immigration. Immigration is the area most vulnerable to the protectionist impulse. This was where a decisive backlash against internationalism occurred in the 1920s, and was accompanied by the hardening of unpleasant and also short-sighted nationalistic arguments.

It is a sensitive political issue, often coupled in popular debates with the "globalization" theme. Indeed the arguments on this issue are very ancient: both Aristotle and Aquinas recognized that some products needed to be traded over long distances, but believed that local production was more moral, because foreigners would disrupt civic life.[7] In every major economy except Japan, the number of foreign-born workers has been rising since the 1980s. In the European Union there are now over 20 million legal immigrants and an estimated 3 million illegal aliens. The most authoritative recent official study, a joint effort by Mexico and the United States, suggested that there are just over 7 million Mexican-born people living in the United States, of whom almost 5 million are legal residents. Illegal immigration has increased as it became easier with mass travel, the removal of bureaucratic restrictions, and the end of Communism.[8]

It is not anti-immigrant sentiment alone that fuels the globalization debate. The most pervasive feature of the new world is a sense of helplessness, produced by altered expectations about what politics can do. Our angst is in large measure so intense because of the way in which the lopsided internationalization (more for capital than for labor) has decisively limited the room for action for governments. The traditional role of states is challenged by globalization. Taxes on capital are limited by the possibility of "exit" (in Albert Hirschman's terminology) resulting from the new

factor mobility. The result is an alteration of the political game, and a reduction in the space for political self-assertion and for privileged elites.

By contrast, the expansion of the state accompanied the first Industrial
Revolution. New wealth gave greater resources to governments, and new
problems called for collective solutions. By the late nineteenth century, a
German economist, Adolph Wagner, even formulated a "law" of the constant growth of state expenditure and of the increasing share of the state in
national income. The organization of the new states, bureaucratic and hi-
erarchical, was mirrored in business organization, with numerous layers of
authority and control.

Such governmental growth in this century was fueled by military expenditure. After the Second World War there was no retrenchment of the public sector. On the contrary, the expansion of the state continued at a faster
rate in the recovery years. Dani Rodrik has recently pointed out the character of the bargain for the great period of postwar trade expansion: that
those states which opened themselves most to trade (small European states
such as Austria, Denmark, the Netherlands, Sweden, as well as Germany)
also embarked on higher state spending on income transfers, in order to
create a safety net to surround the disruptive consequences of the open
trading economy.[9]

Today the same changes that are encouraging businesses to simplify and
abolish hierarchies in order to permit more flexibility, faster responses, and
greater innovation also demand a reorganization of government. It would
be foolish to foresee an end of traditional government, but its role will become much smaller. The past traditions are irrelevant in two critical ways.
First, collective management from the top down—the characteristic behavior of the modern state—will stand in the way of effective institutional
adaptation to global change. Second, transfer payments—increasingly the
business of the late twentieth-century state—are the opposite of wealth
creation.

Indeed in some societies the law of increasing state expenditure, characteristic of the first Industrial Revolution, has already gone into reverse. By
attacking universal entitlement programs, some countries have radically
reduced the share of public expenditure of national income. A recent study
concluded that a reduction of public expenditure in industrialized countries to 30 percent of GDP level would not seriously affect the level of services provided by governments.[10]

In fact a remarkable consensus has emerged, based on trade liberalization, capital account liberalization, stable money (guaranteed by strong and independent central banks), budgetary orthodoxy, the privatization of public-sector enterprise, and (by far the weakest and most unstable area) banking liberalization and deregulation. Sometimes it is called the "Washington consensus" (the term was first used by the economist John Williamson), although this is a misleading label in that the new approach had its roots much more in a series of local responses in developing countries against the failure of previous developmental orthodoxies. The most striking contributions to liberal trade theory were in fact made by economists appalled by their experiences of the controlled trade regime of India: Jagdish Bhagwati and Deepak Lal.

The modern Washington consensus is in this way fundamentally different from the "Geneva consensus" of the interwar period, which was the focus of the bulk of this book. The most important difference does not lie in the power politics of economics (that the Washington consensus is backed by the world's most economically and militarily powerful country, while the Geneva version had to survive on goodwill or hot air). Rather it lies in the difference between an order imposed by treaties and an order built in sustained reflection about appropriate policy—and the gains to be derived from it. It was obviously particularly unfortunate to put the constitution of the League and the International Labour Organization into as vindictive and absurd a treaty as the Versailles peace treaty. But the mistake was characteristic of a world which believed that internationalism had to be politically imposed, rather than internally generated as a consequence of calculations about advantage.

The most astonishing feature of this consensus is that very few argue any longer that their country is a special case. It was once a commonplace that a large country such as Brazil had extensive protection in order to set off its own Brazilian miracle. Indian economists argued about their national peculiarities, which were said to produce a "Hindu rate of growth." Perhaps the summer of 1997 brought the final blow to "special case-ism": the demonstration that east and southeast Asian economies do not have some miraculous key to continued fast growth (as a consequence of an allegedly original approach to the management and regulation of competition by the state). Instead, as elsewhere, extensive state involvement produced misallocation of investment and—unsurprisingly—a collapse of confidence.

Probably the simplest way of summing up the modern orthodoxy is that there is no such thing as a separate economic truth that applies to either developing or developed countries.

Inevitably these ideas do not sit easily with traditional politics. The old politics emphasized the doable, the scope for initiative. The new politics is about the limits on action. Parties explicitly and exclusively devoted to market principles rarely do well in elections. Nor are such parties very good in translating their visions into reality. In Germany, the small, economically liberal FDP (Freie Demokratische Partei) persistently wins the votes of around 5 percent of the electorate. In the recent parliamentary elections in Poland, Leszek Balcerowicz's Freedom Union with 13 percent obtained one of the best-ever election results for a free-market party. One of the striking features of the interwar collapse of global capitalism was its complete inability to generate political toleration, let alone any kind of affection or support. Where a market order survived in the 1930s, it managed to do so only by pretending to be something different: elegiac Anglican romanticism in the case of British Conservatives, planning in the case of U.S. Democrats.

In the past the most effective and sustainable liberal reforms have been introduced by politicians and movements presenting themselves as centrist or leftist: from Ludwig Erhard, who often liked to emphasize rhetorically that his "social market economy" was a third way between Manchesterite liberalism and planned socialism, through Felipe González, Alberto Fujimori (who won by campaigning against the "extreme" neoliberalism of the novelist Mario Vargas Llosa), and Fernando Henrique Cardoso (who was the major theorist of the antiliberal dependency school). Kim dae-Jung, with his strong ties to the labor movement, on this argument is likely to be more effective in introducing a wide-ranging liberal reform than his less popular and more remote and authoritarian predecessor.

The rhetorical offensive against neoliberalism has been the easiest way of introducing market principles. In Europe today, the protests against Anglo-Saxon capitalism have been loudest in France, where there has been a great deal of financial reform and economic restructuring. In Germany, by contrast, there is much less emotional or convincing criticism of the Anglo-Saxon world, but also a greater unwillingness to embark on reform. The essence of the centrist argument today is always concerned with a recognition of "the inevitable," which is usually presented as coming from outside. That is why the transformation of the modern economy by technological advance is now almost always described as "globalization": its foreign origins mean that it cannot be molded or guided by internal political debate.

New Consensus

The extent of the triumph of the new consensus can be judged by an examination of where potential intellectual, ethical, or religious criticisms might originate. There are currently two interpretative models. One suggests that we have arrived at the end of history, the end of conflicts, the end of ideology. Karl Marx was perversely right in predicting the end of class conflict and the withering away of the state, though wrong about the way in which these would be achieved. The alternative suggests that ideas move in great pendulum swings, and that triumphalism invariably provokes a sharp reaction.

But where will that reaction come from? Not, at least for the moment, from a religious critique of secular values. Both Christian and Islamic interpretations of the economy have been shaken or even remolded by the collapse of the Communist alternative.

On the hundredth anniversary of the great encyclical of Leo XII, *Rerum Novarum,* defining the Catholic Church's doctrine in the face of the first Industrial Revolution and asserting the importance of both private property (if used responsibly) and a "just wage," John Paul II issued the encyclical *Centesimus Annus.* It is remarkable in its analysis of the shift in the character of economic activity. After a rough sketch of the history of economic development, it concludes that an order based on land was replaced (during the classical Industrial Revolution) by a system in which the control of capital was paramount; and that this primitive capitalism has now been succeeded by a more fluid and mobile world. Here "the decisive factor is increasingly man himself, that is, his knowledge, especially his scientific knowledge, his capacity for interrelated and compact organization, as well as his ability to perceive the needs of others and to satisfy them."[11] In other words, the modern market economy, the world of choice, is not subject to the structures and problems of classical capitalism.

The interaction between the individual and society depends on a constant human phenomenon, which the church analyzes in terms that the anticlerical and atheist Adam Smith would undoubtedly approve without qualification. Original sin means that the social order will be more stable if it "does not place in opposition personal interest and the interests of society as a whole, but rather seeks ways to bring them into fruitful harmony. In fact, where self-interest is violently suppressed, it is replaced by a burdensome system of bureaucratic control which dries up the wellsprings of initiative and creativity."[12]

From this, an analysis of the state and its role can be deduced. The major function of the state is to provide "sure guarantees of individual freedom and private property, as well as a stable currency and efficient public services."[13] The excessively overstretched state produces ethical as well as economic difficulties. These thoughts have their origins in deep reflection on the character of the collapse of Communist economies. The outcome is a criticism of modern Western welfare states in which ethical and pragmatic considerations overlap.

Islam traditionally has had an ethical code, in which—as in Christian thought—exploitative usury was forbidden, while lending could be rewarded only if there was a participation in risk. It is easy to develop an Islamic system of credit—in fact it is an equity culture—and Western banks can operate so-called Islamic windows quite unproblematically. On the other hand, the attempt since the Second World War to develop a separate science of Islamic economics was heavily dependent—as was liberation theology in the Christian world—on Marxist concepts. The result of the collapse of Marxism has consequently also been a deep crisis in the attempt to define anti-Western Islamic economics. It may therefore not come as a surprise that modern Iran is as much a part of the new consensus about the market economy as Brazil or India.

If religion is not likely to be a fruitful source of criticism, will there be a reaction against this modern consensus? There are at least four reasons for thinking that a violent rejection is inevitable. In shorthand, these are: the nostalgia of the ci-devants, the protest of the hand-loom weavers, the Zhirinovsky reaction, and the banana-skin effect.

1. The political implications of the new world are anti-elitist: they make the position of an entrenched elite defending privileges generated through state control of economic activity increasingly untenable. This group neither deserves much of our sympathy, nor is it likely to be very successful in hanging onto the doctrines that made it powerful. Indeed its main hope is now lawlessness—the phenomenon of nomenklatura privatization, whereby in the anarchy of the transformation process the old elite builds up a property position for the future. The threat in former Marxist states,

from the former Soviet Union to Africa, is not a revival of Marxism, but the likelihood of elite-sponsored chaos. There is a precise analogy with the aristocracy of pre-industrial Europe, the ci-devants (dispossessed nobles) of the French Revolution. Where this group clung to political power alone, as in France, it was rapidly overwhelmed. But where, as in Britain or parts of Germany, noblemen used the remnants of political power to move into the new industrial activities, and developed coal mines and steel mills, they were easily able to secure and guarantee their continuation as a social order. The only way for the old elite to rescue itself was by shifting from a monopoly of political power to one of economic power. This is the lesson that much of the nomenklatura has quite effectively learned.

2. More important, in a process of rapid technical and economic transformation it may be clearer who the losers are than who the eventual gainers will be (since inevitably no one can predict what sort of occupations and activities will emerge or whether he or she personally will be any good at them). Thus there is always a potential for a revolt of the losers. Like the similarly displaced hand-loom weavers of nineteenth-century Europe, who also found it very hard to envisage where their precarious future might lie, those displaced by today's technology are unlikely to be able to reshape politics.

3. There is a sort of schadenfreude that wants this cooperative process of mutually beneficial development to collapse, not because anyone will gain significantly from the crash but rather so that the costs can be imposed on some hate figure. This might be termed the Zhirinovsky reaction. Vladimir Zhirinovsky is not much of a politician, but he is a fine inventor of malicious aperçus. One of his most revealing is the question he asks of Russians: "Why should we create suffering for ourselves? We should create suffering for others."[14] It is surprising and perhaps gratifying how rare this reaction is, or how widely appreciated it is that the world economy is not a simple zero-sum game. Even in the peculiarly dramatic and colorful world of Russian politics, Zhirinovsky is treated as a clown, not a prophet.

4. When unexpected and unpleasant events take place, many blame the "system" as a whole and begin a search for alternatives. This is the "banana-skin" effect. We slip, and then we start to curse the whole world. Slipping on the banana skin is sometimes unavoidable. It is quite conceivable—indeed it is inevitable—that the new economic consensus will be challenged by dramatic crises, fiscal and financial. Market economies are dynamic and disruptive. And there is an underlying political problem.

In particular, states are faced by contradictory pressures: on the one hand, to reduce tax levels, because of the enhanced mobility of factors of production; and on the other traditional considerations requiring additional expenditure. Since the 1970s, the international capital markets have made it easier to finance deficits. They react sharply to unsustainable fiscal policies—not immediately, at the first signs of problems, but only at the last moment, with the result that the integrated world is likely to see more and more generalized financial and banking panics of the type currently experienced in Asia.

But is the liberalized economy really a "system"? Or is it not rather, as some critics who like the idea of more order sometimes complain, a "non-system." The character of the liberal economy lies in its governance only by general rules or laws, which do not envisage or intend specific or discriminatory outcomes. It might be said that the more any order is unplanned and the result of chance interactions, ideas, and developments, the less likely there is to be a coordinated effort to overthrow it. The more complex a system is, the less simple-minded ideas of planned alternatives are likely to appeal: centralization looked much more attractive and efficient in an era when industry was dominated by the production of a few basic goods.

New Panics

From the summer of 1997 to the summer of 1998, Asia dominated the financial headlines. There followed in 1998 an autumn of panic about the possibility of a truly global contagion. After 1997, many Americans and Europeans gloated about the end of the "Asian Miracle." Asian economies have indeed been shaken by a major crisis of confidence, one that contains the risk of a prolonged deflationary spiral. But it is already clear that the response will be greater liberalization of financial markets, the end of below-market interest credits, and an opening to foreign investors. There is no reason why growth cannot resume quite quickly—much more quickly than in Latin America, after the traumatic debt crises of the 1980s.

The Asian debate has been misleading as to where the fundamental problems lie in the relationship between markets and states. The greatest risk to the world economic order emanates from two opposing directions: from some of the richest and oldest industrial societies, and in societies as yet largely untouched by the globalization revolution. In geographical terms, Europe and Africa present the greatest dangers. In the former, there is too little flexibility in regard to expectations of what the state should do, and too much of a tendency to put reform proposals outside the pale of acceptable political discourse. These states rely on their credibility—on the confidence of the markets—to such an extent that they can prolong the outbreak of a severe fiscal crisis for the longest time. This perception stops politicians from reacting and innovating, even when the diagnosis of the malaise is unmistakable. The markets are less inclined to punish deficits and irresponsible behavior because market-makers are conventional and do not like to think the impossible. The result is that when and where crises occur here, they will be late and appear completely insoluble within the confines of the existing political order and current political expectations.

In Latin America or east Asia, markets are vigilant and blow up quickly as a result of inappropriate policy. The demonstration effects are readily apparent, and other emerging markets rapidly learn the lessons about the need for consistent policy. By contrast, the reserve of confidence in Europe creates a blockage of reforms.

In the other area, in the poorest economies, markets do not trust states at all, and the consequence is a profound current crisis of governability, in which the prerequisites for economic development are often destroyed. Here is another parallel with the original Industrial Revolution, which was politically far less problematical in its heartland, in western Europe and then the United States, than where its impact was more recent and explosive, and far more linked with political resentments: in eastern Europe and Russia, and in the colonial world.

The sustainability of the global economy depends on effective political reform in these two areas: in short, in a rethinking of both the European and the African models of development. The pursuit of a notion of a special route for development—the wrong approach to policy and to the role of the state—has badly damaged African economic and political stability. Frighteningly, the same diagnosis applies to continental Europe.

There is also an important political and constitutional element here. The nation-state was not a creature of the era of industrialism, but its existence helped to facilitate economic change by providing a stable legal framework. Now it is also worth preserving as an essential element of political order. But its future is threatened by the absence of reform. It will survive only if the expectations about what politics can do are reduced. Otherwise there will be an inexorable pressure to look to supranational institutions to impose an order where national governments are increasingly failing—to cut subsidies, to restore fiscal stability, to regulate banking. Already the European Union is being widely instrumentalized as a source of necessary discipline that states cannot impose on their own initiative. This phenomenon has produced across the continent disenchantment both with politics and with Europe itself. Such a mood will make any coming explosion more difficult to resolve.

The disenchantment with politics is reflected in the increasing prevalence of corruption scandals. It is no longer simply a matter of corruption as a way of life in the peculiar circumstances of post-Communist transition economies, notably Russia. In western Europe, the end of the Cold War broke some bands that had previously held political systems together. Ideology became less important, and many people began cynically to see in politics just a mechanism for distributing the spoils of political power. Italy has gone furthest along the path of de-ideologization and political disintegration, in that the two most influential governing parties of the Cold War era, the Christian Democrats and the Socialists, simply disappeared in mushrooming corruption scandals. Ministerial corruption ("sleaze") was a critical element in the widespread loss of confidence in the British Conservative party in the 1990s. Similar scandals continue to bring down ministers in France. A party financing scandal in Germany looks as if it could develop to almost Italian proportions and seriously weaken, if not destroy, the preeminent parties of the Bonn Republic, the Christian Democrats and the Social Democrats.

What makes the late twentieth century unique is the depth of skepticism with regard to the previous answer (a strong state) to the sin of globalization. The answer that Martin Luther gave in the German Reformation— the strengthening of the state and public power—was essentially the answer of the late nineteenth century also. It became the orthodoxy in the mid-twentieth century after wars and the Great Depression boosted state activities. But now the states look politically more unattractive—more sinful—than the markets.

We also have a very different view of what the sin of globalization involves. Most of the world has dramatically changed its attitude to economic and financial action. George Soros' criticism of modern financial capitalism rests on the observation that there exist fewer and fewer common values than bind a society together and that there has been a "general failure of politics both on the national and the international level."[15] One striking demonstration of the transformation of values is the way in which financial villainy is treated. This had been the stock story in the demonization of capitalism in the nineteenth and first half of the twentieth centuries. Are there really financial villains left in the world? The 1990s is much more forgiving. Nick Leeson, the Singapore trader whose activities brought down the venerable Barings Bank in 1995, is portrayed in film as an amiable man caught up in something much bigger. Michael Milken's insider trading is much less important to us than his invention of a new from of finance ("junk bonds") that drove a great part of the dynamism of the U.S. economy in the 1990s.

Speculation can really be quite positive in its effects, and more and more frequently is judged in this way. George Soros, who put together a "war chest" of £19 billion in the attack on the parity of the pound sterling within the European Monetary System's Exchange Rate Mechanism in 1992, and is estimated to have made a profit of £1 billion on what became more and more of a one-way bet, is generally treated as a hero rather than a villain. It is not simply that he is a reflective and interesting thinker, or that he has given large sums of money for educational and social projects in central and eastern Europe. It is rather that many recognize that the attack on the pound was actually a benevolent action, which ended a crazy exchange-rate regime. The financial humiliation of the British government in 1992 was not followed, as that of 1967 had been, by any outbursts against the "gnomes of Zurich." Instead it provoked a burst of intense self-criticism among the politicians, who had to acknowledge their responsibility for their mistaken policies. As one of the chief figures involved in the débacle, Norman Lamont, who had been chancellor of the Exchequer, put it in his resignation speech, "The trouble is that they [the government] are not even very good at politics, and they are entering too much into policy decisions. As a result, there is too much short-termism, too much reacting to events, and not enough shaping of events."[16] The lesson was that governments could no longer decide the fate of economies.

The de-demonization of finance is part of a democratization of financial activity. We are like the heroes or villains of the past when we tap e-trades into our home computers. As a consequence, we have a completely different concept of financial sin from that which stimulated those nineteenth-century critiques of capitalism analyzed in the first chapter. Marx's and Wagner's demons are now quite commonplace characters. It is no longer a question of mysterious gods of high finance in top hats: we are all part of the system.

Are there then alternative answers to the problems that may be caused by global chaos? It is commonplace to suggest that a new international order, and the threat of disorders on the capital markets, require a new international regulatory regime.

New Organization

One of the differences between the world of the late twentieth century and the world of depression economics is the complexity and strength of international organizations. To what extent is such a complicated system an effective protection mechanism? After all, in the 1920s there had been a highly sophisticated and at the same time visionary approach to the international order. All international economic movements could be subject to international surveillance and even control. Financial flows across frontiers were to be managed by central-bank cooperation, orchestrated by the Bank for International Settlements. The League of Nations would supervise economic stabilization and negotiate the removal of barriers to the flow of goods. The International Labour Organization would harmonize conditions of work, remove "unfair competition," and thus manage global labor markets. The generous and certainly exaggerated expectations vested in the new institutional arrangements were soon bitterly disappointed. The BIS was much too small, the World Economic Conferences were a fiasco, and the ILO an irrelevant sideshow.

The clearest case for the desirability of a role for international institutions is when there has been a failure of the state to perform basic functions. In some very poor countries a quite different question about the state and its role arises to that gripping the problematic welfare states of the industrial world. Good rule, stability, and respect for law and the law-making process are preconditions for effective economic reform and advance. But how can it be extended to these areas where at present there are anarchy and a disintegration of state structures? Some cynics might ask why the rest of the world should even care about the integration of other lands into a functioning world economy. One answer is that this is primarily a moral obligation, concerned with the realization of human potential. But the urgent need for a response can also be grounded in pragmatism or self-interest. For if these societies cannot export goods and participate in international society, they will not remain simply self-contained in a ghetto of misery and inhumanity. They will export their problems: their terrorism, their violence, and even their diseases.

International institutions will be crucial in resolving the crises arising here. They can provide a substitute for a domestic order that is not in place. An elaboration of the elements of the modern economic consensus makes clear the extent to which it reaches well beyond the simply technical spheres of economic management and into highly sensitive political areas. Of course, during the Cold War era economic assistance was frequently linked to political criteria: indeed the major economic crisis that in 1956 brought the IMF back into the center of the world financial system, Suez, was basically political in origin. Decisions in the 1970s to support Rumania or Yugoslavia followed a fundamentally political logic (as these were the planned economies furthest politically from the Soviet Union), as did the extensive assistance to Egypt or Zaire. Some Europeans complained that "Washington," a close and unhealthy working relationship between the U.S. administration and the Bretton Woods institutions, was illegitimately paying for American policies with "other people's money."[17]

The post–Cold War world has a quite different politics: no longer a line-up of East versus West, in which pro-western regimes automatically obtain support, regardless of levels of efficiency and competence and probity, but rather a much more interventionist stance in which the logic that associates economic and political change is taken much more seriously. The result has been the forcing of a much quicker pace of economic reform in some states (such as Egypt, which until the early 1990s largely resisted attempts to liberalize); the disintegration of the political order in others (the collapse and defeat of Mobutu's Zaire); and descent into the status of international pariah for others (Nigeria after the execution of Ken Saro-Wiwa). The striking change in this area is that there is no longer an acceptance of domestic political inefficiency, corruption, or oppression.

The collapse of the Communist economies or (in the case of China) their transformation into market economies was the last stage in the creation of the new consensus. The consequence has been an increasing homogeneity of political outlook, as well as of the economic order. Indeed, one key insight is that the two are linked: that economic efficiency depends on a functioning civil society, on the rule of law, and on respect for private property.

The most visible product of the new political environment is the concern of the Bretton Woods institutions with "governance." In August 1997 a new set of Guidance Notes from the IMF's Executive Board instructed the staff that in policy advice the IMF "has assisted its member countries in creating systems that limit the scope for ad hoc decision making, for rent seeking, and for undesirable preferential treatment of individuals or organizations." The IMF suggested that "it is legitimate to seek information about the political situation in member countries as an essential element in judging the prospects for policy implementation."[18]

The new political outlook had already been reflected in a number of very high-profile decisions of international institutions in 1996–97. Military spending had never been a topic of explicit discussion in the era of the Cold War. Now, in a number of cases, notably Pakistan and Rumania, it became a quite central element in Fund discussions. Corruption is now explicitly addressed—in Africa, but also in the case of Indonesia's crony capitalism. So too is democracy, although (unlike the European Bank for Reconstruction and Development) there is no reference to democracy in the Bretton Woods Articles of Agreement. Serbia was barred from the IMF on the basis of such a political argument. In the case of Croatia, in July 1997, the IMF withheld the release of a $40 million tranche of structural assistance for privatization, not because of any direct problems with the privatization program, but because of "the unsatisfactory state of democracy in Croatia."[19]

There had been some links with human-rights issues in the past—in Poland, where the membership application was held up in the 1980s after the imposition of martial law and the internment of political dissenters; and, more discreetly and subtly, in South Africa in the 1980s, where apartheid was attacked as an inefficient labor practice. But the scale of the discussion of political issues in the mid- and late 1990s is quite novel. The gradual extension of the IMF into politics is an immediate result of the new consensus about economic practice, and of a new world political order that it has helped to produce. But it reflects something more profound—a realization increasingly shared throughout the world that the world economy and world institutions can be better guarantors of rights and of prosperity than some governments, which may be corrupt and rent-seeking and militaristic.

There are many obvious problems in regard to the new position. One of the most fundamental is the political counterpart to the criticism expressed by Paul Volcker for Fund economic programs: "When the Fund consults with a poor and weak country, the country gets in line. When it consults with a big and strong country, the Fund gets in line. When the big countries are in conflict, the Fund gets out of the line of fire."[20] Dealing with military expenditure, corruption, and undemocratic practices is easier for international institutions in the cases of small countries such as Croatia or Rumania, or even in isolated states such as Pakistan or Nigeria. But it is likely to be hard and controversial in large states with substantial military and economic potential, such as Russia or China. In other cases, it will be interpreted as a flagrant attempt to impose Western values in the hope of restraining or even crippling potential competitors (the criticism frequently voiced by Mahathir Mohamad).

Second, there is the question of institutional capacity for implementation. Some recent programs and statements also go into the question of economic organization: the dismantling of cartels, the improvement of accounting practices, and banking supervision. It is easy to see the macroeconomic effects of the organizational or structural flaws criticized by the IMF. On the other hand, correcting them takes the IMF into completely new areas, in which it has no expertise. It is clearly experienced in fiscal affairs and in advising on central bank policy, but not in wide-ranging reforms of the financial sector and certainly not in accountancy. Many critics will wonder whether the specification and implementation of such advice are not better left to other institutions or to the concerned firms themselves.

Third, and most fundamentally, this process of adding new expectations will create a dangerous momentum of its own. Part of the package under discussion in the late 1990s in the U.S. Congress for an IMF quota increase involves the integration of environmental and labor standards into Fund programs. The same issues, once enunciated by the president of the United States, led to the débacle of the Seattle meeting of the WTO. Such demands reflect an expectations trap. The more the IMF is seen to extend its mandate, the more it will be expected to do; and inevitably also the less it will be able to live up to the demands. The consequence of this perception of failure is already clear in the mounting skepticism, even in the mainstream of political life, about the continued viability of the IMF. In order to counter such opposition, it will need to resist institutional overstretch: to ensure that its mandate is limited, clearly defined, and subject to an assessment of results.

Since the outbreak of the Asia crisis in the summer of 1997, critiques of the IMF have exploded, from almost every political direction. Common to many of the criticisms is the idea that the existence of international institutions constitutes a "moral hazard." States do not follow good policies, because they think that they will be bailed out. But more important, investors have no incentive to be prudent, because they believe that if they lend to a major country, they will be bailed out by the international community because it is frightened by the global implications of financial panics. It might be thought that this argument applies only to sovereign debt, for instance to the purchases in 1994 of Mexican government dollar-denominated short-term securities. But it does not require too much political ingenuity to see that lending to a large industry or bank in a big country, especially with good political connections, may be based on similar calculations. The government in the recipient country will be too anxious or too weak or too corrupt to let big companies fail, and they therefore have an implicit government guarantee. In this interpretation, which is very widespread, Mexico in 1994–95 provided a bad precedent, which encouraged the very rapid capital inflows to the Asian economies in the two subsequent years.

Another way of formulating the overstretch critique is to argue that the IMF and other international institutions are strengthening states that are incapable of efficient and just economic action. Such a point is most obvious in the case of failed states or states engulfed in civil war. The civil war in Tajikistan in the early 1990s was sometimes described as a struggle between rival gangs to control the fax machine connected with the IMF and the World Bank—and thus with money. A similar point has been made about ethnic conflict and genocide in Rwanda: the struggle for control of government was so important because it led to aid and thus power.

Such thinking often also lies behind the moral-hazard critique in the case of states that function much better: the incentives of the international system may lead them away from good policy.

The expectations overstretch that has partly crippled the IMF—or at least sent it into a profound phase of self-criticism and self-doubt—is even more characteristic of the brief history of the World Trade Organization. Trade issues are more politically sensitive than international monetary arrangements, for the reasons suggested in the foregoing analyses of trade and monetary policies in the depression era. Whereas money works abstractly and anonymously, the consequences of trade flows are immediately visible to every consumer. Trade is as a result much more a part of the political process. Resistance to globalism can easily be translated into trade policy terms: for rich industrial countries, resistance means using fair trade, labor standards, and environmental considerations to block imports from poorer countries that cannot meet ambitious and costly targets. For the developing world, such Western preconditions are hypocritical, masking a new protectionism in a cloak of concern about the international order. In fact the international institutions are, in this interpretation, being used as a lever to force an unfair globalism on the world. The handling of the Seattle WTO meeting by the United States—the lack of an effective agenda on the part of the chair, U.S. Trade Representative Charlene Barshefsky, and the apparent embracing of the cause of labor standards protection by the U.S. president—are all taken as evidence of the duplicity of the U.S. commitment to an international regime.

Here again the story of the depression era offers a grim warning. The international system—the politics of reparations and war debts, and the mechanisms devised to handle those political problems—became demonized as the source of international disorder. It was the unilateral protectionism of the United States in the Hawley-Smoot tariff that gave the most powerful of the early warning signals to financial markets in 1929 and helped to precipitate the financial contagion that provided the trigger mechanism in the collapse of globalization. The scale of financial movements has increased (but not, as many commentators would have it, incomparably) from those of the interwar world, creating a greater inherent vulnerability. To give some idea of the magnitudes involved, a capital outflow of less than $1 billion brought down Germany in 1931 (4 percent of GDP) and precipitated a world crisis; almost $30 billion in short-term capital flowed out of the United States in 1971 (less than 3 percent of GDP), destroying the Bretton Woods system; and over $100 billion (over 10 percent of GDP) flowed out of the Asian crisis economies in 1996 and 1997.[21]

In dealing with the consequences of globalization, there have been historically two institutional defense mechanisms. The first set out to develop new compensation mechanisms within existing political systems, on a state and national level. The second saw the process as a universal one, recognized the limitations on localist responses, and correspondingly tried to generate rules that went beyond the national level. Inevitably, in the second process, a good deal of national interest filtered through in a new guise, as a solution to a general, universal, and global challenge. Before the First World War, in the classic era of globalization and belief in progress, the former defensive mechanism was most politically successful and appealing. It gradually brought with it, through tariffs, monetary policy regulation, and immigration legislation, a series of obstacles to globality. After the

First World War, confronted with these obstacles, there was considerable energy and commitment behind an attempt to explore the second answer (as there was also after the Second World War). But after 1918, the international vision was hopelessly overburdened with expectations, and provoked a much more bitter backlash that radicalized the attempt to find national solutions.

Can such a backlash occur again? The case for optimism rests, perhaps curiously, on the extent of our disillusionment with institutions, both national and international. At the beginning of the new millennium, nobody would write about the United Nations or—more importantly for this argument—the IMF or the WTO with the passion and the commitment of the 1920s idealists who dreamed about the League of Nations and the Bank for International Settlements (although the president of the World Bank made a point of telling protesters in Prague calling for the abolition of his organization that he admired "their passion and their commitment").[22] Wilsonian rhetoric sounds jaded and passé. We have very reduced expectations of what institutions can offer. But the same disillusionment affects our view of national institutions and their capacity to respond to globalization and its problems.

The obviously political types of reaction against globalization—fascism, Stalinism, and their economic manifestations in managed trade and the planned economy—are forever discredited. There is in consequence little proclivity to see a political answer as solving the dilemmas of globalism and globalization. The French protesters against Seattle used the term *souverainisme* for the defense of the nation-state. But it is a defense that without any rationale will hardly appear attractive. National sovereignty, without a systematically worked out ideological justification and without any clear demonstration or proof of its success, is nothing more than an empty shell.

At present there is the beginning of an antiglobalist coalition, based on hostility to immigration (because of concerns about the labor market), a belief in capital controls (in order to prevent shocks emanating from the financial sector), and skepticism about global trade. There is plenty of anger against a multiplicity of targets—the acronym jungle of multinational corporations, international financial institutions, global capital, the new billionaires . . . But no one has shown convincingly how that anger makes sense or how it can be used productively in formulating alternative strategies. There is no coherent intellectual package that links the resentment. It is incoherent and allusive—in short, postmodern. It may, however, produce some policy initiatives.

Is there a model of antiglobal success? Some commentators see Mahathir's Malaysia as offering a path for nonorthodox economic success, based on state direction, capital controls, and anti-American rhetoric. But he is not as globally seductive as were Hitler and (especially) Stalin in the 1930s.

The absence of these two features—the intellectual cement and the specific model of national success—explains why the pendulum is so slow in swinging back from globality. But it does not and cannot explain why it will not swing.

NOTES
INDEX

$\blacklozenge \ \blacklozenge \ \blacklozenge$

Notes

1. Introduction

1. Joseph Stiglitz, "The Role of International Financial Institutions in the Current Global Economy," address to the Chicago Council on Foreign Relations, 27 February 1998; Paul Krugman, *The Return of Depression Economics* (New York: W. W. Norton, 1999), p. 166.
2. George Soros, *The Crisis of Global Capitalism: Open Society Endangered* (New York: Public Affairs, 1998), pp. 103, 134.
3. John Gray, *False Dawn: The Delusions of Global Capitalism* (London: Granta Books, 1998), p. 196.
4. Thomas Friedman, *The Lexus and the Olive Tree: Understanding Globalization* (New York: Farrar Straus, 1999), p. 269.
5. Kevin H. O'Rourke and Jeffrey G. Williamson, *Globalization and History: The Evolution of a Nineteenth-Century Atlantic Economy* (Cambridge, Mass.: MIT Press), 1999.
6. I have dealt extensively with the International Monetary Fund (IMF) in Harold James, *International Monetary Cooperation since Bretton Woods* (New York: Oxford University Press and IMF, 1996).
7. IMF, "External Evaluation of IMF Surveillance," Washington, D.C., 2000.
8. O'Rourke and Williamson, *Globalization and History*, p. 93.
9. Joseph A. Schumpeter, "The Instability of Capitalism," *Economic Journal* 38 (1928): 361, 386; also Richard Swedberg, *Schumpeter: A Biography* (Princeton: Princeton University Press, 1991), p. 83.
10. José Ortega y Gasset, 1933 lecture, in *Gesammelte Werke*, vol. 3 (Stuttgart: Deutsche Verlags-Anstalt, 1955), pp. 463–464. I owe this reference to Lionel Gossman.
11. Martin Luther, "Trade and Usury," in *Luther's Works: The Christian in Society*, ed. Walther I. Brandt, vol. 45 (Philadelphia: Muhlenberg Press, 1962), pp. 245–246.

12. Quoted in Thomas Brady, *The Politics of the Reformation in Germany: Jacob Sturm (1489–1553) of Strasbourg* (Atlantic Highlands, N.J.: Humanities Press International, 1997), p. 13.

13. Luther, "Trade and Usury," p. 258.

14. This is a point now very frequently made in historically informed literature on globalization: see Paul Hirst and Grahame Thompson, *Globalization in Question*, 2d ed. (Cambridge: Polity Press, 1999), pp. 19–65.

15. Theodor Fontane, *Der Stechlin* (1899; reprint, Cologne: Könemann, 1994), p. 5.

16. W. Arthur Lewis, *Growth and Fluctuations, 1870–1914* (London: Allen and Unwin, 1978), p. 181; Dudley Baines, *Emigration from Europe* (Cambridge: Cambridge University Press, 1995), p. 1.

17. Brinley Thomas, *Migration and Economic Growth* (Cambridge: Cambridge University Press, 1954); idem, *Migration and Urban Development: A Reappraisal of British and American Long Cycles* (London: Methuen, 1972).

18. Jeffrey G. Williamson, "Globalization, Convergence, and History," *Journal of Economic History* 56 (1996): 277–306; O'Rourke and Williamson, *Globalization and History*.

19. See Maurice Obstfeld and Alan M. Taylor, "The Great Depression as a Watershed: International Capital Mobility over the Long Run," in *The Defining Moment: The Great Depression and the American Economy in the Twentieth Century*, ed. Michael D. Bordo, Claudia D. Goldin, and Eugene N. White (Chicago: Chicago University Press, 1998), pp. 353–402; Maurice Obstfeld, "The Global Capital Market: Benefit or Menace," *Journal of Economic Perspectives* 12 (1998): 9–30.

20. See Robert C. Feenstra, "Integration of Trade and Disintegration of Production in the Global Economy," *Journal of Economic Perspectives* 12 (1998): 33.

21. Helmut Böhme, *Deutschlands Weg zur Grossmacht: Studien zum Verhältnis von Wirtschaft und Staat während der Reichsgründungszeit 1848–1881* (Cologne: Kiepenheuer, 1966), p. 94.

22. A point made by Ernest Gellner, *Nations and Nationalism* (Oxford: Basil Blackwell, 1983).

23. Adolph Wagner, *Die Ordnung des österreichischen Staatshaushalts* (Vienna: C. Gerold's Sohn, 1863).

24. On the relationship between external opening and an extension of governmental activity, see Dani Rodrik, *Has Globalization Gone Too Far?* (Washington, D.C.: Institute of International Economics, 1997).

25. E. E. Williams, *Made in Germany* (London: W. Heinemann, 1896), p. 11.

26. Paul Kennedy, *The Rise of the Anglo-German Antagonism, 1860–1914* (London: Routledge, 1980), p. 300.

27. Peter Flora et al., *State, Economy, and Society in Western Europe, 1815–1975*, vol. 1 (Frankfurt: Campus, 1983), pp. 381–382, 393.

28. Quoted in Michael Stürmer, *Das ruhelose Reich: Deutschland 1866–1918* (Berlin: Severin und Siedler, 1983), p. 49.

29. John Bodnar, *The Transplanted: A History of Immigrants in Urban America* (Bloomington: Indiana University Press, 1985), p. 93.

30. Quoted in Jeremy Adelman, *Frontier Development: Land, Labour and Capital on the Wheatlands of Argentina and Canada* (Oxford: Oxford University Press, 1994), p. 151.

31. See Max Weber, *Landarbeiterfrage, Nationalstaat, und Volkswirtschaftspolitik: Schriften und Reden, 1882–1889*, ed. Wolfgang J. Mommsen and Rita Aldenhoff, in Bayerische Akademie der Wissenschaften, *Max Weber Gesamtausgabe* I/4, 1 (Tübingen: Mohr, 1993), p. 183.

32. Quoted in Christoph Klessman, "Long-Distance Migration, Integration and Segregation of an Ethnic Minority in Industrial Germany: The Case of the 'Ruhr-Poles,'" in *Population, Labour and Migration in 19th- and 20th-Century Germany*, ed. Klaus J. Bade (Leamington Spa: Berg, 1987), p. 108.

33. Weber, *Landarbeiterfrage, Nationalstaat, und Volkswirtschaftspolitik*, p. 183.

34. Carlos Marichal, *A Century of Latin American Debt Crises* (Princeton: Princeton University Press, 1989).

35. Michael Bordo and Barry Eichengreen, "Is Our Current International Economic Environment Unusually Crisis Prone?" in *Capital Flows and the International Financial System* (Sydney: Reserve Bank of Australia, 1999), pp. 18–74.

36. Karl Helfferich, *Die Reform des deutschen Geldwesens nach der Gründung des Reiches*, vol. 2 (Leipzig, 1899), pp. 128–130, 136.

37. Charles Goodhart, *The Evolution of Central Banks* (Cambridge Mass.: MIT Press, 1988).

38. Alphonse Raffalovitch, *L'abominable vénalité de la presse, d'après les documents des archives russes* (Paris: Librairie du Travail, 1931); Michael D. Bordo and Hugh Rockoff, "The Gold Standard as a 'Good Housekeeping Seal of Approval,'" *Journal of Economic History* 56 (1996): 389–428.

39. Niall Ferguson, *The World's Banker: The History of the House of Rothschild* (London: Weidenfeld and Nicolson, 1998), pp. 628–630.

40. Jean Strouse, *Morgan: American Financier* (New York: Random House, 1999), p. 587.

41. See Hans Neisser, "Der internationale Geldmarkt vor und nach dem Krieg," *Weltwirtschaftliches Archiv* 29 (1929): 185.

42. Karl von Lumm, "Diskontpolitik," *Bank-Archiv* 11 (1912): 164.

43. See Dieter Ziegler, *Das Korsett der "Alten Dame": Die Geschäftspolitik der Bank of England, 1844–1913* (Frankfurt: Fritz Knapp, 1990).

44. *Berliner Actionair,* 6 and 23 November 1907.
45. *Volkswirtschaftliche Wochenschrift* (Vienna), 28 March 1907.
46. Raab in Reichstag, 15 January 1908, in *Stenographische Berichte über die Verhandlungen des Deutschen Reichstages,* vol. 229 (Berlin: Norddeutsche Buchdruckerei und Verlags-Anstalt, 1908), p. 2445.
47. Ibid., 14 January 1908, p. 2400.
48. Karl Marx, *Capital: A Critical Analysis of Capitalist Production,* trans. Samuel Moore and Edward Aveling, 3 vols. (London: Lawrence and Wishart, 1970–1974), 1: 714–715.
49. Ibid., p. 707.
50. Ibid., 3: 545.
51. Krugman, *The Return of Depression Economics,* pp. 118–19.
52. Quoted in Strouse, *Morgan,* p. 574.
53. John Kenneth Galbraith, "Introduction" to Robert Shaplen, *Kreuger: Genius and Swindler* (New York: Alfred A. Knopf, 1959), p. ix.
54. Lionel Robbins, *The Great Depression* (London: Macmillan, 1934), p. 63.
55. Marx, *Capital,* 3: 668–669.
56. *Lord Salisbury on Politics: A Selection from His Articles in the Quarterly Review, 1860–1883,* ed. Paul Smith (Cambridge: Cambridge University Press, 1972), pp. 47, 356–357. The article quoted was first published under the title "Disintegration" in October 1883.
57. A. J. Grant and Harold Temperley, *Europe in the Nineteenth Century (1789–1914)* (London: Longmans, 1927), p. 558.
58. Helmut Schmidt, "Vorsicht, Finanzhaie," *Die Zeit,* 8 October 1997, p. 3.
59. See Mark Mazower, *Dark Continent: Europe's Twentieth Century* (New York: Alfred A. Knopf, 1998).
60. Albrecht Ritschl, "Deutschlands Krise und Konjunktur 1924–1934: Binnenkonjunktur, Auslandsverschuldung und Reparationsproblem zwischen Dawes-Plan und Transfersperre" (Manuscript, 1997), p. 106.

2. Monetary Policy and Banking Instability

1. Graciela L. Kaminsky and Carmen M. Reinhart, "The Twin Crises: The Causes of Banking and Balance-of-Payments Problems," Board of Governors of the Federal Reserve System International Finance Discussion Papers no. 544 (March 1996).
2. Angela Redish, "The Latin Monetary Union and the Emergence of the International Gold Standard," in *Monetary Regimes in Transition,* ed. Michael Bordo and Forrest Capie (Cambridge: Cambridge University Press, 1993), pp. 68–85; Giulio Gallarotti, *The Anatomy of an International Monetary System* (New York: Oxford University Press, 1995); Barry Eichengreen and Marc

Flandreau, "The Geography of the Gold Standard," in *Currency Convertibility: The Gold Standard and Beyond,* ed. Jorge Braga de Macedo, Barry Eichengreen, and Jaime Reis, vol. 3 of *Explorations in Economic History* (London: Routledge, 1996), pp. 113–143.

3. Peter Temin, *Lessons from the Great Depression* (Cambridge, Mass.: MIT Press, 1989); Barry Eichengreen, *Golden Fetters: The Gold Standard and the Great Depression, 1919–1939* (New York: Oxford University Press, 1992).

4. John Kenneth Galbraith, "Introduction," in Robert Shaplen, *Kreuger: Genius and Swindler* (New York: Alfred A. Knopf, 1959), p. ix.

5. William Adams Brown, *The International Gold Standard Reinterpreted, 1914–1934* (New York: National Bureau of Economic Research, 1940), p. 749.

6. Per Jacobsson to Sir Otto Niemeyer, 30 November 1932, Bank of England Archive, London (hereafter BE) OV50/4. He added: "Unfortunately it is only too true that most experts are afraid of their masters to a quite appalling degree."

7. "Notes on Currency Questions," August 1924, League of Nations Archive, Geneva (hereafter LN) S123 (Salter Papers).

8. Montagu Norman to J. P. Morgan, 19 November 1927, BE G1/307.

9. Jacobsson, "Notes on a Conversation with Sir Otto Niemeyer," 13 December 1933, BE OV50/6.

10. Norman, preface to C. H. Kisch and W. A. Elkin, *Central Banks: A Study of the Constitution of Banks of Issue* (London, 1928), p. vi.

11. Compendium, "Principles of Central Banking," 1936, quoting Norman in 1921, BE OV50/8.

12. Benjamin Strong to Norman, 1 May 1927, BE G1/421.

13. Hjalmar Schacht to Norman, 6 November 1933, BE G1/415.

14. Niall Ferguson, *The Pity of War* (London: Allen Lane, 1998), p. 324.

15. Elizabeth Wiskemann, *Czechs and Germans: A Study of the Struggle in the Historic Provinces of Bohemia and Moravia* (London: Oxford University Press and Royal Institute of International Affairs, 1938), pp. 142–143.

16. For a detailed survey, see League of Nations, *The Financial Reconstruction of Austria* (Geneva, 1926) and *The Financial Reconstruction of Hungary* (Geneva, 1926); also Nicole Piétri, *La Société des Nations et la reconstruction financière de l'Autriche, 1921–1926* (Geneva: Centre Européen de la Dotation Carnegie pour Paix Internationale, 1970).

17. League of Nations, *Financial Reconstruction of Hungary,* p. 9.

18. Ibid., pp. 9, 18.

19. See Louis Pauly, "The League of Nations and the Foreshadowing of the International Monetary Fund," Princeton Essays in International Finance no. 201 (International Finance Section, Department of Economics, Princeton University, 1996).

20. Salter to Niemeyer, 14 April 1927, LN S123.

21. See Hans O. Schötz, *Der Kampf um die Mark 1923/4* (Berlin: de Gruyter, 1987).

22. Paul Warburg to Owen Young, 21 March 1924, Federal Reserve Bank of New York Archive, New York (hereafter FRBNY).

23. Sir Charles Addis to Frederick Leith-Ross (British Treasury), 28 July 1929, BE G1/1.

24. Bank for International Settlements (BIS), *Fifth Annual Report*, 1934–36, quoted in Eichengreen, *Golden Fetters*, p. 263.

25. Conversation between Pierre Quesnay and Norman, 24 April 1930, BE OV5/1.

26. Addis to Norman, 16 October 1929, BE G1/1. See also "Bank für internationalen Zahlungsausgleich," *Neue Zürcher Zeitung*, 30 January 1930.

27. Roger Auboin, "The Bank for International Settlements, 1930–1955," Princeton Essays in International Finance no. 22 (International Finance Section, Department of Economics, Princeton University, 1955).

28. Niemeyer memorandum, n.d., BE G1/1.

29. Norman to Addis, 19 October 1929, BE G1/1.

30. "Bank für internationalen Zahlungsausgleich," *Neue Zürcher Zeitung*, 30 January 1930.

31. E.g., Francis Rodd to Harry A. Siepmann, 2 September 1931, BE G1/4.

32. Niemeyer memorandum, BE G1/1.

33. Siepmann memorandum on telephone conversation with Rodd, Bank for International Settlements (hereafter BIS), 12 August 1930, BE G1/2.

34. HAS [Siepmann], note on telephone conversation with Rodd, 10 August 1930, BE G1/2.

35. Quesnay to Siepmann, attaching memorandum by Simon, 29 October 1930, BE OV4/84.

36. Memorandum (no signature), "Kindersley scheme," 2 February 1931, BE OV4/84.

37. Clément Moret to Gates McGarrah, 27 February 1931, BE OV4/84.

38. See Barry Eichengreen and Richard Portes, "After the Deluge: Default, Readjustment, and Readjustment during the Interwar Years," in *The International Debt Crisis in Historical Perspective*, ed. Barry Eichengreen and Peter Lindert (Cambridge, Mass.: MIT Press, 1989), pp. 12–47; also Barry Eichengreen and Richard Portes, "The Anatomy of Financial Crises," in *Threats to International Financial Stability*, ed. Richard Portes and Alexander K. Swoboda (Cambridge: Cambridge University Press, 1987), pp. 10–58; John T. Madden, *America's Experience as a Creditor Nation* (New York: Prentice-Hall, 1937), pp. 111–113.

39. Jacobsson, "Problems of International Financing," May 1936, BE OV50/6.

40. Gates McGarrah, cable to Thomas W. Lamont and Seymour Parker Gilbert, 18 March 1931, FRBNY 797.3 BIS.

41. Norman to George Harrison, 3 March 1931, BE OV4/84.

42. Report of Francqui subcommittee, 7 May 1931; McGarrah to Norman, 22 April 1931; BIS Board meeting, 18 May 1931; all BE OV4/84.

43. Charles H. Feinstein and Catherine Watson, "Private International Capital Flows in the Inter-War Period," in *Banking, Currency, and Finance in Europe between the Wars*, ed. Charles H. Feinstein (Oxford: Oxford University Press, 1995).

44. W. Arthur Lewis, "World Production, Prices and Trade, 1870–1960," *Manchester School of Economic and Social Studies* 20 (1952): 130.

45. F. G. Conolly memorandum (BIS), "International Short Term Indebtedness," October 1936, BE OV50/6 ($ = 5.165 Swiss francs).

46. Carl-Ludwig Holtfrerich, *The German Inflation, 1914–1923: Causes and Effects in International Perspective* (Berlin: de Gruyter, 1986), pp. 178, 288.

47. Feinstein and Watson, "Private International Capital Flows," p. 115.

48. League of Nations Economic Committee, Report on 36th session, 31 October 1930.

49. League of Nations, *World Economic Survey, 1932–33* (Geneva, 1933), pp. 137–138.

50. Rudolf Nötel, "Money, Banking, and Industry in Interwar Austria and Hungary," *Journal of European Economic History* 13, no. 2 (1984): 162.

51. Philip Cottrell, "1931: The Collapse of the Credit-Anstalt," University of Leicester, manuscript.

52. *The Banker,* 1929, p. 82.

53. G. W. F. Bruins report, 9 July 1931, BE OV 5/3.

54. Norman to Harrison, 25 May 1931, BE OV32.

55. Note, 15 May 1931, Banque de France Archive, Paris (hereafter BF), Austria file.

56. Conseil Général Procès-Verbaux, 13 July 1931, BF.

57. Charles P. Kindleberger, *The World in Depression* (Berkeley: 1986), p. 147.

58. Van Hengel report, 19 November 1932, LN C87; Deloitte Plender Binder to Austrian minister of finance, enclosing audited account of Creditanstalt (Schedule F), 3 October 1931, LN C88.

59. Rost van Tonningen to Kienböck and Rost to Frankenstein, 6 and 22 April 1932, LN C95.

60. *Financial Times* (London edition), 25 August 1998, p. 3. The IMF estimates the fiscal cost of the bank crises in Asian countries as higher than this level: 32 percent for Thailand, 29 percent for Indonesia, 18 percent for Malaysia, and 17.5 percent for Korea; International Monetary Fund, *World Economic Outlook and International Capital Markets: Interim Assessment* (Washington, D.C., 1998), p. 88.

61. Dieter Stiefel, *Die grosse Krise in einem kleinen Land* (Vienna: Böhlau, 1988), pp. 3 ff.

62. See Alice Teichova and Dieter Mosser, "Investment Behavior of Industrial Joint-Stock Companies and Industrial Shareholding by the Österreichische Credit-Anstalt," in *The Role of Banks in the Interwar Economy*, ed. Harold James, Hakan Lindgren, and Alice Teichova (Cambridge: Cambridge University Press, 1991), pp. 122–157.

63. Diane Kunz, *The Battle for Britain's Gold Standard, 1931* (London: Croom Helm, 1987), p. 47.

64. *L'avenir*, 10 October 1931.

65. *Annuaire statistique hongrois* (Budapest: Government Printing Office, various dates). See also Ivan T. Berend and Gyorgy Ranki, *Hungary: A Century of Development* (Newton Abbott: David and Charles, 1974), p. 146.

66. *Annuaire statistique hongrois* (Budapest: Government Printing Office, 1931), p. 125.

67. Michael C. Kaser, *The Economic History of Eastern Europe, 1919–1975*, vol. 2 (Oxford: Oxford University Press, 1986), p. 223.

68. HAS [Siepmann], note of conversation with Dr. Popovics, 9–10 February 1931; Popovics conversation with Per Jacobsson, 1 April 1931; both in BE, OV33/79.

69. Ibid.

70. Per Jacobsson (BIS), Report on the Budget and Exchequer Position in Hungary, April 1931, BE OV33/79.

71. McGarrah to Moret, 22 April 1931, BF, Hungary file; Popovics cable to Norman, 6 April 1931, BE G1/306.

72. Note, "Position of Hungarian Banks on the Principal Creditor Countries," 23 January 1932, BE OV33/80.

73. Per Jacobsson interview with Dr. Sándor Wekerle, 30 March 1931, BE OV33/79.

74. *The Banker*, April 1930, p. 38.

75. Harrison memorandum, 3 July 1931, FRBNY 2690.2.

76. Harrison cable to Norman, 8 July 1931, BE OV32.

77. Erika Jorgensen and Jeffrey Sachs, "Default and Renegotiation of Latin American Foreign Bonds in the Interwar Period," in Eichengreen and Lindert, *International Debt Crisis*, pp. 51–52.

78. Quoted in Ilse Mintz, *Deterioration in the Quality of Foreign Bonds Issued in the United States, 1920–1930* (New York: National Bureau of Economic Research, 1951), pp. 66, 81.

79. Robert Kindersley, "British Overseas Investments in 1932 and 1933," *Economic Journal* 44 (1934): 367.

80. Cleona Lewis, *America's Stake in International Investment* (Washington, D.C.: Brookings Institution, 1938), pp. 632–644.

81. Mintz, *Deterioration*.

82. Jorgensen and Sachs, "Default and Renegotiation," p. 54.

83. Brian R. Mitchell, *International Historical Statistics: The Americas and Australasia* (London: Macmillan, 1983), pp. 552–553, 820–821.

84. Jorgensen and Sachs, "Default and Renegotiation," p. 58.

85. Arturo O'Connell, "Argentina into the Depression: Problems of an Open Economy," in *Latin America in the 1930s: The Role of the Periphery in World Crisis,* ed. Rosemary Thorp (New York: St. Martin's Press, 1984), p. 208.

86. Mitchell, *International Historical Statistics,* p. 777.

87. Barrie A. Wigmore, *The Crash and Its Aftermath: A History of Securities Markets in the United States, 1929–1933* (Westport, Conn.: Greenwood Press, 1985), p. 205.

88. Albert Fishlow, "Lessons from the Past: Capital Markets during the 19th Century and the Interwar Period," *International Organization* 39 (1985): 383–439.

89. Carlos F. Díaz-Alejandro, "Latin America in the 1930s," in Thorp, *Latin America in the 1930s,* pp. 17–49.

90. Rosemary Thorp, *Progress, Poverty, and Exclusion: An Economic History of Latin America in the 20th Century* (Washington, D.C.: Inter-American Bank, 1998), pp. 113–117.

91. Díaz-Alejandro, "Latin America in the 1930s," p. 24; José Manuel Campa, "Exchange Rates and Economic Recovery in the 1930s: An Extension to Latin America," *Journal of Economic History* 50 (1990): 626–631.

92. See Pierluigi Ciocca and Gianni Toniolo, "Industry and Finance in Italy, 1918–1940," *Journal of European Economic History* 13, special issue (1984): 130–131.

93. John Kenneth Galbraith, *The Great Crash* (Harmondsworth: Penguin, 1961), p. 38.

94. See Sidney Pollard, *The Gold Standard and Employment Policies between the Wars* (London: Methuen, 1970); Robert W. D. Boyce, *British Capitalism at the Crossroads* (Cambridge: Cambridge University Press, 1987); Kunz, *Battle for Britain's Gold Standard.*

95. Milton Friedman and Anna J. Schwartz, *Monetary Trends in the United States and the United Kingdom and Their Relation to Income, Prices, and Interest Rates, 1867–1975* (Chicago: University of Chicago Press, 1982), pp. 289–290; also Allan H. Meltzer, *Keynes's Monetary Theory: A Different Interpretation* (Cambridge: Cambridge University Press, 1988), pp. 32–34.

96. Quoted in Alec Cairncross and Barry Eichengreen, *Sterling in Decline: The Devaluations of 1931, 1949, and 1967* (Oxford: Basil Blackwell, 1983), p. 64.

97. Committee of Treasury, 27 July 1931, BE G14/316.

98. See Robert S. Sayers, *The Bank of England, 1891–1944,* vol. 1 (Cambridge: Cambridge University Press, 1976), pp. 323–330.

99. Harrison to Nornan, 18 May 1931, BE OV32.

100. On Kleinworts see Stephanie Diaper, "Merchant Banking in the Interwar Period: The Case of Kleinwort Sons & Co.," *Business History* 28 (1986): 69–71.

101. Banks' Clearing House, Totals of Outstanding Foreign Exchange Contracts, 21 July 1931, BE C43/75: German forward purchases of foreign exchange amounted to £19,633,340, Austrian purchases to £2,347,833, and Hungarian purchases to £1,026,267.

102. Harlow and James to Chief Cashier, Bank of England, 7 October 1930, BE C43/75.

103. Frederick Hyde diary, entries for 15 and 21 July 1931, Hongkong and Shanghai Bank Corporation, Midland Bank archive.

104. Minutes of meeting (Beaumont Pease), 24 September 1931; minutes of meeting (McKenna), 25 September 1931; both in BE G15/3019.

105. *The Economist*, Banking Supplement, 14 May 1932, p. 4.

106. Sir William Goode to Prime Minister Ramsay MacDonald, 18 September 1931, BE OV48/9.

107. *Echo de Paris,* 20 September 1931.

108. "Very Secret, No Distribution," 20 September 1931, British Public Records Office (hereafter PRO) Cab. 60 (31).

109. See Barry Eichengreen and Olivier Jeanne, "Currency Crisis and Unemployment: Sterling in 1931," Centre for Economic Policy Research Discussion Paper no. 1898 (London, June 1998).

110. Quoted in Andrew Boyle, *Montagu Norman: A Biography* (London: Cassel, 1967), pp. 267–268.

111. [Siepmann?,] Conversation with Lord Passfield, 8 September 1931, BE OV48/9.

112. Ben Bernanke, "Nonmonetary Effects of the Financial Crisis in the Propagation of the Great Depression," *American Economic Review* 73 (1983): 257–276.

113. See Elmus Wicker, *The Banking Panics of the Great Depression* (Cambridge: Cambridge University Press, 1996), p. 92.

114. Milton Friedman and Anna J. Schwartz, *Monetary History of the United States, 1867–1960* (Princeton: Princeton University Press, 1967), p. 317.

115. Critics of the Federal Reserve system's policies make two points: that there would have been enough gold in the U.S. system to allow an expansion of the monetary base; and that the outflows of 1931 and 1932 were not analogous to the central European or British crises. After September 1931, it is claimed, most of the conversions were by other central banks, responding to losses from the sterling devaluation (but the drain was still interpreted as a dollar weakness); in the spring of 1932, it is said, there cannot have been a general panic, as Canada, South America, and the Far East were all still shipping gold to the United States and not participating in the European withdrawals. The

clearest exposition of this critical case is in Michael D. Bordo, Ehsan U. Choudhri, and Anna J. Schwartz, "Was Expansionary Monetary Policy Feasible during the Great Contraction? An Examination of the Gold Standard Constraint," National Bureau of Economic Research Working Paper no. 7125 (Cambridge, Mass., May 1999).

116. Herbert Stein, *The Fiscal Revolution in America* (Chicago: University of Chicago Press, 1969), p. 37.

117. Quoted in William J. Barber, *From New Era to New Deal: Herbert Hoover, the Economists, and American Economic Policy, 1921–1933* (Cambridge: Cambridge University Press, 1985), p. 120.

118. Stein, *Fiscal Revolution,* p. 33.

119. Burgess to Harvey telephone call, 22 March 1932, FRBNY C261.

120. Hambro to Harvey telephone call, 30 May 1932 (memorandum of 2 June 1932), FRBNY 3117.2.

121. Crane note, 2 June 1932, FRBNY 3117.2.

122. Friedman and Schwartz, *Monetary History,* p. 423.

123. Barry A. Wigmore, "Was the Bank Holiday of 1933 Caused by a Run on the Dollar?" *Journal of Economic History* 47 (1987): 745.

124. Peter Temin and Barry Wigmore, "The End of One Big Deflation," *Explorations in Economic History* 27 (1990): 483–502.

125. Wicker, *Banking Panics,* pp. 108 ff.

126. Wigmore, "Bank Holiday of 1933," p. 749.

127. Barber, *From New Era to New Deal,* p. 142.

128. Wicker, *Banking Panics,* p. 125.

129. Kenneth S. Davis, *FDR: The New York Years, 1928–1933* (New York: Random House, 1985), pp. 371, 367.

130. Samuel I. Rosenman, comp., *The Public Papers and Addresses of Franklin D. Roosevelt,* vol. 2: *The Year of Crisis, 1933* (New York: Random House, 1938), p. 264.

131. Estimate of foreign short-term funds in Paris, 24 October 1933, BE OV45/6; Cobbold memorandum on visit to Paris, 24 October 1933, BE OV 45/83.

132. Memorandum, "French Gold," 19 July 1931, BE OV45/5.

133. Charles Cariguel to Crane telephone call, 15 July 1932, FRBNY C261.

134. *Les nouvelles financières et économiques,* 3 June 1932.

135. Cariguel to Crane telephone call, 20 April 1933, FRBNY C261.

136. League of Nations, *Public Finance, 1935* (Geneva, 1935), France, p. 4.

137. Quoted in Gordon Wright, *Rural Revolution in France: The Peasantry in the Twentieth Century* (Stanford: Stanford University Press, 1964), pp. 13–14.

138. Conseil Général Procès-Verbaux, 26 February 1931, BF. These figures were never released to the Chamber of Deputies.

139. Moret to finance minister, 19 March 1931, BF B84.

140. HAS [Siepmann] memorandum for Mr. Powell, 12 August 1930, BE OV45/81.

141. Moret to Norman telephone call, 28 October 1930, BE 45/81.

142. Conseil Général Procès-Verbaux, 27 November 1930, BF.

143. See Fernand de Brinon, "Le franc et la politique," *L'information*, 10 May 1933.

144. Ministry of Commerce to Finance Ministry, 21 May 1931; Report of Comité régional, 13 February 1931; both in BF B84.

145. Conseil Général Procès-Verbaux, 17 February 1932, BF.

146. Jean Bouvier, "The French Banks: Inflation and Economic Crisis, 1919–1939," *Journal of European Economic History* 13, no. 2 (1984): 50.

147. Conseil Général Procès-Verbaux, 6 December 1928, BF.

148. Ibid., 6 February 1933.

149. Ibid., 6 April 1933.

150. Ernest Rowe-Dutton memorandum, 7 May 1934, BE OV45/7; Conseil Général Procès-Verbaux, 29 March 1934, BF.

151. Service Nationale de Statistiques and Institut de Conjoncture, *Mouvement économique en France de 1929 à 1939* (Paris: Imprimerie Nationale, 1941), p. 203.

152. Figures calculated from statistics in BF B30.

153. Cariguel to Crane telephone call, 5 March 1935, FRBNY C261.

154. Cariguel to Crane telephone call, 15 April 1935, FRBNY C261.

155. See Kenneth Mouré, "Une eventualité absolument exclue: French Reluctance to Devalue, 1933–1936," *French Historical Studies* 15 (1988): 479–505.

156. Rowe-Dutton, note of conversation with Robert Lacour-Gayet, 28 May 1935, BE OV45/8.

157. *Journal des finances*, 29 November 1935.

158. L. Werner Knoke to Cariguel telephone call, 16 May 1935, FRBNY 261.

159. Marc Perrenoud, "Banques et diplomatie suisse à la fin de la Deuxième Guerre mondiale," *Schweizerisches Bundesarchiv Studien und Quellen* 13–14 (1988): 17; Légation suisse aux Pays Bas, 1 July 1933, Swiss National Archive, Bern (hereafter SNA) E2001 (c) 3/147.

160. Interpellation 138, 7 December 1936; Konferenz betreffend Kapitalanlagen im Ausland, 28 January 1937, both in SNA 6100 (a) 14/814.

161. Schulthess to Finanzdepartement, 16 May 1935, SNA E6100 (a)/691.

162. Robert U. Vogler, "Das Bankgeheimnis: Seine Genese im politisch-wirtschaftlichen Umfeld" *Schweizer Monatshefte* 80, no. 3 (2000): 37–43.

163. Protokoll der interdepartementalen Konferenz zur Besprechung unsere wirtschaftlichen und finanziellen Beziehungen zu Deutschland, 23 May 1932, SNA E2001 (c) 3/146.

164. S.E.D. to Finanzdepartement, 7 June 1934, SNA E2001 (c)/524.

165. Meeting in Nationalbank, 4 February 1933, SNA E7800/1/99.

166. See Ginette Kurgan-van Hentenryk, "Finance and Financiers in Belgium," in

Finance and Financiers in European History, ed. Youssef Cassis (Cambridge: Cambridge University Press, 1992), pp. 317–335; and Guy Vanthemmsche, "State, Banks, and Industry in Belgium and the Netherlands," in James, Lindgren, and Teichova, *Role of Banks in Interwar Economy,* pp. 104–121.

167. Richard T. Griffiths, ed., *The Netherlands and the Gold Standard, 1931–193: A Study in Policy Formation and Policy* (Amsterdam: NEHA, 1987), pp. 201–202.

168. Ibid., p. 96.

169. Pierre Renou, *La dévaluation du franc suisse: ses causes, ses effets, son enseignement* (Bordeaux: Delmas, 1939).

170. Miles Fletcher, "Japanese Banks and National Eonomic Policy 1920–1936," in James, Lindgren, and Teichova, *Role of Banks in Interwar Economy,* pp. 254–255.

171. Eleanor M. Hadley, "The Diffusion of Keynesian Ideas in Japan," in *The Political Power of Economic Ideas: Keynesianism across Nations,* ed. Peter A. Hall (Princeton: Princeton University Press, 1989), pp. 292–294; Shinju Fujihira, "Conscripting Money: Total War and Fiscal Revolution in the Twentieth Century" (Ph.D. diss., Princeton University, 2000).

172. Caroline M. Betts, Michael D. Bordo, and Angela A. Redish, "Small Open Economy in Depression: Lessons from Canada in the 1930s," *Canadian Journal of Economics* 29 (1996): 1–36.

173. Ian M. Drummond, "Why Canadian Banks Did not Collapse in the 1930s," in James, Lindgren, and Teichova, *Role of Banks in Interwar Economy,* pp. 232–250.

174. Governors' meeting, 11 December 1932, BE OV5/6.

175. *Report of the Gold Delegation of the Financial Committee* (Geneva: League of Nations, 1932), p. 24.

176. Bonn, Mlynarski, and Chalendar to President of Gold Delegation, 12 January 1932; Jung to Trip, 8 January 1932; both in LN R2962.

177. Crane memorandum, 12 November 1931, FRBNY 797.41.

178. Kaminsky and Reinhart, "The Twin Crises." The most thorough recent survey of the literature is Graciela L. Kaminsky, Saul Lizondo, and Carmen M. Reinhart, "Leading Indicators of Currency Crises," *IMF Staff Papers* 45 (1998): 1–48.

3. Tariffs, Trade Policy, and the Collapse of International Trade

1. W. Arthur Lewis, "World Production, Prices and Trade, 1870–1960," *Manchester School of Economic and Social Studies* 20 (1952): 105–138.

2. Calculated from Alfred Maizels, *Industrial Growth and World Trade* (Cambridge: Cambridge University Press, 1963).

3. League of Nations, *World Production and Prices, 1937/8* (Geneva, 1938). See

also Douglas A. Irwin, "The GATT in Historical Perspective," *American Economic Review* 85, no.3 (May 1995): 324.

4. League of Nations, *World Production and Prices, 1925–1932* (Geneva, 1933), p. 39.

5. John Maynard Keynes, "National Self-sufficiency," *Yale Review,* June 1933; Dennis Holme Robertson, "The Future of International Trade," *Economic Journal* 48, no. 189 (1938): 1–14. See also Werner Sombart, *Die deutsche Volkswirtschaft im 19. Jahrhundert* (Berlin: G. Bondi, 1909).

6. Economic Policy Committee, 24 April 1933, in *Documents on German Foreign Policy, 1918–1945, Series C: The Third Reich, The First Phase* (Washington, D.C.: U.S. Government Printing Office, 1957), doc. 182, p. 337.

7. Robertson, "Future of International Trade," p. 9.

8. Maizels, *Industrial Growth and World Trade,* p. 192.

9. Committee on Industry and Trade, *Survey of Overseas Markets* (London, 1925).

10. Maizels, *Industrial Growth and World Trade,* p. 228.

11. Heinrich Liepmann, *Tariff Levels and the Economic Unity of Europe: An Examination of Tariff Policy, Export Movements and the Economic Integration of Europe, 1913–31* (London: G. Allen and Unwin 1938), p. 165.

12. Klaus E. Knorr, *World Rubber and Its Regulation* (Stanford: Stanford University Press, 1945).

13. This sort of calculation is the basis of the analysis of trade offered by Beth A. Simmons, *Who Adjusts? Domestic Sources of Foreign Economic Policy during the Interwar Years* (Princeton: Princeton University Press, 1994), p. 176.

14. Anne O. Krueger, "The Political Economy of a Rent-seeking Society," *American Economic Review* 64, no. 3 (June 1974): 291–303. Charle Kershaw Rowley and Robert D. Tollison, "Rent-seeking and Trade Protection," in *Protectionism and Structural Adjustment,* ed. Heinz Hauser (Grüsch: Verlag Rügger, 1986), pp. 141–166; Bruno S. Frey, *International Political Economics* (Oxford: Basil Blackwell, 1984).

15. Simmons, *Who Adjusts?* pp. 198–202.

16. John A. C. Conybeare, "Tariff Protection in Developed and Developing Countries: A Cross-sectional and Longitudinal Analysis," *International Organization* 37, no. 3 (Summer 1983): 441–467; Stephen D. Krasner, "State Power and the Structure of International Trade," *World Politics* 28, no. 3 (April 1976): 317–343.

17. See Harry G. Johnson, "An Economic Theory of Protectionism, Tariff Bargaining and the Foundation of Customs Unions," *Journal of Political Economy* 73 (1965): 256–283; Bruno S. Frey and Friedrich Schneider, "International Political Economy: A Rising Field," *Economia Internazionale* 37, no. 3 (1984): 3–42.

18. Daniel Verdier makes an intriguing case for the nondeterminancy of political

outcomes on trade issues in democracies: *Democracy and International Trade: Britain, France, and the United States, 1860–1990* (Princeton: Princeton University Press, 1994).

19. Brian R. Mitchell, *European Historical Statistics: The Americas and Australasia* (London: Macmillan, 1983).

20. Pierre Barral, *Les Agrariens français de Méline à Pisani* (Paris: A. Colin, 1968), p. 223.

21. See Frank William Taussig, *The Tariff History of the United States* (New York: G. P. Putnam's Sons, 1931). Taussig played a key role in working out the Democratic position on tariff reduction.

22. Liepmann, *Tariff Levels and Economic Unity,* pp. 58–59.

23. Arthur Fischer Bentley, *The Process of Government: A Study of Social Pressures* (Chicago: University of Chicago Press, 1908).

24. Quoted in Daniel Rodgers, *Contested Truths: Keywords in American Politics since Independence* (New York: Basic Books, 1987), p. 181.

25. Elmer Schattschneider, *Political Pressures and the Tariff: A Study of Free Private Enterprise in Pressure Politics as Shown in the 1929–1930 Revision of the Tariff* (New York: Prentice-Hall, 1935), p. 86.

26. Robert A. Pastor, *Congress and the Politics of U.S. Foreign Economic Policy, 1929–1976* (Berkeley: University of California Press, 1980), p. 80.

27. See Charles S. Maier, *Recasting Bourgeois Europe: Stabilization in France, Germany, and Italy in the Decade after World War I* (Princeton: Princeton University Press, 1975).

28. See Karl-Heinrich Pohl, *Weimars Wirtschaft und die Aussenpolitik der Republik, 1924–1926* (Düsseldorf: Droste Verlag 1979), especially pp. 278 ff.

29. Posse to Ritter, 26 July 1927, in *Akten zur Deutschen Auswärtigen Politik: Aus dem Archiv des Auswärtigen Amtes,* Series B, vol. VI (Göttigen: Vandenhoeck und Ruprecht, 1974), doc. 68, pp. 139–41.

30. Ritter to Posse, 5 July 1927, ibid., doc. 6, pp. 15–16.

31. Posse to Ritter, 12 July 1927, ibid., doc. 25, pp. 51–54.

32. Liepmann, *Tariff Levels and Economic Unity,* pp. 116–117; Bernhard Harms, *Strukturwandlungen der Weltwirtschaft* (Jena: Fischer, 1927).

33. Liepmann, *Tariff Levels and Economic Unity,* p. 117.

34. H. J. Hutchinson note, "Safeguarding of Industries: Commercial Motor Vehicles," Public Record Office, London (hereafter PRO), T172/1513.

35. Charles Kindleberger, "Commercial Policy between the Wars," in *Cambridge Economic History of Europe,* vol. 7 (Cambridge: Cambridge University Press, 1989), p. 167; John Bell Condliffe, *The Reconstruction of World Trade: A Survey of International Economic Relations* (New York: W. W. Norton, 1940).

36. League of Nations, *The World Economic Conference, Geneva, May 1927, Final Report* (Geneva, 1927), p. 31.

37. See Johnson, "An Economic Theory of Protectionism."

38. Speech by Colijn, 14 January 1931, LN R2668.

39. See Hal B. Lary and Wayne C. Taylor, *The United States in the World Economy: The International Transactions of the United States during the Interwar Period* (Washington, D.C.: Bureau of Foreign and Domestic Commerce, 1943), pp. 171–172.

40. Joseph Marion Jones Jr., *Tariff Retaliation: Repercussions of the Hawley-Smoot Bill* (Philadelphia: [n.p.], 1934), p. 87.

41. Ibid., pp. 108, 122.

42. Resolution, 9 November 1929, LN R3589.

43. Quoted in Jones, *Tariff Retaliation,* p. 265.

44. On the failure of Briand, see Robert D. Boyce, "Britain's First 'No' to Europe: Britain and the Briand Plan," *European Studies Review* 10, no. 1 (January 1980): 18–45.

45. Leith-Ross to de Bordes, 19 December 1931; Ritter to de Bordes, 17 December 1931; both in LN S69.

46. Federation of British Industry resolution, 10 February 1932, PRO T172/1513.

47. PRO Cab. CP 41 (32); discussed at cabinet meeting of 27 April 1932, Cab. 9 (32).

48. W. J. Clarke (director of National Federation of Iron and Steel) to Chamberlain, 19 February 1932; Maj.-Gen. Alfred Knox, M.P. for Wycombe, to Chamberlain, 9 February 1932; both in PRO T172/1513.

49. See Forrest Capie, *Depression and Protectionism: Britain between the Wars* (London: Allen and Unwin, 1983), pp. 77–95; and, on the IDAC, Clemens Wurm, *Business, Politics, and International Relations: Steel, Cotton, and International Cartels in British Politics, 1924–1939* (Cambridge: Cambridge University Press, 1993).

50. Quoted in Capie, *Depression and Protectionism,* p. 25.

51. Quoted in Richard Norman Kottmann, *Reciprocity and the North Atlantic Triangle, 1932–1938* (Ithaca: Cornell University Press, 1968), p. 21.

52. See David L. Glickman, "The British Imperial Preference System," *Quarterly Journal of Economics* 61, no. 3 (May 1947): 439–470; Donald MacDougall and Rosemary Hutt, "Imperial Preference: A Quantitative Analysis," *Economic Journal* 64, no. 254 (June 1954): 233–257.

53. Cabinet meeting, 15 March 1933, PRO C18/33.

54. Cabinet meeting, 28 November 1932, PRO C47/32.

55. Cabinet meeting, 27 August 1932, RO C46/32.

56. League of Nations, *Review of World Trade, 1936* (Geneva, 1936), p. 42.

57. Report and Draft Resolution submitted by the Second Committee to the Assembly, 23 September 1931, LN R2915.

58. David Marquand, *Ramsay MacDonald* (London: Jonathan Cape, 1977), p. 721.

59. Hoesch cable, 20 December 1930; Curtius to Hoesch, 29 December 1930;

both in Politisches Archiv des Auswärtigen Amtes, Bonn (hereafter PA/AA), W21A.

60. Castle memorandum, 29 October 1930, State Department 462.00, R266/5027, National Archives, Washington, D.C. (hereafter NA).

61. Second meeting of Monetary Subcommittee, 1 November 1932, LN R2672.

62. Third meeting of Preparatory Committee, 7 November 1932, LN R2671.

63. Organizing Committee note, 22 November 1932, LN R2670.

64. *The Guardian,* 26 October 1932.

65. Posse to Berger, 12 January 1933, PA/AA W21A.

66. Pietro Stoppani, "First reflections on the Preparatory Commission's Task in regard to international trade," 26 October 1932, LN R2671.

67. Meeting, 7 November 1932, LN R2671.

68. Stimson to MacDonald, 27 January 1933, PRO 30/69/678.

69. The best treatment of the conference is Patricia Clavin, *The Failure of Economic Diplomacy: Britain, Germany, France, and the United States, 1931–36* (London: Macmillan, 1996).

70. Hoesch cable, 5 April 1933, PA/AA W21A/6.

71. *Foreign Relations of the United States, 1933,* vol. 1 (Washington, D.C.: U.S. Government Printing Office, 1953), p. 621.

72. Memorandum, "Dem Herrn Reichsminister vorzulegen für die Unterredung mit Norman Davis," 10 April 1933, PA/AA W21A/6.

73. Aussenminister to Staatssekretär in der Reichskanzlei, 11 April and 4 May 1933, PA/AA 21A/6 and 21A/7.

74. *Documents on German Foreign Policy,* doc. 312, quotations pp. 563–564, 567.

75. Krogmann cable, 7 July 1933, PA/AA 21A/12.

76. *New York Times,* 4 May 1933.

77. *Washington Post,* 16 May 1933.

78. Report of German delegation, 15 July 1933, PA/AA 21A/14.

79. Pastor, *Congress and Foreign Economic Policy,* p. 83.

80. Hull to H. Wallace, 25 December 1934, Hull Papers, reel 50.

81. H. Clay memorandum on conversation with Riefler, 16 June 1936, BE OV31/27.

82. Dodd to Hull, 19 May 1934, Hull Papers, reel 11.

83. T. W. Page to Hull, 25 January 1933, Hull Papers, reel 9.

84. Hull memorandum, 1 June 1934, Hull Papers, reel 50.

85. See Thomas Ferguson, "From Normalcy to New Deal: Industrial Structure, Party Competition, and American Public Policy during the Great Depression," *International Organization* 38, no. 1 (1984): 86–92. A much more skeptical view is presented by Stephan Haggard, "The Institutional Foundations of Hegemony: Explaining the Reciprocal Trade Agreements Act of 1934," *International Organization* 42, no. 1 (1988): 91–120.

86. Pastor, *Congress and Foreign Economic Policy,* p. 91; Lawrence H. Chamber-

lain, *President, Congress, and Legislation* (New York: Columbia University Press, 1946), pp. 131–132.

87. Henry J. Tasca, *The Reciprocal Trade Policy of the United States: A Study in Trade Philosophy* (Philadelphia: University of Pennsylvania Press, 1938).

88. *U.S. Congressional Record*, 4 February 1937.

89. Memorandum: "Situation of the Cotton Industry," 19 April 1935, Hull Papers, reel 33, 63/274.

90. Kottmann, *Reciprocity*, p. 217.

91. Tim Rooth, *British Protectionism and the International Economy: Overseas Commercial Policy in the 1930s* (Cambridge: Cambridge University Press, 1993), pp. 288–289.

92. Memorandum, 27 October 1933, BE OV31/23.

93. Daniels to Hull (and Roosevelt), 17 August 1934, Hull Papers, reel 11.

94. See especially Richard Overy, *War and Economy in the Third Reich* (Oxford: Oxford University Press, 1994), pp. 93–118.

95. See Dietrich Eichholtz, "Das Expansionsprogramm des deutschen Finanzkapitals am Vorabend des zweiten Weltkriegs," in *Der Weg in den Krieg*, ed. Dietrich Eichholtz and Kurt Pätzold (Cologne: Pahl-Rugenstein 1989), pp. 1–40.

96. See League of Nations, *World Economic Survey, 1934/5* (Geneva, 1935), pp. 176–178.

97. Second meeting of Ministry of Agriculture and Fisheries Committee, 22 April 1933, PRO MAF 40/12.

98. Morgenthau cable for Wallace, 5 July 1933, in *Foreign Relations of the United States, 1933*, 1: 808–809.

99. Richard C. Snyder, "Commercial Policy as Reflected in Treaties from 1931 to 1939," *American Economic Review* 30, no. 4 (December 1940): 792.

100. Albert O. Hirschman, "Statistical Study of the Trend of Foreign Bilateral Trade toward Equilibrium and Bilateralism," in *Studies in the Surplus Approach: Political Economy* 4, no. 1 (1988): 111–124.

101. Pier Francesco Asso, "Bilateralism, Trade Agreements, and Political Economics in the 1930s: Theories and Events Underlying Hirschman's Index," ibid., pp. 85, 95.

102. Rooth, *British Protectionism*, pp. 126–43.

103. Ansprache des Reichsbankpräsidenten Dr. Hjalmar Schacht auf dem 8. Allgemeinen Bankiertag zu Berlin am 10. Mai 1938, Bavarian State Archive, Munich, MWi 414, pp. 6–7.

104. Howard Sylvester Ellis, *Exchange Control in Central Europe* (Cambridge, Mass: Harvard University Press, 1941), pp. 128–129.

105. Alan S. Milward, "The Reichsmark Bloc and the International Economy," in *The "Führer State": Myth and Reality*, ed. Gerhard Hirschfeld and Lothar Kettenacker (Stuttgart: Klett-Cotta, 1981), p. 378.

106. Royal Institute of International Affairs, *South-Eastern Europe: A Brief Survey* (London: Oxford University Press, 1940), p. 121. See also Ellis, *Exchange Control in Central Europe.*

107. See Philippe Marguerat, *Le IIIe Reich et le pétrole roumanin, 1938–1940* (Leiden: A. W. Sijthoff, 1977).

108. Ellis, *Exchange Control in Central Europe,* quoted in Larry Neal, "The Economics and Finance of Bilateral Clearing Agreements," *Economic History Review* 32, no. 3 (1979): 395.

109. Milward, "Reichsmark Bloc," p. 401.

110. Robert M. Spaulding, *Osthandel and Ostpolitik: German Foreign Trade Policies in Eastern Europe from Bismarck to Adenauer* (Providence: Berghahn, 1987), pp. 263–265.

111. Ibid., p. 257.

112. Albert O. Hirschman, *National Power and the Structure of Foreign Trade* (Berkeley: University of California Press, 1945), pp. 29–34.

113. Ibid., p. 39.

114. Douglas A. Irwin and Barry Eichengreen, "Trade Blocs, Currency Blocs, and the Reorientation of World Trade in the 1930s," *Journal of International Economics* 36 (1995): 1–24.

115. Henry Kissinger, *Diplomacy* (New York: Simon and Schuster, 1994), pp. 290–291.

116. League of Nations, *Prices and Production, 1937/8* (Geneva, 1938), pp. 84–85.

117. League of Nations, *Review of World Trade, 1938* (Geneva, 1938), p. 34.

118. Erika Jorgensen and Jeffrey Sachs, "Default and Renegotiation of Latin American Foreign Bonds in the Interwar Period," in *The International Debt Crisis in Historical Perspective,* ed. Barry Eichengreen and Peter Lindert (Cambridge, Mass.: MIT Press, 1989), pp. 48–85.

119. Report of the Finance Ministry, 13 June 1931, BE OV 102/1.

120. PA/AA Argentinien Finanzen 16/1.

121. Board of Trade, "Draft first report of the Subcommittee for Exchange Restrictions in South and Central America," 2 February 1933, BE OV 102/2.

122. *The Economist,* 22 October 1932; R. Gravil and T. Rooth, "A Time of Acute Dependence: Argentina in the 1930s," *Journal of European Economic History* 7 (1978): 347.

123. Sir Otto Ernest Niemeyer (1883–1971), from 1927 adviser to the Governor, Bank of England, from 1932 director of BIS.

124. Clay to Osborne, 4 February 1933, BE OV102/2.

125. Niemeyer cable to Hambro, 9 February 1933, BE G1/401.

126. Niemeyer cable to Hambro, 27 February 1933, BE G1/402.

127. Niemeyer cable to Hambro, 28 January 1933, BE G1/403. See in general Alberto Hueyo, *La Argentina en la depresion mundial* (Buenos Aires: Liberia editorial "El Ateneo," 1938).

128. Niemeyer cable to Hambro, 19 February 1933, BE G1/403.

129. C. Hambro memorandum, 20 March 1933, BE OV102/2.

130. Kelly interview with Argentine Ambassador, 30 August 1933, PRO 371/16534; also Gravil and Rooth, "A Time of Acute Dependence," p. 365.

131. Cabinet meeting, 15 March 1933, PRO C18/33.

132. Gravil and Rooth, "A Time of Acute Dependence," p. 350.

133. Prebisch to Ritter, 7 August 1934, HaPol Ritter Argentinien, Bd. 1, PA/AA.

134. *Rivista de economía argentina* 36 (1936): 233, 228.

135. Memorandum by Schwarte (IG Farben), 27 January 1937, Handakten Clodius, PA/AA.

136. German embassy to Auswärtiges Amt, 22 July 1936; Schlotterer memorandum, 15 December 1936; both in Argentinien Handel 13, PA/AA.

137. Kiep Aktennotiz, 5 November 1936; Thermann (German minister in Buenos Aires) cable to Auswärtiges Amt, 6 November 1936; both in HaPol Ritter, Argentinien, Bd. 2, PA/AA.

138. See for instance the list of complaints in Schlotterer to Fricke, 13 January 1937, ibid.

139. Thermann Aufzeichnung, 18 August 1940, Kriegsgerät Argentinien, PA/AA.

140. D. W. Giffin, "The Normal Years: Brazilian-American Relations, 1930–1939" (Ph.D. diss., Vanderbilt University, 1962), p. 200.

141. League of Nations, *Review of World Trade, 1938,* p. 54.

142. Ritter notes on interview with Brazilian ambassador, 15 October 1936, Brazilien Handel 11/1, PA/AA.

143. Ritter interview, 6 August 1936; Fricke memorandum, 5 October 1936; both in Brazilien Handel 13/2, PA/AA.

144. Stanley E. Hilton, *Brazil and the Great Powers, 1930–1939: The Politics of Trade Rivalry* (Austin: University of Texas Press, 1975), p. 105.

145. *New York Times,* 2 January 1937.

146. *Wall Street Journal,* 17 July 1937.

147. Hilton, *Brazil and the Great Powers.*

148. Confidential report, Bankers Trust Company, March 1938, Brazilien Handel 12, Bd. 1, PA/AA.

149. Ritter cable to Auswärtiges Amt, 14 July 1938, ibid.

150. First meeting of Latin America conference, 12 June 1939, Clodius Handakten Argentinien 5, PA/AA.

151. Niemeyer at second session of Committee on Clearing Agreements, 25–30 March 1935; Loveday to H. R. Cummings, 3 May 1935; both in LN R4422.

152. A. P. Rosenholz, *Fifteen Years of the Foreign Trade Monopoly of the U.S.S.R.* (Moscow: Cooperative Publishing Society of Foreign Workers in the U.S.S.R, 1933), p. 5.

153. Interview in 1927, quoted in J. D. Yanson, *Foreign Trade in the U.S.S.R.* (New York: Putnam, 1935), p. 24.

154. Quoted in Edward H. Carr and Robert W. Davies, *Foundations of a Planned Economy, 1926–1929,* vol. 1 (Harmondsworth: Penguin, 1974), p. 750.

155. Ibid., p. 747.

156. Yanson, *Foreign Trade,* p. 57.

157. Ibid., p. 55.

158. Jacob Viner, *International Trade and Economic Development* (Glencoe, Ill.: Free Press, 1952), p. 109.

159. Nicolas Spulber, *The Soviet Economy: Structures Principles Problems* (New York: W. W. Norton, 1969), pp. 255–269.

160. Yanson, *Foreign Trade,* p. 30.

161. Quoted in Richard B. Day, *The "Crisis" and the "Crash": Soviet Studies of the West (1917–1939)* (London: New Left Books, 1981), p. 202.

162. Paul R. Gregory, *Before Command: An Economic History of Russia from Emancipation to the First Five-Year Plan* (Princeton: Princeton University Press, 1994), p. 129.

163. Carr and Davies, *Foundations,* p. 757.

164. Glenn A. Smith, *Soviet Foreign Trade: Organization, Operations, and Policy, 1918–1971* (New York: Praeger, 1973), p. 16.

165. Yanson, *Foreign Trade,* p. 120; Harold James, *The Reichsbank and Public Finance in Germany, 1924–1933* (Frankfurt: Fritz Knapp, 1985), p. 309; Hartmut Pogge von Strandmann, "Industrial Primacy in German Foreign Relations? Myths and Realities in Russian-German Relations at the End of the Weimar Republic," in *Social Change and Political Development in Weimar Germany,* ed. Richard Bessel and Ernst J. Feuchtwanger (London: Croom Helm, 1981), p. 94.

166. James, *Reichsbank and Public Finance,* p. 308; Andrew J. Williams, *Trading with the Bolsheviks: The Politics of East-West Trade, 1920–39* (Manchester: Manchester University Press, 1992), p. 161.

167. Spaulding, *Osthandel and Ostpolitik,* p. 268.

168. Robert Conquest, *The Great Terror: Stalin's Purges of the 1930s* (Harmondsworth: Penguin, 1971), pp. 220–258.

169. Isaac Deutscher, *Stalin: A Political Biography* (London: Oxford University Press, 1949), pp. 340–341.

170. Vladislav Zubok and Constantine Pleshakov, "The Soviet Union," in *The Origins of the Cold War in Europe: International Perpectives,* ed. David Reynolds (New Haven: Yale University Press, 1994), pp. 60, 62.

171. Calculated from U.S. Bureau of the Census, *Statistical Abstract of the United States* (Washington, D.C.: U.S. Department of Commerce, 1949); League of Nations, *Review of World Trade, 1938,* p. 60.

172. See also Folke Hilgerdt, "The Approach to Bilateralism—A Change in the Structure of World Trade," *Index Svenska Handelsbanken* 10 (1935): 175–188; Kindleberger, "Commercial Policy between the Wars," pp. 188–190.

173. See John S. Odell, *U.S. International Monetary Policy: Markets, Power, and Ideas as Sources of Change* (Princeton: Princeton University Press, 1982); Stephen D. Krasner, "United States Commercial and Monetary Policy: Unraveling the Paradox of External Strength and Internal Weakness," in *Between Power and Plenty: Foreign Economic Policies of Advanced Industrial States,* ed. Peter J. Katzenstein (Madison: University of Wisconsin Press, 1978); Joanne S. Gowa, "Public Goods and Political Institutions: Trade and Monetary Policy Processes in the United States," *International Organization* 42, no. 1 (1988): 15–32.

4. The Reaction against International Migration

1. Barry Eichengreen and Timothy J. Hatton, "Interwar Unemployment in International Perspective: An Overview," in *Interwar Unemployment in International Perspective,* ed. Eichengreen and Hatton (Dordrecht: Kluwer, 1988), pp. 6–7.

2. David Marquand, *Ramsay MacDonald* (London: Jonathan Cape, 1977), p. 537.

3. Barry Eichengreen and Jeffrey Sachs, "Exchange Rates and Economic Recovery in the 1930s," *Journal of Economic History* 45 (December 1985): 925–946; Ben Bernanke and Harold James, "The Gold Standard, Deflation, and Financial Crisis in the Great Depression: An International Comparison," in *Financial Markets and Financial Crises,* ed. R. Glenn Hubbard (Chicago: University of Chicago Press, 1991); Ben Bernanke and Kevin Carey, "Nominal Wage Stickiness and Aggregate Supply in the Great Depression," *Quarterly Journal of Economics* 111 (August 1996): 852–883; Michael D. Bordo, Christopher J. Erceg, and Charles L. Evans, "Money, 'Sticky Wages,' and the Great Depression," NBER Working Paper 6071, June 1997.

4. Barry Eichengreen, *Golden Fetters: The Gold Standard and the Great Depression, 1919–1939* (New York: Oxford University Press, 1992), p. 16.

5. George S. Bain and Robert Price, *Profiles of Union Growth: A Comparative Statistical Portrait of Eight Countries* (Oxford: Blackwell, 1980), pp. 88, 123, 133, 142.

6. A. M. Endres and K. E. Jackson, "Policy Responses to the Crisis: Australasia in the 1930s," in *Capitalism in Crisis: International Responses to the Great Depression,* ed. W. R. Garside (London: Pinter, 1993), pp. 157, 161.

7. R. G. Gregory, V. Ho, L. McDermott, and Jim Hagan, "The Australian and

U.S. Labour Markets in the 1930s," in Eichengreen and Hatton, *Interwar Unemployment in International Perspective*, pp. 397–420.

8. Anthony P. O'Brien, "A Behavioral Explanation for Nominal Wage Rigidity during the Great Depression," *Quarterly Journal of Economics* 104 (November 1989): 719–736.

9. Lionel Robbins, *The Great Depression* (London: Macmillan, 1934), pp. 60–61.

10. Edwin Cannan, "The Post-War Unemployment Problem," *Economic Journal* 40, no. 157 (March 1930): 45–55; Jacques Rueff, "Les variations du chomage en Angleterre," *Revue politique et parlementaire* 125 (1925).

11. David K. Benjamin and Levis A. Kochin, "Searching for an Explanation of Unemployment in Interwar Britain," *Journal of Political Economy* 87 (June 1979): 441–478.

12. Barry Eichengreen, "Unemployment in Interwar Britain: New Evidence from London," *Journal of Interdisciplinary History* 27 (Autumn 1986): 335–358.

13. W. R. Garside, *British Unemployment, 1919–1939: A Study in Public Policy* (Cambridge: Cambridge University Press, 1990), p. 101.

14. Knut Borchardt, "Constraints and Room for Manoeuvre in the Great Depression of the Early Thirties: Towards a Revision of the Received Historical Picture," in *Perspectives on Modern German Economic History and Policy* (Cambridge: Cambridge University Press, 1991), pp. 143–160; Theo Balderston, *The Origins and Course of the German Economic Crisis, 1923–1932* (Berlin: Haude and Spener, 1993), p. 16.

15. Balderston, *Origins and Course*, pp. 36–43; Johannes Bähr, *Staatliche Schlichtung in der Weimarer Republik: Tarifpolitik, Korporatismus, und industrieller Konflikt zwischen Inflation und Deflation, 1919–1932* (Berlin: Colloquium Verlag, 1989).

16. Quoted in John W. Gregory, *Human Migration and the Future: A Study of the Causes, Effects and Control of Emigration* (London: Seley Service, 1928), p. 113.

17. Michael A. Bernstein, *The Great Depression: Delayed Recovery and Economic Change in America, 1929–1939* (New York: Cambridge University Press, 1987), pp. 84, 92.

18. Peter Temin, *Did Monetary Forces Cause the Great Depression?* (New York: W. W. Norton, 1976), pp. 66–67, citing George C. Galster, "Immigration Activity and Construction Activity in the 1920s" (Paper, Massachusetts Institute of Technology, 1972).

19. See Claudia Goldin, "The Political Economy of Immigration Restriction in the United States, 1890 to 1921," in *The Regulated Economy: A Historical Approach to Political Economy*, ed. Claudia Goldin and Gary D. Libecap (Chicago: University of Chicago Press, 1994), pp. 223–257.

20. *Proceedings of the World Population Conference* (London: Edward Arnold, 1927), p. 276.

21. Arthur M. Carr-Saunders, *World Population: Past Growth and Present Trends* (Oxford: Oxford University Press, 1936), p. 196.

22. Quoted in John W. Follows, *Antecedents of the International Labour Organization* (Oxford: Clarendon Press, 1951), p. 3.

23. James T. Shotwell, ed., *The Origins of the International Labor Organization*, 2 vols. (New York: Columbia University Press, 1934), 1: 4.

24. Follows, *Antecedents*, p. 24.

25. Hartmut Pogge von Strandmann, ed., *Walther Rathenau: Industrialist, Banker, Intellectual and Politician: Notes and Diaries, 1907–1922* (Oxford: Oxford University Press, 1985), p. 224.

26. Shotwell, *Origins*, 1: 17.

27. Ibid., pp. 225–226.

28. Francis Graham Wilson, *Labor in the League System: A Study of the International Labor Organization in Relation to International Administration* (Stanford: Stanford University Press, 1934), pp. 334–335.

29. Quoted in address of Albert Thomas, "International Migration and Its Control," *Proceedings of the World Population Conference*, 1927, p. 262.

30. Shotwell, *Origins*, 2: 180–181.

31. Quoted in Wilson, *Labor in the League System*, p. 284.

32. Quoted in ibid., p. 285.

33. SNA E 6351 (F) 1, 521.

34. Carr-Saunders, *World Population*, p. 158.

35. René Del Fabbro, *Transalpini: Italienische Arbeitswanderung nach Süddeutschland im Kaiserreich 1870–1918* (Osnabrück: Rasch, 1996), p. 84.

36. The most detailed account of the link between inflation experience and wage bargaining is to be found in Balderston, *Origins and Course*. See also Bähr, *Staatliche Schlichtung*.

37. Thomas, "International Migration," quotations pp. 256–257, 264.

38. Brian R. Mitchell, *European Historical Studies, 1750–1970* (London: Macmillan, 1978), p. 29.

39. Stephen Kotkin, *Magnetic Mountain: Stalinism as a Civilization* (Berkeley: University of California Press, 1995), p. 34.

40. Louise Young, *Japan's Total Empire: Manchuria and the Culture of Wartime Imperialism* (Berkeley: University of California Press, 1998), pp. 213, 231.

41. Claudio G. Segrè, *Fourth Shore: The Italian Colonization of Libya* (Chicago: University of Chicago Press, 1974), pp. 83, 93, 95.

42. Hans Grimm, *Volk ohne Raum* (Munich: Alobert Langen, 1928), pp. 10–11.

43. Quoted in Ian Kershaw, *Hitler, 1889–1936: Hubris* (New York: W. W. Norton, 1999), p. 249.

44. *Hitler's Secret Book*, trans. Salvator Attanasio (New York: Grove Press, 1961), p. 19.

45. Kershaw, *Hitler*, p. 442.

46. Rainer Zitelmann, *Hitler: Selbstverständnis eines Revolutionärs* (Stuttgart: Klett, 1987), pp. 311–317.

47. Klaus Hildebrand, *Das vergangene Reich: Deutsche Aussenpolitik von Bismarck bis Hitler 1871–1945* (Stuttgart: DVA, 1995), p. 638.

48. "Poland's Efforts to Obtain a Common Frontier with Hungary," *National Minorities* 1 (January–March 1939): 41–45.

49. Joseph Roth, *Die Kapuzinergruft* (Bilthoven: De Gemeenschap, 1938), p. 207.

5. The Age of Nationalism versus the Age of Capital

1. Klaus A. Langweit, ed., *Hitler: Reden, Schriften, Anordnungen*, vol. 5, pt. 1: *Februar 1925 bis Januar 1933* (Munich: Saur, 1996), p. 284.

2. John Galsworthy, *The Forsyte Saga* (New York: Scribner, 1933), p. 665.

3. Martin Gregor-Dellin, ed., *Richard Wagner: Mein Denken* (Munich: Piper, 1982), p. 174.

4. Gerald D. Feldman, *The Great Disorder: Politics, Economics and Society in the German Inflation, 1914–1924* (New York: Oxford University Press, 1993), pp. 200–202.

5. Helen B. Junz, "Report on the Pre-War Wealth Position of the Jewish Population in Nazi-Occupied Countries, Germany, and Austria," in Independent Committee of Eminent Persons, *Report on Dormant Accounts of Victims of Nazi Persecution in Swiss Banks* (Bern: Staempfli, 1999), p. A-180.

6. André Bouton, "Note sur l'état dans l'Ouest de l'opinion concernant les finances publiques," February 1936, BF Devaluation file IX.

7. Ministry of Finance archive (hereafter FFM), B18675.

8. Etat-Major de l'Armée, 2e Bureau, 2 April 1936, FFM B18675.

9. Cobbold note, 29 January 1935, BE OV45/84; Tannery to Norman, 8 May 1936, BF England.

10. *Humanité*, 22 and 5 November 1935.

11. *Le petit parisien*, 13 April 1936.

12. *Journal officiel de la République Française: Débats parlementaires, Chambre des Députés*, 15e legislature, 34e séance, 3 December 1934, p. 2947.

13. René Girault, "Léon Blum, la dévaluation, et la conduite de la politique extérieure de la France," *Relations internationales* 13 (1978): 98; also Robert Frankenstein, *Le prix du réarmement français, 1935–1939* (Paris: Publications de la Sorbonne, 1982), pp. 130–131.

14. John Morton Blum, *From the Morgenthau Diaries: Years of Crisis, 1928–1938* (Boston: Houghton Mifflin, 1959), pp. 155–159.

15. Ernest Rowe-Dutton to Sigismund Waley, 19 July 1937, BE OV45/12.
16. Gold Movements, 18–31 May 1936, BF B30.
17. Rowe-Dutton to Waley, 14 May 1936, BE OV 34/10. *Commentaires*, 24 November 1935, claimed that Paribas (as well as Lazards) was sympathetic to devaluation.
18. Report of Inspector Général Bloch, 1937, BF B34.
19. Frankenstein, *Le prix du réarmement français*, p. 129.
20. On the connections between these events, see ibid., p. 137.
21. Jean Bouvier, "The French Banks, Inflation, and the Economic Crisis, 1919–1939," *Journal of European Economic History* 13, no. 2, special issue (1984): 72.
22. Note (unsigned) on Paris visit, 8 December 1937, BE OV45/86.
23. On the relative insignificance of the Tripartite Pact, except as a political statement of solidarity with Britain and the United States, see Ian Drummond, *London, Washington, and the Management of the Franc, 1936–1939* (Princeton: Princeton University Press, 1979).
24. Blum, *Morgenthau Diaries*, pp. 457–459.
25. HAS [Siepmann], note on telephone call from Leith Ross (Treasury), 4 March 1937, BE OV45/11.
26. Cobbold memorandum: "Some views expressed by M. Jean Monnet this afternoon," 8 July 1937, BE OV45/12.
27. Frankenstein, *Le prix du réarmement français*, pp. 74–83.
28. Drummond, *London, Washington, and the Franc*, pp. 45–46.
29. Lacour memorandum, 15 July 1938, BF B34.
30. N. E. Young, note on interview with Charles Rist, 23 May 1939, BE OV34/86.
31. See Frankenstein, *Le prix du réarmement français*, p. 101.
32. Gottfried Haberler, *Prosperity and Depression: A Theoretical Analysis of Cyclical Movements* (Geneva: League of Nations, 1939); Ragnar Nurkse, *International Currency Experience: Lessons from the Inter-War Period* (Geneva: League of Nations, 1944).
33. John Maynard Keynes, "National Self-Sufficiency," in *Collected Writings of John Maynard Keynes*, vol. 21: *Activities, 1931–1939* (London: Macmillan, 1982), p. 236; translated and published as "Nationale Selbstgenügsamkeit," in *Schmollers Jahrbuch* (Munich: Duncker and Humblot, 1934), pp. 565–566. On the German translation, see Knut Borchardt, "Keynes' Nationale Selbstgenügsamkeit von 1933," *Zeitschrift für Wirtschafts- und Sozialwissenschaften* 108 (1988): 271–284.
34. Arthur Salter, *Recovery: The Second Effort* (London: G. Bell, 1932).
35. André Gide, *The Journals*, trans. Justin O'Brien, vol. 4 (New York: Alfred A. Knopf, 1951).
36. Thomas Balogh, "The National Economy of Germany," *Economic Journal* 48 (September 1938): 460–497; idem, *The Dollar Crisis, Causes and Cures: A*

Report of the Fabian Society (Oxford: Blackwell, 1950); idem, "Welfare and Freer Trade—A Reply," *Economic Journal* 61 (March 1951): 72–82; idem, *Germany: An Experiment in "Planning" by the "Free" Price Mechanism* (Oxford: Blackwell, 1951), pp. 58–72; idem, *The Irrelevance of Conventional Economics* (London: Weidenfeld and Nicolson, 1982), pp. 2–3. See also Harry G. Johnson, *Economic Nationalism in Old and New States* (Chicago: University of Chicago Press, 1967), pp. 131–132 ("The infiltration of ideas from Central Europe into the Anglo-Saxon tradition did a great deal to implant the habit of thinking in nationalist rather than cosmopolitan terms into the Western economic tradition and to establish the fictional concept of the nation as an economic entity endowed with consistent objectives and a consensus in favor of realizing them by national economic policy").

6. Conclusion

1. Thomas Friedman, *The Lexus and the Olive Tree: Understanding Globalization* (New York: Farrar Straus, 1999), pp. 207–210.
2. Most prominently, Roger Bootle, *The Death of Inflation: Surviving and Thriving in the Zero Era* (London: Nicholas Brealey, 1996).
3. Marina v. N. Whitman, *New World, New Rules: The Changing Role of the American Corporation* (Boston: Harvard Business School Press, 1999), pp. 9, 209.
4. Quoted in "Malaysia Acts on Market Fall," *Financial Times,* 4 September 1997.
5. For a discussion of this debate, see Branko Milanovic and M. Lundberg, "Globalization and Inequality: Are They Linked, and How?" World Bank, Washington, D.C., 2000; Vincent Mahler, David Jesuit, and Douglas Roscoe, "Exploring the Impact of Trade and Investment on Income Inequality," *Comparative Political Studies* 32 (May 1999). A much more alarmist view is found in Adrian Wood, *North-South Trade, Employment, and Inequality* (Oxford: Oxford University Press, 1994).
6. Patrick Low, *Trading Free: The GATT and U.S. Trade Policy* (New York: Twentieth Century Fund Press, 1995), p. 247.
7. Douglas A. Irwin, *Against the Tide: An Intellectual History of Free Trade* (Princeton: Princeton University Press, 1996), p. 19.
8. *New York Times,* 31 August 1997, pp. A1, A6.
9. Dani Rodrik, *Has Globalization Gone Too Far?* (Washington, D.C.: Institute for International Economics, 1997).
10. Vito Tanzi and Ludger Schildknecht, "The Growth of Government and the Reform of the State in Industrial Countries," IMF Working Paper 95/130, Washington, D.C., December 1995.

11. *Centesimus Annus* (1 May 1991), http://www.vatican.va/holy_father/ john_paul_ii/encyclicals/documents/hf_jp_ii_enc_01051991_centesimus_ annus_en.html, sec. 33.

12. Ibid., sec. 25.

13. Ibid., sec. 48.

14. As quoted by Chrystia Freeland, "Blood Sweat and Tears—For Others," *Financial Times*, 9 December 1993.

15. George Soros, *The Crisis of Global Capitalism: Open Society Endangered* (New York: Public Affairs, 1998), p. 102.

16. Quoted in Philip Stephens, *Politics and the Pound: The Conservatives' Struggle with Sterling* (London: Macmillan, 1996), p. 285.

17. Klaus Engelen, "Angst and Anger: Why Germans Hate the IMF and the World Bank," *International Economy*, October 1988.

18. *IMF Survey* 26/15, 5 August 1997, pp. 233–236.

19. *Financial Times*, 31 July 1997.

20. Paul Volcker and Toyoo Gyohten, *Changing Fortunes: The World's Money and the Threat to American Leadership* (New York: Times Books, 1992), p. 143.

21. Harold James, *The German Slump: Politics and Economics, 1924–1936* (Oxford: Oxford University Press, 1986), p. 294, on the reduction of German short-term borrowing by 3 million RM in the year preceding the 1931 crisis; idem, *International Monetary Cooperation since Bretton Woods* (New York: Oxford University Press, 1996), p. 214, on the outflow of $29.6 billion in 1971; Joseph Stiglitz, "Must Financial Crises Be This Frequent and Painful?" in *The Asian Financial Crisis: Causes, Contagion and Consequences*, ed. Pierre-Richard Agénor, Marcus Miller, David Vines, and Axel Weber (Cambridge: Cambridge University Press, 1999), p. 390, on an outflow of $109 billion.

22. James Wolfensohn, quoted in *The Guardian* (London), 27 September 2000.

Aachen, Congress of (1818), 174
Abyssinia, 183
Addis, Sir Charles, 42
Agricultural interests, 111–113
Agricultural prices, 57, 65, 102, 104, 113, 129, 145–146
Angell, Norman, 12
Anti-Semitism, 188–189
Aquinas, Thomas, 206
Aranha, Oswaldo, 155–157
Argentina, 12, 64–65, 67–68, 145–146, 177; banks, 66; central bank, 36, 151; depression, 146–152; Roca-Runciman agreement, 132, 147–149; trade policies, 146–147
Asia: financial and economic crisis of 1997, 17, 26, 32, 65, 200, 208, 213–214, 220–222; wage conditions, 176–177
Auriol, Vincent, 193–194
Australia, 12, 28–29, 63, 126; immigration, 15; wage bargaining, 171
Austria: Anschluss (1938), 184, 195; bank crisis, 53–57, 71, 98–99; budget, 56; exchange control, 46–47; League of Nations stabilization, 36, 38; Nationalbank, 20, 141; trade policy, 126, 141

Bähr, Johannes, 171
Bailouts, 56
Balcerowicz, Leszek, 209
Balderston, Theo, 171
Balfour Committee, 107
Balogh, Thomas, 198

Bankers Trust, 86
Bank for International Settlements (BIS), 5, 41–48, 97, 217; decline in 1930s, 95
Bank of England, 20, 35, 45, 69–70, 190; and devaluation, 73–74; and private banks, 72–73
Bank of United States, 76
Banque de France, 20, 54, 73, 84, 190; and devaluation, 87; internal structure, 192, 194; links with commercial banks, 85–86, 195–196
Barings, 20, 216
Barshefsky, Charlene, 222
Belgium: bank problems, 51; gold standard, 91–92; stabilization, 40
Benjamin, David, 170
Bennett, Richard, 121, 125
Bentley, Arthur Fischer, 114
Bernanke, Ben, 169
Bilateralization of trade, 140, 163–166
Binder, Hamlyn, 55
Blanqui, Jérome, 175
Blum, Léon, 191, 194–195
Bodenkreditanstalt, 53–54, 71
Bolivia, 152; default, 46, 64, 66, 146
Bonar Law, Andrew, 118
Bonnet, Georges, 195
Borah, William, 135
Borchardt, Knut, 171
Boyce, Robert, 68
Brazil, 3, 26, 28, 100, 126; bank problems, 66; central bank, 36; depreciation and default, 46, 64–66, 73; trade policies, 144, 146, 152–157

Bretton Woods conference (1944), 43, 166, 205

Briand, Aristide, 25, 122

Brüning, Heinrich, 92, 128

Brussels conference (1920), 36

Buchanan, Patrick, 202

Bülow, Bernhard von, 132

Bülow tariff, 101

Bulgakov, Mikhail, 163

Bulgaria, 142–143

Caldwell and Company, 76

Canada: central bank, 36, 195; immigration, 15–16, 174; and imperial preference, 125–126; protectionism, 121, 125–126; and world depression, 94–95, 116, 145–146

Cannan, Edwin, 170

Capital flight, 50, 61–62, 82, 85–86, 187–189, 195–196

Capital flows: and crises, 2–3, 16, 19–20, 31–32, 45–46, 95, 98–100, 222; long-term, 17, 48–49, 63, 103; short-term, 42, 48–50, 103

Caprivi, Leo von, 15

Cardoso, Fernando Henrique, 209

Carey, Kevin, 169

Cariguel, Charles, 87

Cartels, international, 139–140

Castle, William, 128

Central banks, 17–18; and BIS, 43; and economic crises, 96–97; independence, 35–37, 41, 52, 208; as villains of depression, 97

Chamberlain, Neville, 124–126, 131

Chevalier, Michel, 13, 26

Chile, 36, 145, 157; default, 46, 64, 66–67, 146

China, 16, 172, 177

Clay, Henry, 148

Cleveland, Grover, 173

Cobden, Richard, 13, 26

Colijn, Hendrik, 92, 121

Colombia, default, 46, 64, 67

Condliffe, J. B., 119

Connally, Thomas T., 80

Construction and economic activity, 173

Copper, 139

Corruption, 215–217

Counter-Reformation, 8–10

Crane, J. E., 87

Creditanstalt, 54–56

Cuba, 67, 136

Czechoslovakia, 111, 184; stabilization, 37–39; trade policy, 107–108, 126, 144

Daladier, Edouard, 83–84, 195

Danat Bank (Darmstädter- und Nationalbank), 61–63, 71

Daniels, Josephus, 137

Davenport, C. B., 174

Davis, Norman, 129

Dawes plan, 39–40, 42, 141

Democratic politics, 110–115, 140, 165

Denmark, 40, 126, 140

Dependency theory, 143

Deutsche Bank, 61, 63

Díaz-Alejandro, Carlos, 67

Dollfuss, Engelbert, 131

Duclos, Jacques, 191

Economist, 72, 129

Egypt, 48, 68; cotton exports, 112, 144

Eichengreen, Barry, 33, 69, 169, 196

Einzig, Paul, 91

Elliott, Walter, 124

Ellis, Howard, 142

El Salvador, 67

Estonia, 126

Federal Reserve System, 40, 76; and BIS, 43; creation, 19; New York Bank, 61–62, 77, 79–80; open market operations, 78, 80

Federation of British Industry, 114, 118, 124

Feinstein, Charles, 50

Feis, Herbert, 136

Finland, 140

First World War, 25, 168; and depression, 5; and finance, 37, 117; and labor militancy, 35, 175; and national production, 110, 188–189

Fontane, Theodor, 10

Fordney-McCumber Tariff Act, 28, 102, 116–118

Fournier, Pierre, 193

France, 57; bank weakness, 84–86; budget policies, 15, 83–84, 88, 194–195; and

capital flight, 49–50, 82, 189–191;
    currency stabilization, 37, 40; and
    empire, 146; and Germany, 39, 114, 119,
    167; and Great Britain, 41–42, 54;
    immigration, 179–181; trade policy and
    protectionism, 110–112, 118–119, 126
Francqui, Emile, 47
Fugger, Jakob, 9
Fujimori, Alberto, 209

Galbraith, John Kenneth, 22–23, 68
Galsworthy, John, 188
Geddes, Sir Eric, 37
General Agreement on Tariffs and Trade,
    110, 166, 204–205
Genoa conference (1922), 33–34, 42, 93
Germain-Martin, Louis, 83
Germany, 2, 37, 64; banking crises, 59–63,
    71, 99; budget problems, 15, 62; customs
    union with Austria, 123; external debt,
    6–16, 70; and gold standard, 33;
    immigration, 16, 176, 180–181; recovery
    and rearmament, 197–198; short-term
    debt, 49; stabilization (1924), 39–40;
    trade with Argentina, 151–152; trade
    protection, 100, 113, 117–118, 126, 136,
    141–145; trade with Brazil, 153–155;
    trade with Soviet Union, 161; wages, 169,
    171
Gide, André, 197
Gilbert, Seymour Parker, 47
Glass, Carter, 80
Glass-Steagall Act (1932), 81
Gnägi, Gottfried, 89
Goebbels, Joseph, 189
Göring, Hermann, 138, 151
Gold standard, 17–18, 33–35, 65, 73–74,
    79–82, 87–89, 91–92, 94, 96, 169
González, Felipe, 209
Goode, Sir William, 72
Grandi, Dino, 182–83
Gray, John, 4
Great Britain: banking problems, 70–74, 98;
    and bilateralism, 164–166; budget, 69–
    70; as short-term debtor, 49–50;
    stabilization (1925), 68–69; trade policy
    and protection, 110, 118, 123–125, 129,
    136; trade with Argentina, 132; wages
    and unemployment, 170–171, 181

Greece, 46, 126, 142
Grimm, Hans, 183
Grosz, George, 25
Grundy, Joseph, 112

Haberler, Gottfried, 196
Habsburg empire, 9, 51–52, 111, 119, 185
Haider, Jörg, 202
Hajdu, Zoltan, 53
Harrison, George, 37, 61, 71, 77, 79, 97
Harvey, Sir Ernest, 70
Hawley-Smoot Tariff Act (1930), 29, 102,
    112–114, 116, 121–122, 134, 222
Herriot, Edouard, 83–84, 191
Hilferding, Rudolf, 171
Hirschman, Albert, 144–145
Hitler, Adolf, 106, 133, 134–135, 141, 183–
    184, 224
Honduras, 67
Hoover, Herbert, 78–79, 81, 112, 130, 170
Hopkins, Sir Richard, 69–70
Hülse, Ernst, 44
Hueyo, Alberto, 148, 150
Hugenberg, Alfred, 132
Hull, Cordell, 109, 132–136, 138, 156–157,
    166
Hungary: and anti-Semitism, 189; banks,
    52–53; currency losses, 58; foreign
    indebtedness, 57–59, 71; League of
    Nations stabilization, 36, 38–39; trade
    policy, 107–108, 111, 119, 142–143

India, 177
Inflation, 7, 34–35, 37, 39, 117, 198
Inoue Junnosoke, 93
Interest groups, 109, 111–112, 114–115,
    124–125, 134–135, 137–138, 165
International Labour Organization, 5, 176–
    177, 181, 208, 217
International Monetary Fund (IMF), 5, 25,
    43, 39, 100, 166, 218–221
International Trade Organization, 166
Inukai Tsuyoshi, 94
Ireland, 11
Islam, 210–11
Istituto di Ricostruzione Industriale, 68
Italy: bank problems, 53, 68; demography,
    182; emigration, 172–173, 179–180, 182;
    stabilization, 40; trade policy, 126

Jacobsson, Per, 34–35, 47, 95
Janssen, Albert, 96
Japan: banks, 93; and depression, 43, 93–94;
    emigration, 172, 182–183; recovery and
    rearmament, 198; trade and trade policy,
    107, 121, 126, 136, 138–139; wages and
    costs, 136, 175, 177
John Paul II, 210
Jorgensen, Erika, 146
Jung, Guido, 97

Kanitz, Count, 20
Kellogg, Frank, 25
Keynes, John Maynard, 6, 43, 123, 197,
    204
Keynesianism, 26
Kim dae-Jung, 209
Kindersley, Sir Robert, 45–46, 72
Kindleberger, Charles, 55, 119
Kissinger, Henry, 145
Kleinworts, 71–72
Kochin, Levis, 170
Korea, 32
Kreuger, Ivar, 22, 47–48
Krugman, Paul, 3, 22
Kulenkampff, J. A., 151
Kunz, Diane, 69

Labeyrie, Ernest, 192–193
Lacour-Gayet, Robert, 88
Lafontaine, Oskar, 200
Lamont, Thomas W., 47, 64
Latvia, 47, 68
Lausanne conference (1932), 128
Laval, Pierre, 92
Layton, Sir Walter, 129
Lazards, 71–72, 192–193
League of Nations, 25–26, 35, 51, 157, 179,
    217; and Austria, 57; financial
    stabilizations, 25, 38–39; and Hungary,
    59; and labor policy, 176; and trade
    policy, 109, 119–121
Leeson, Nick, 216
Lehideux, Roger, 192
Leith-Ross, Sir Frederick, 129–131, 140
Lenin, Vladimir Ilyich, 158
Leo XIII, 210
Le Pen, Jean-Marie, 202
Lewis, W. Arthur, 104–105, 119

Ley, Robert, 151
Libya, 151
Long Term Capital Management, 3
Luther, Hans, 61–62
Luther, Martin, 8–10, 24, 215

MacDonald, Ramsay, 71–72, 123–124, 127–
    129, 131, 168–169
Macedo Soares, José Carlos de, 155
Machiavelli, Niccolò, 8–9
Mahathir Mohamad, 3, 202, 224
Malaysia, 3, 202
Manchuria, 182–183
Mannheimer, Fritz, 190
Mant, Sir Reginald, 96
Marchandeau, Pierre, 195–196
Marx, Karl, 21–25
McDonald's, 2, 12
McGarrah, Gates, 44, 47
McKenna Committee, 50
Méline, Jules, 112
Mexico, 46, 56, 68, 98, 206
Meyer, Eugene, 80, 97
Midland Bank, 72
Mikoyan, A. I., 159
Milken, Michael, 216
Mills, Ogden, 79, 97
Milward, Alan, 143
Mitchell, Charles, 63–64
Mitterrand, François, 200
Mönick, Emanuel, 88, 191–192
Moggridge, Donald, 68
Moret, Clément, 46–47, 54–55, 84–85
Morgan, J. P., 18, 56, 86
Morgenthau, Henry, 194–195
Most-Favored-Nation Clause, 105–106,
    117–118, 120, 122–123, 130
Mussolini, Benito, 25, 121, 134–135, 182–
    183
Musy, Jean-Marie, 90

Napoleon III, 43
Nationalism, 13–14, 26, 29–30, 187–189
Netherlands, 7, 43, 47, 51, 61; bank crises,
    89, 91; devaluation, 92
Neurath, Konstantin von, 132
Niemeyer, Sir Otto, 44, 148, 152, 157
Norman, Montagu, 35–37; and Austria, 54–
    55; and BIS, 41, 45–46; and financial

crisis (1931), 69–70, 73–74; mental collapse, 73; view of statistics, 95
Norway, 11
Nurkse, Ragnar, 6, 196

O'Brien, R. L., 135
O'Rahilly, Alfred, 178–179
O'Rourke, Kevin, 4, 6, 11
Ortega y Gasset, José, 7
Oslo convention (1930), 123
Ottawa conference (1932), 125–126, 129–130, 147, 149
Ouchy convention (1932), 123
Oustric scandal, 84–85
Owen, Robert, 174–175

Panama, 67
Paraguay, 152
Pâtenotre, Raymond, 87
Peru, and debt defaults, 64, 67, 146
Poland, 47, 111, 126, 209; agricultural laborers, 16; emigration, 16, 180, 184–185; trade policies, 116, 144
Pollard, Sidney, 68
Popocics, Sándor, 57
Posse, Hans, 130
Prebisch, Raúl, 149, 151, 198
Puttkamer, Robert von, 16
Pyatakov, Grigori, 162

Quesnay, Pierre, 43, 44, 54

Rašin, Alois, 38
Rathenau, Walther, 175
Reciprocal Trade Agreements Act, 135–136
Reconstruction Finance Corporation, 81
Reformation, 8–10
Reichsbank, 18–20, 28, 61–63, 131
Reichsverband der Deutschen Industries, 114–115
Reparations, 38–42, 61, 128, 141
Reynaud, Paul, 87, 191
Ricardo, David, 204
Rist, Charles, 88, 195
Ritter, Karl, 156
Robbins, Lionel, 23, 170
Robertson, Dennis, 106
Roca, Julio, 148–149
Rockefeller, John D., 134

Rodrik, Dani, 207
Roosevelt, Franklin Delano, 81–82, 131–134, 152, 192
Roosevelt, Theodore, 18, 22
Roth, Joseph, 185
Rothschilds, 18, 20, 54, 71
Rubber, 27, 42, 108
Rueff, Jacques, 170
Rumania, 38, 142, 146
Runciman, Sir Walter, 124, 126, 148–149
Russia, 3, 18, 26, 200; commercial monopoly, 122, 158–163; inflation, 37; as model, 21, 160–161, 163, 198, 224
Rwanda, 221

Sachs, Jeffrey, 146, 169
Sackett, Frederick, 128
Salisbury, Lord (Robert Cecil), 24–25
Salter, Sir Arthur, 35, 197
Samuel, Sir Herbert, 124, 126
Schacht, Hjalmar, 28, 37, 131–133, 141, 190
Schachtianism, 133, 141, 163, 166
Schiller, Friedrich, 131
Schmidt, Helmut, 26
Schroeders bank, 71–72
Schumpeter, Joseph, 6
Schwartz, Anna, 69, 76–77
Sciarra, Marco, 9
Scotland, 21
Siepmann, Harry, 74
Simon, Sir John, 124
Singer sewing machines, 12
Smith, Jeremiah, 38
Snowden, Philip, 70, 124
Société Générale, 51
Sombart, Werner, 106, 199
Soros, George, 3, 203, 215–216
South Africa, 40
Souza Aranha, Olavo Egydio de, 154–155
Soviet Union. *See* Russia
Spain, 7, 43, 45
Stalin, Joseph, 158–163, 224
Stevenson rubber plan, 27, 42, 108
Stiglitz, Joseph, 3
Stimson, Henry, 97, 130
Stoppani, Pietro, 130
Strakosch, Sir Henry, 96
Strong, Benjamin, 36–37, 40–41
Sugar, 139

Sweden, 136
Switzerland, 43–44, 51, 61; bank crises and capital flight, 89–91; bank secrecy, 90; devaluation, 92; immigration, 179; trade policy, 121–122, 127, 141
Swope, Gerald, 134

Tajikistan, 221
Takahashi Korekiyo, 94
Tardieu, André, 112, 123
Tea, 139
Teagle, Walter, 134
Temin, Peter, 33–34, 69
Thailand, 32
Thomas, Albert, 181–182
Thomas, Brinley, 11
Torrens, Robert, 106
Trade unions, 111, 170–171
Tripartite Pact (1936), 194–195
Trotsky, Leon, 158
Turkey, 46, 47, 142; bank runs, 68

Unemployment, 70, 74, 78, 168–169, 171
United States: bank exposure to central Europe, 59; banking crises, 76–82; budget problems, 77–79, 81–82; capital export, 33, 48–50, 60, 63–64, 133, 137, 148, 157; and crisis of 1907, 18–19; and gold standard, 81–82; immigration, 15, 172–174; labor unions, 170; Securities and Exchange Commission, 63; stock crash (1929), 29, 76–82; trade policy, 107, 113–114, 121, 131–137; trade with Brazil, 155–157; trade with Soviet Union, 161
Universal banks, 51–53
Uruguay, 65–67

Vandenberg, Arthur, 135
Van Tonningen, Rost, 57

Varga, Eugen, 160
Vargas, Gétulio, 153, 155–156
Vargas Llosa, Mario, 89
Versailles Treaty (1919), 28, 101, 113, 176, 208
Villermé, Louis René, 175
Viner, Jacob, 160
Volcker, Paul, 4, 219

Wages and wage costs, 11, 69, 74, 117, 169–170, 180–181, 203
Wagner, Adolph, 14, 207
Wagner, Richard, 23–25
Warburg, Paul, 40
"Washington consensus," 200, 207–208
Washington Hours of Work Convention, 178
Watson, Catherine, 50
Webb, Sidney (Lord Passfield), 74
Weber, Max, 16
Wicker, Elmus, 76
Wilhelm II, 175
Williams, E. E., 15
Williamson, Jeffrey, 4, 6, 11
Williamson, John, 208
Wilson, Harold, 23
Wilson, Woodrow, 101, 173
World Bank, 223
World Economic Conference: of 1927, 109, 119–120; of 1933, 97, 109, 128–133, 139
World Population Conference (1927), 181
World Trade Organization, 5, 166, 205, 221; Seattle meeting, 1–2, 4, 220

Young, Owen, 41
Young plan and loan (1929), 41–42, 141
Yugoslavia, 39, 46; trade policy, 142–143

Zhirinovsky, Vladimir, 202, 212
Zimmermann, Alfred, 38